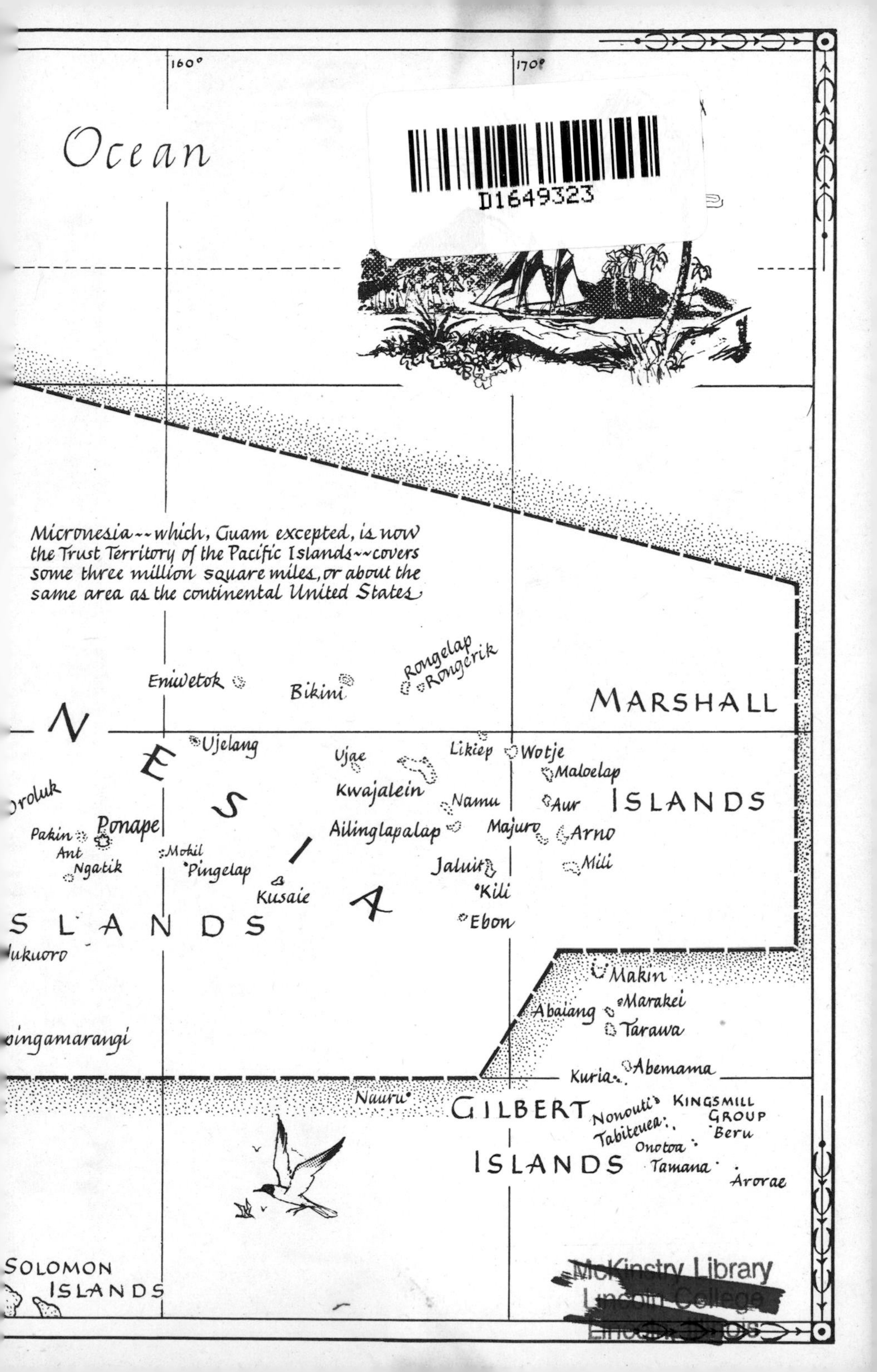

160°
170°
Ocean
Micronesia--which, Guam excepted, is now the Trust Territory of the Pacific Islands--covers some three million square miles, or about the same area as the continental United States
Eniwetok
Bikini
Rongelap
Rongerik
MARSHALL
ISLANDS
Ujelang
Ujae
Likiep
Wotje
Maloelap
Kwajalein
Namu
Aur
Ailinglapalap
Majuro
Arno
Jaluit
Mili
Kili
Ebon
Ponape
Pakin
Ant
Ngatik
Mokil
Pingelap
Kusaie
N E S I A
S L A N D S
Makin
Marakei
Abaiang
Tarawa
Kuria
Abemama
Nauru
GILBERT
ISLANDS
KINGSMILL
GROUP
Nonouti
Tabiteuea
Beru
Onotoa
Tamana
Arorae
SOLOMON
ISLANDS

A Reporter in Micronesia

Other books by E. J. Kahn, Jr.

THE ARMY LIFE

G. I. JUNGLE

MCNAIR: EDUCATOR OF AN ARMY

THE VOICE

WHO, ME?

THE PECULIAR WAR

THE MERRY PARTNERS

THE BIG DRINK

A REPORTER HERE AND THERE

THE STRAGGLERS

THE WORLD OF SWOPE

A REPORTER IN MICRONESIA

by E. J. Kahn, Jr.

W · W · NORTON & COMPANY · INC ·

NEW YORK

FIRST EDITION

Library of Congress Catalog Card No. 66-13686

A good part of the contents of this book originally appeared, in somewhat different form, in *The New Yorker*.

Published simultaneously in Canada by
George J. McLeod Limited, Toronto

Printed in the United States of America

1 2 3 4 5 6 7 8 9 0

Contents

Photos from Trust Territory Information Office

A Reporter in Micronesia

1.

The American Period

THE SUM OF AN AREA'S FAMILIAR PARTS IS BY NO means its identifiable whole. To many Americans who served in the Pacific during the Second World War, the names of Peleliu, Saipan, and Kwajalein are and will always be memorable. Bikini and Eniwetok are names of the nuclear age. But there are few people anywhere who are aware that all these places are currently incorporated in a sprawling entity called the Trust Territory of the Pacific Islands, over which, for the last twenty years, the United States—as an administering authority technically responsible to the United Nations—has held firm sway. Nowhere, and at no time, has America had a comparable opportunity to demonstrate how its resources, skills, and techniques can be used to make an underdeveloped region become, in the contemporary phrase, emergent.

The Trust Territory, sometimes known as Micronesia, embraces the land and the lapping waters of the Marshall Islands, the Caroline Islands, and all of the Mariana Islands except Guam, which has been a full-fledged, non-trust territory of the United States since the end of the Spanish-American War. The Trust Territory is divided into six far-flung administrative districts: the Marianas, the Marshalls, and, within the Carolines, Palau, Yap, Truk, and Ponape. Descriptively, Micronesia can be made to sound vast or insignificant, depending on the mood of the describer. There are more than two thousand islands in the Trust Territory, a few of them the peaks of largely submerged and quiescent volcanoes, but the majority of them segments of coral atolls. Ninety-six of them are inhabited, but inasmuch as most of the entire lot are of exceedingly modest dimensions, they would if lumped together constitute a land mass merely seven hundred miles square—one-tenth the size of Fiji or one-half the size of Rhode Island. (Nearly all of Micronesia is above the Equator, and its name means "small islands"; Polynesia, below the Equator, means "many islands," but the names could be reversed and still be applicable.) Water included, the Territory covers nearly three million square miles of the earth's surface, and would accordingly occupy just about as much of the range of vision of an orbiting astronaut as the continental United States, but the total population of Micronesia is only ninety thousand—one-fifth the population of Fiji or one-tenth that of Rhode Island. The distances that separate the components of Micronesia, and the time it ordinarily takes to get from one spot there to another, are enough to dismay almost anyone but an astronomer. In the jet age, a Micronesian with three days' business to conduct on some outlying atoll (there are no jets in Micronesia) may have to allot three months to the task. In 1964, a visiting United Nations mission described the region as "a Territory whose geographical dispersion and remoteness makes every undertaking more costly, probably, than in any other area of the world." The most routine of undertakings is apt to be uncommonly challenging. Early in October of the following year one Micronesian newspaper was exhorting its readers, "Do your Christmas shopping now! Only seventy-nine days left until Christmas!"

Micronesians, not surprisingly, are a maritime people. Many of them use the fathom as a unit of linear measurement for land, which, little of it though they have, is far and away their most precious possession. Most of them are friendly, attractive, intelligent folk, and they are so tractable, despite all the explosions that have ruffled their environment in modern times, that hardly anybody pays much attention to them. Indeed, of all the areas on earth in which America has an interest—fiduciary or otherwise—Micronesia is probably the least known. It simply doesn't pay nowadays to be peaceful. A nation that is geared to react swiftly to the thrusts of angry enemies and the shifts of doubtful neutrals often understandably hasn't the time to think much about docile friends. Micronesians, during the generation in which they have been our wards, have given us practically no trouble, and trouble spots are the ones that usually get the national attention and the appropriations as well. In the phrase one often hears around Washington these agitated days, "The wheel that squeaks is the one that gets greased."

Inhabitants of the Trust Territory often make wry little jokes about themselves, and a much-repeated one is a two-liner that begins "What do you think about Micronesia?" and ends "Mike who?" Micronesians are ruefully aware that scarcely anyone beyond Tobi, Mili, Farallon de Pajaros, and Kapingamarangi—respectively, the western, eastern, northern, and southern outposts of the Trust Territory—has the faintest notion of who they are or where they live. Some of the comparatively few Micronesians who have visited the United States have found it handy to carry maps, to help them answer questions about where in the world they hail from.

The ranking Catholic prelate in the Trust Territory is a Jesuit Bishop, Vincent J. Kennally, a resident of Truk, which is the hub of the eastern Carolines, and, with a population of more than twenty thousand, is the most crowded of the six districts. Bishop

Kennally, who was born in Dorchester, Massachusetts, and went to Boston College, has spent most of his time in Micronesia since 1946. In Rome for the Ecumenical Congress, he had an audience with Pope Paul. Emulating the pride and chauvinism that most native-born Micronesians display toward their Territory, the Bishop told His Holiness that his diocese—the Vicariate of the Carolines and Marshalls—covered two million square miles, more than that of any other Bishop on earth. "And just where might those places be?" the Pope inquired politely. Bishop Kennally, who didn't happen to have a map with him, began to describe his bailiwick. When he finished, Pope Paul sighed and said, "These days I have to study more geography than theology."

Tosiwo Nakayama, who is an assistant administrator of the Truk district government, the President of the House of Delegates of the Congress of Micronesia, and, like many Micronesians, the son of a Japanese father, said not long ago to a committee of the Congress' predecessor body, the Council of Micronesia, "If we look at the Territory, there are certain problems that face us. There is the factor of distance, the vast physical distance between districts. We have six districts in a large area of ocean. This in itself creates a problem. How to overcome the problem of distance. All of us know from experience that because of these distances we have another problem, that of communication. Also deriving from the problem of distance is another one, of transportation. Because of distance, lack of communication, lack of transportation, there have developed different languages, different beliefs, different customs."

Because of these differences, there is a good deal of clannishness, suspiciousness, and competitiveness among the districts. Not only do the natives of each generally believe, and assert, that theirs is beyond doubt the best of all six, but Americans who have spent any amount of time in Micronesia tend to fall into a similar way of thinking. The Indiana-born captain of a ship that plied Trukese waters would make it clear to all who crossed his gangplank that as far as he was concerned Truk was the cynosure of Micronesian districts; and the captain had an articulate parrot who'd been trained to second the motion. In Saipan, the principal Trust Territory island in the Marianas chain and at present the seat of the Territory's headquarters, the natives, who like their kin on Guam are called Chamorros, look down upon all non-Chamorros, and there have been enough altercations between Saipanese and Carolinians (most of these Palauans and Trukese) to make the local police force deem it prudent to assign two constables to every car that cruises around the urban settlements of Saipan on Saturday nights and pay days. Not long ago, it was necessary for the Catholic church in Chalan Kanoa, the main postwar municipality of Saipan, to hold separate services for Chamorro and Carolinian parishioners: the two groups declined to sing hymns, even in Latin, in unison. The Marshallese, for their part, frequently side with the Chamorros in regarding all Carolinians as peculiar because they wear brighter-colored clothing than do other Micronesians and indulge in perfume.

Distances between districts notwithstanding, Micronesians are a peripatetic lot. In the center of the Yap district, for instance, there is a settlement of several hundred migrant Palauans who live pretty much by themselves, if not exactly in the South Seas counterpart of a ghetto, and who do not enjoy entirely harmonious relations with their Yapese hosts. Recently, a Yapese leader, a man with a college degree from an American university, was discussing this non-fraternal state of affairs with a visitor, and went on at some length about the disparaging views his fellow Yapese held toward the colony of outlanders. Then he paused. "Of course *I* don't feel that way," the Yapese said. "Some of my best friends are Palauans."

In order to achieve cohesiveness, compassion, and comprehension in Micronesia today, the learning of English is being vigorously encouraged. It seems a reasonable enough proposition, inasmuch as an American veneer—albeit still a thinnish coat on many of the islands—is gradually being applied to practically all of Micronesian life. Quite a few of the islands remote from the six district centers, and some of the centers as well, still cling resolutely to their time-honored customs (in Yap it is considered the height of bad local taste to step over the legs of a reclining man; in Truk only a boor would pat a child on the head; in Palau it is a terrible gaffe to ask a man, "How is your father?"), but they may all be fighting a losing battle against the American way of life. There are Boy Scouts troops on Saipan, and the Little League has infiltrated Ponape. Yap has a dog-leashing ordinance, Truk has one-way traffic during peak hours, the Marshalls have a radio program called "Coffee Break," and Palau, where there are a good many caves, has a restaurant called Cave Inn. Some young-girl Micronesian dancers, who used to dance for the fun of it, will no longer perform for foreigners with cameras unless they are paid two dollars a head—or, to get right down to it, two dollars a bare bosom. In the summer of 1964, presumably hoping to instill in Micronesian bosoms of both sexes a veneration for thrift, the American administration announced that indigenes were eligible to buy United States Savings bonds. The response was inconclusive; in six months, a single Micronesian invested in a single twenty-five-dollar bond. Moreover, although there are less than a dozen post offices throughout Micronesia, the place has zip codes. A letter mailed from Koror, the capital of Palau 96940, to Colonia, the capital of Yap 96943, could hardly go astray, since they are the only communities in their respective districts that have any formal postal service, and the mail planes and ships go directly between these ports. Nonetheless, Micronesians in both places who engage in correspondence seem pleased to enjoy zip-code status and take pains to append numbers to their envelopes, thereby incurring the risk of having these misdelivered to Truk, which is 96942.

Lately, too, Stateside school teachers have been encouraging their native pupils to join them in celebrating emphatically non-Micronesian holidays, like Thanksgiving. The natives love holidays, often regarding any one that comes along as a legitimate excuse for a four-day spree; on the eve of a really big holiday, like Christmas, some Marshallese, most of whom are Christians, are apt to move from their island to a relative's island, taking all their worldly goods along, and to stay for several months. In Truk, the strains of "Adeste Fidelis" ring out, rendered in Trukese, and in Saipan, where the supply of authentic evergreens is negligible, plastic Christmas trees are obtainable. Thirty-four dollars and seventy-eight cents for a six-footer, twenty-six dollars and nine cents for a five-footer.

Micronesians are often confused with Polynesians and Melanesians. Melanesians are generally dark-skinned (*melas* is Greek for "black") and fuzzy-haired; the Papuans of New Guinea are a good example. Polynesians are lighter-skinned, have features more Caucasian than Negroid, and have settled mainly in the South Pacific islands, from New Zealand east to Samoa and thence to Hawaii. But Kapingamarangi and Nukuoro, two of the most southerly atolls within the geographical area called Micronesia, were occupied many years ago by migrant Polynesians. At Nukuoro, Santa Claus makes three annual appearances—on Christmas Eve, Christmas Day, and the day after. Instead of a waddling old man, the Nukuoroan version of St. Nick is a lively monster composed of two or three men, and its entrance into the local church (Nukuoroans are very religious) is heralded by such a barrage of firecrackers that some of the impressionable youth in the community usually dive in fright through the church windows. Fortunately, the island has no glass.

Thanksgiving, though, is something again. The inhabitants of the Trust Territory take in their easygoing stride outlandish tales involving all sorts of strange creatures, who can build mountains, tame winds, and perform other feats that might stump Superman, but the idea of Pilgrims and Indians is somewhat beyond them—all that business of white men crossing oceans in small boats, landing on alien rocks, stuffing turkeys, and baking pumpkin pies. But Micronesians are forever trying to be agreeable, and if the Americans want to observe Thanksgiving, that is fine with them. They have evolved their own explanations for that holiday, however. One story goes that God created the coconut, breadfruit, and pandanus trees—each producing only one fruit annually. But late one November sometime long, long ago—any informed American can give you the exact date—God changed His mind and created varieties of the three essential trees that bore multiple fruit, as they have continued to ever since. And to commemorate His happy afterthought, Micronesians accordingly celebrate Thanksgiving—for four days, naturally.

Among other imported concepts, democracy is being plugged hard these days in Micronesia, and it is on the whole being warmly received, though not without some confusion. Micronesians usually like unanimity and have long tolerated autocracy, so they find it hard to grasp why a vote on any issue of, say, fifty to forty-nine should be deemed decisive. Why should any one man's ballot tip the scales?, they sometimes wonder. How can *that* be democratic? Asked not long ago how he felt about majority rule, one Micronesian chief said, "If there are five people and only four want to do it, we do not do it. Only when all five want it, then we do it."

The Trust Territory abounds with hereditary chiefs, some of them men of considerable distinction and most of them men of considerable power. When one outlying atoll in the Marshalls was urged in 1964 to move into the modern political mainstream and elect itself a municipal council, its leaders were leery. They didn't want to do anything that would seem disrespectful to their chief or might lessen his authority. The Americans who were advising them then suggested that in that case they elect their chief to the council. They did, but whenever anything controversial came up he refused to vote, declining to take sides against anyone because, as he put it, "All these people are my children." The council's deliberations came to a standstill. Nobody else would vote, either, not knowing how the chief felt and not wishing to take a chance on disagreeing with him.

Still another local chief, whose domain is an outlying island in the Truk lagoon with a population of less than two thousand, moved in an entirely different direction. Having got the word that it was fashionable to emulate American customs, and having read in a seventh-grade civics book about the way the United States was run, he set up a cabinet of his own, with a Secretary of State, a Secretary of Defense, a Secretary of Health, Education, and Welfare, and so on, and he decreed further that before anybody could go out and pick coconuts on an island the chief controlled several miles away a passport would have to be obtained.

In Koror, which in the pre-1945 days was the seat of the Japanese territorial government and where nowadays there is a stronger affinity for the Japanese than in any other part of Micronesia, it is not uncommon to hear an early-rising Palauan greet the dawn by whistling "God Bless America." One can only guess whether or not there are ironic overtones. In any event, the American influence is unquestionably manifest throughout Micronesia. A couple of years ago, a University of Connecticut anthropologist, the late Edwin Grant Burrows, collected a batch of home-grown native love songs from Ifalik, a fairly remote atoll in the Yap district. Among the romantic ballads that Mr. Burrows bagged was one that went, in part, "I am caught fast as with an American fishhook," and another—it sounded more like Abe Burrows—in which a lover wooing a girl intoned, "You are like an American flag in my heart."

There are septuagenarian Micronesians who look like savages but are proficient not only in one or several of their native tongues but also in Spanish, German, Japanese, and English. The versatility of their speech reflects the variousness of their subjugation. Not long ago a Yapese elder—his body streaked with tattoos, his teeth blackened by betelnut, his clothing merely a carmine breechclout called a *thu*, an ornamental comb in his hair indicative of his dignity, and the stone blade of a hand-fashioned mattock casually slung, in Yapese fashion, over one sinewy shoulder—told an inquiring visitor, "You know, we've learned in our day to be Spanish, and we've learned to be German, and we've learned to be Japanese, and now we're learning to be American, but . . ."—here he paused to spit out a bright red arc of betelnut juice, not so much for dramatic effect as because his mouth was full—"what should we be preparing to learn to be next?"

Micronesians are among those few earthly groups of men who by geographical accident are so isolated that they have had to learn and practice self-sufficiency; yet there is no living Micronesian who has not known foreign domination. Historians like to give names to eras. Micronesia has no formal historians, but its inhabitants customarily refer to their region's most recent phases as The Spanish Period, The German Period, The Japanese Period, and The American Period.

2.

Other Peoples' Squabbles

MICRONESIANS HAVE A MIXED RACIAL BACKGROUND—being a blend, most ethnologists agree, of Mongoloid, Caucasoid, Negroid, and Melanesian strains. Just how the Micronesians got where they are no one knows for sure. It is generally believed, though, that as far back as the year B.C. 1200 their ancestors thought nothing of undertaking a trip of several hundred miles in open outrigger canoes over uncharted seas. The survivors of such bold exploratory voyages presumably founded today's societies, which have had to do a good deal of surviving themselves. In years past, there was nothing much more to cope with than typhoons, famines, fratricidal wars, and a bit of cannibalism. Despite these deterrents, Micronesia flourished; a century ago, what are now the Trust Territory islands boasted a population that has been estimated at more than two hundred thousand, over twice what it is today. The numbers diminished in part because of the importation of assorted Western scourges. Some of these were introduced by more than one nation, but the major credit for smallpox is usually ceded to Spain, for leprosy to Germany, for dysentery to England, for venereal diseases to the United States, and for tuberculosis to Japan. Firearms constituted a joint effort.

The Spaniards were first on the scene. Following Magellan's landing at Guam, in 1521, Spain moved in on the Marianas, which were then known as the Ladrones, or Islands of Thieves. Magellan thought up that name; in his view, the native Chamorros were inexcusably sticky-fingered. Spanish missionaries rechristened these islands in honor of their queen, the wife of Phillip IV. (The Carolines were named for Charles II, Phillip's son, the Marshalls for an Englishman who visited them in 1788.) Other early voyagers, chiefly Portuguese and Dutch, cruised in Micronesian waters, but they gave the islands themselves a wide berth. It is said that one ship of indeterminate origin sailed into the Ponape harbor in 1603, but sailed right out again after a glance at the menacing-looking cliff that juts up at one end of the main island there. By the early nineteenth century, the Russians were around, too, and Ponape and its adjacent islands are still sometimes called the Senyavins, after a Russian vessel that nosed its way among them.

From the mid-nineteenth century on, it was the Spanish, Germans, British, Japanese, and Americans who were most in evidence. There are comparatively few Micronesians anywhere, probably, who do not carry in their blood some alien genes; in Palau, one of the ranking native dowagers, who had a German forebear somewhere along the line, has white skin. The American contingent included some New England whaling men, but the majority were hard-core Protestant missionaries, less interested in conquest or commerce than in conversion. There were Spanish missionaries, too—Catholics, of course—often accompanied by garrisons of soldiers recruited from the Philippines.

By 1873, Spain had extended its sphere of influence westward from the Marianas to Yap and Palau, and eastward to Truk and

Ponape. That year, Spain summarily decreed that any trader of another nationality who wanted to do business in the area would have to stop off first at Manila and buy a Spanish permit. The Germans who came to Micronesia were mainly businessmen. They were the pioneer exporters of copra, the dried meat of the coconut, which, ever since a German merchant began to trade profitably in it in 1864, has been Micronesia's principal source of outside income. The Germans wanted no part of any such licensing arrangement as the Spanish had prescribed, and the British backed up the Germans.

For a dozen years after 1873 there was considerable wrangling back and forth about who had what prerogatives. As far as the Spanish were concerned, Germany was pretty much welcome to the Marshall Islands, which were the farthest away from Manila and had gone discouragingly Protestant to boot. Germany, though, was restive, and in 1885 a landing party ran up the Kaiser's colors on a flagpole at Yap, where their very presence was, in Spanish eyes, anathema.

Things got to the point where Pope Leo XIII was asked to step in as an arbiter. He upheld the Spanish claim to Micronesia, but he mollified the Germans by granting them trading, coaling, and fishing rights, with no nonsense about permits. The *détente* was short-lived. The Spanish-American War finished off Spain as a Pacific power, and being also pressed for cash, Spain was glad, in 1899, to sell everything it controlled in Micronesia to Germany for four and a half million dollars. The Spanish did retain a coaling station in Ponape, where they had set up their Carolinian headquarters. They have not yet exercised their fueling privilege. Under the Germans, the site that had been reserved for the station became a hospital. Under the Japanese, it became a village for Okinawan workers. Under the Americans it is a housing compound for administrative personnel. Not far from it, nowadays, live some Maryknoll Sisters who teach at a Catholic mission school. Ponape wags like to say that the nuns are keeping a watchful eye on the spot for General Franco, in case he ever wants to assert his right to it.

In all the hauling and tugging that went on, Micronesians had hardly any say about the disposition of their region. They were, and are, an agreeable lot, but from time to time they made it clear to the presiding foreigners that they could be pushed just so far. When the Spanish reigned in Ponape, there were periodic skirmishes between their troops and the permanent population. When the Germans took over, their resident governor in Ponape announced that all able-bodied men would have to work fifteen days a year without pay—half the fruits of their labor going to their own chiefs, and half to him.

Few Ponapeans objected to toiling for the chiefs, whose word had always been their law in any event, but working gratis for a European was another matter. In 1909 the residents of the municipality of Sokehs balked at their fifteen-day stint. The next year the German governor ordered them to make amends by putting in thirty days. Again they refused, and a fight broke out. The Germans won, having the better weapons. They executed seventeen Sokehs resisters and exiled the rest of the community to Palau, a thousand miles away. It was a severe punishment to inflict on Micronesians, one of whose contemporary chiefs expressed their attitude toward their homes when he said, "Even though I travel on all the islands, my own island will remain in my head. No one can make me forget it." The outcast group was ultimately repatriated to Sokehs in 1922 by the Japanese.

Every big change in the administration of Micronesia has resulted from a war in which there was no issue that directly affected any Micronesian. The outbreak of the First World War disposed of the Germans. The Japanese, ostensibly on behalf of the Allies but actually in furtherance of their own territorial cupidity, moved in and took over. Germany was too busy elsewhere to resist. Few Micronesians regretted that particular switch. For one thing, the new overlords were Asian and were nonwhite. For another, some of the Germans around had behaved fairly high-handedly. In the Marshalls, when the natives bought imports from them—dress goods, utensils, tobacco, beer, or whatever—some of the German merchants had a double-standard scale of charges. There was one price for cash sales, and another for goods paid for in copra. The copra price was much the steeper, and since few of the natives had much cash, that was the one they usually had to pay. Moreover, the German governor in Palau had found it diverting to hold public executions of malcontent indigenes on a main thoroughfare of Koror. He had designated one large tree a hanging tree, and had had iron rungs imbedded in its trunk—they are there still—to facilitate elevating his victims to the desired branch.

The Japanese were far from strangers to Micronesia. As early as 1891 *their* first trader had gone to Truk. A somewhat scuffed statue of him is still there on the island of Dublon, the Japanese headquarters for that district. Dublon is rather scuffed itself today, but at the height of the Japanese regime it had a network of paved roads, a hotel, two geisha houses, a large seaplane base, and a theater at which traveling circuses from Tokyo went through their acrobatic paces.

The Japanese rule over Micronesia was a *de facto* one throughout that war, and although to quite a few Micronesians it came to fall considerably short of being *de gustibus*, at Versailles the Allies made it *de jure*. Woodrow Wilson's apprehensions that the Peace Conference might produce something less than open covenants openly arrived at were heightened when he learned at Versailles that the other members of the Big Four—France, Great Britain, and Italy—had already given their blessing to a covert war-time agreement between Japan and England that all German possessions in the Pacific north of the Equator were, once the fighting ended, to be administered by the former, and all those south of it by the latter. (Kapingamarangi, the southernmost point in Micronesia, lies just one degree above the Equator.) The United States never did formally approve of that partition. However, not being a member of the League of Nations, it was in no position to vote one way or the other when, in December, 1920, Japan was granted a League mandate over Micronesia, and was instructed to "promote to the utmost the material and moral well-being and the social progress of the inhabitants of the territory."

The mandatory power was further enjoined to keep the islands free of slavery, forced labor, and liquor; and to refrain from establishing any military or naval bases. In 1922, the United States, shrugging at a *fait accompli*, endorsed the agreement. (That year, the Japanese substituted a civilian territorial administration for the military one that had been there since the start of the war.) The United States did make one demand. One of our principal channels of communication with the Orient had been by means of a cable that ran from Guam to Manila to Shanghai. There was another cable running from Guam to Shanghai by way of Yap, and wanting an alternative in case something happened to the first cable, we insisted on having access to Yap. (Some American isolationists screamed at our wishing to get involved in any place so far away and so preposterously named.) The Japanese agreed readily enough, but they never honored their pledge. It all became academic anyway when the Yap cable station was destroyed by a typhoon in 1925.

Aside from the stipulation about slavery, the Japanese soon began disregarding the entire confining bill of particulars laid down by the League, and after withdrawing from that body in 1935 Japan didn't feel obliged to let anybody know what it was up to in Micronesia. No military or naval bases? For any country with long-range expansionist goals, Micronesia was strategically irresistible. Truk, which Japan picked as the site of a major naval base, not only had a commodious lagoon forty miles wide, but, lying just about in the center of the mandated area, it was handily located—twenty-two hundred miles southeast of Tokyo Bay, three thousand miles north of Sydney, Australia, twenty-one hundred miles east of Manila, and six hundred and fifty and thirty-six hundred miles away, respectively, from the American bases at Guam and Pearl Harbor.

But the military usefulness of the area was only one of Micronesia's charms. Japan's economy needed all the bolstering it could get. The names, in English translation, of three successive Japanese companies that operated in Micronesia are indicative of Japan's shifting attitude toward it. First of all, in 1914, there was the South Seas Trading Company. In 1921, along came the South Seas Development Company, and finally, in 1936, the South Seas Exploitation Company. This last had twenty subsidiary companies, which, among many other enterprises, caught and processed fish, grew and canned pineapple, grew and refined sugar cane (Japan built several railroads just to carry this product from fields to factories), and cultivated pearls.

The Exploitation Company had an initial capitalization of ten million dollars, and on this was returned a handsome annual profit of twenty-two percent. Its head office was at Koror, outside of which Palauan community the Japanese carved agricultural terraces on the hills. They also constructed an elaborate Shinto shrine, which was dedicated in 1940, with a special representative of the Emperor in attendance. Koror itself became a stylish Oriental metropolis with a population of thirty thousand and factories that manufactured beer and fireworks. Koror had public baths, laundries, dressmakers, tailors, masseurs, barber shops, butcher shops, and drug stores. There were forty-one ice dealers, seventy-seven geisha girls, one fortune-teller, and fifty-five restaurants, thirteen of them considered upper-class. Palauans had never seen anything like it before, and they haven't since, either.

Micronesians who could afford to were allowed to patronize these establishments, and they developed a taste for rice, a cereal non-native to the area, as well as for its accompanying soy sauce, which sells briskly in the Trust Territory today in gallon lots. (Pickled radishes are another holdover favorite.) But the new order of things was established mainly for the satisfaction of the Japanese in residence. Of all the nations that have had a go at running Micronesia, Japan is the only one that has seriously undertaken to colonize the place. By the start of the Second World War, the mandated area contained some fifty thousand Micronesians. They were outnumbered by outsiders—seventy thousand of these in all, including Okinawans and Koreans brought in by the Japanese as laborers.

The natives were made emphatically aware of their presumed inferiority. Brutality is common in Asia, and while there was a good deal of slapping and pummeling, and an occasional beheading, the Japanese were on the whole not terribly much more abusive to their involuntary hosts than most Asians are to other Asians. But the Micronesians, in the Japanese view, were even lower than Koreans, who to most Japanese represent the bottom of the human heap. Sometime Japanese officials would characterize Micronesians as "*tomi*," a word whose separate elements mean "native" and "nothing." Sometimes they would refer to them, whatever their ethnic background, as "*kanakas*," a Polynesian word for "persons." Despite bruised feelings, however, there were a lot of jobs available to Micronesians, and throughout the area there was an unaccustomed hum of activity. Some Micronesians are inclined to look back nostalgically at the geishas and the glitter. They do not miss the slaps, but they miss the hustle and bustle. In Koror especially, natives comparing the frenetic Japanese Period with the infinitely more relaxed American Period that succeeded it confess that they are unable to understand how we won the war.

The League of Nations had merely given Japan a mandate, but there was nothing transitory about the Japanese approach to their dominion. Practically everything they built was built to last, and their term of occupancy is sometimes also known in Micronesia as The Concrete Period. (The American Period is The Corrugated Tin Period.) Bishop Kennally's residence in Truk is part of the Xavier High School, a territory-wide parochial school that occupies the premises of a Japanese wartime communications station. The building has stone walls three feet thick, a roof six feet thick in part, and steel window shutters. But such fortifications were not for Micronesians, whose homes, often ramshackle and tindery affairs of wood and straw and thatch, were not designed to withstand bombs and shells.

For generations, moreover, before the foreigners came in, Micronesians had subsisted quite satisfactorily—many still do—on what the bountiful environment provides: coconuts, bananas, taro, breadfruit, yams, pandanus, fish, and shellfish, to cite the staples. Once the Second World War broke out, it proved difficult for Micronesians to satisfy the new tastes they had acquired from the Japanese, what with American planes and warships constantly harassing Japan's supply lines. What did get through to the islands the Japanese reserved pretty much for their own colonists and armed forces. With hostilities in full swing, furthermore, there was no more attention paid to the League of Nation's attitude toward forced labor. One hundred and seventy-nine natives from the main island of Ponape were shipped to Kusaie, nearly three hundred miles southeast, in the summer of 1943, to work on army installations, and they didn't get back home for more than two years. All Yapese males between the ages of eleven and fifty spent a comparable stretch of time constructing, mostly by hand, an air strip for fighter planes. When the United States bombed it to rubble, they spent another year putting it back together.

Noncombatants though they were, hundreds of Micronesians died when their islands were invaded or bombed. (One of the first postwar requests that the Trukese made of their new administering authority was that if there had to be a Third World War, would the United States please hold it somewhere else.) Where there was ground fighting, the destruction was very nearly total. The pride of Saipan, for example, was the Japanese-built city of Garapan, which on the eve of the war had a population of twenty-nine thousand and amenities comparable to those of Koror and Dublon. After the invasion of Saipan there was nothing left of Garapan. Other war-torn cities have risen from their ashes. Garapan is still nothing. Just about all that remains of its former glory is a larger-than-life-size bronze statue of the founder of the sugar-cane industry there. Now bullet-riddled, he stands forlornly in what was once a manicured botanical garden, but now is a tangle of undergrowth infested with African snails, still another Japanese legacy.

There has been much tampering with the ecological balance of Micronesia. The first foreign ships brought rats. The Spanish once imported monitor lizards to kill the rats, and when the lizards multiplied they brought in poisonous tree toads to kill them, and now the toads have spread all over. So have the rats. As for the African snails, they came to the Marianas in 1939, imported by an Okinawan whose wife had tuberculosis and who thought that eating them would cure her. Some of them moved on to Guam in a shipload of yams and have been there ever since. They reproduce at an astonishing rate; they are hermaphroditic, and a single one of them can theoretically have forty thousand offspring in a year. In 1960, the United States authorities brought in carnivorous snails from Kenya to fight the original snail population, but it has been a losing battle. Recently, the Marianas district legislature appropriated two thousand dollars for extermination—ten cents for each three-gallon bucket of African snails. There is also a local bounty of a nickel a rat.

There was no ground fighting in Koror, but when our Marines moved in to occupy the city some of them, in a highly charged emotional state because of the reverses they'd suffered at nearby Peleliu and Angaur, demolished most of the city anyway, including the water works and the power plant. That was more than twenty years ago, and the United States and Japan have since become friendly, but Koror doesn't yet have the kind of public utilities it had before the Palauans inadvertently got into the middle of somebody else's fight. In the Ponape district, where there was no ground fighting at all, the Japanese custodians of a botanical garden were fearful that when the Americans landed they would destroy the rare species they'd been propagating. So on the eve of the conquerors' arrival, the custodians affixed to every tree and shrub, which had theretofore borne appropriate name tags in Latin and Japanese, a third tag bearing their English identifications. The place got pretty well trampled notwithstanding.

The scars of war remain in Micronesia, although tropical foliage forms quick obliterating blankets. In some parts of the territory half-hearted attempts have been made to clean up the debris, and in others full-hearted attempts, but it may be many more years, if ever, before all of Micronesia looks serene again. Some of the souvenirs have their picturesque aspects, like the remnants of Zero fighter planes, perhaps two dozen in all (the jungle growth makes precise counting difficult), that fringe the Yap air strip. Some rusted relics are misleading; they are the hulks of ships that have gone aground on treacherous Micronesian reefs *since* the war. Some are plain ugly, and, one would think, eradicable. At Angaur, for instance, the United States has a spick-and-span Coast Guard station (an outpost of a long-range navigational guidance system), with tidy buildings and flower beds, and movies every night, sometimes double features. But the nearest beach, a pleasant cove only a few hundred feet away, is still littered with the garbage of war.

As on so many other one-time battlefields, unexploded bombs and other potentially death-dealing live ammunition are still to be found in parts of Micronesia. (There is still stuff from the First World War in France.) The incumbent administration has neither the skills nor the funds to cope with this dangerous situation. On Saipan, after the war, our armed forces tried to get rid of a lot of unexpected ammunition all at once by blowing up a dump. Things didn't go exactly according to plan, and as a result live ammunition was spewed in every which direction, without all of it being detonated. The area in which most of it lies is supposed to be off limits, but Micronesians love explosives. They like to fish with them, and in preparing to blow up fish not infrequently blow off their own hands. On Saipan, to the despair of the American authorities, small boys in search of shiny playthings persist in hammering brass burling bands off live shells they encounter. On the island of Babelthuap in the Palau district, a native family raised hell when an American demolition team tried to cart off four live bombs they'd been using as supporting pillars of their homes. An unexploded bomb, its tail fins visible above the ground, remains where it fell, a minute's walk away from a beach where residents of Koror take their children swimming. A single small bare stick marks the spot. Many Palauans and Americans alike agree that this is perhaps an inadequate warning signal, and that somebody probably ought to do something about this hazard sometime soon.

3. Under the Charter

At the outset of the war in the Pacific, it became evident that if the United States won it would have to move at least temporarily into the vacuum created by the departure of the Japanese (whom we naturally had no intention of leaving *in situ*). Inasmuch as Micronesia was mostly water, the Navy seemed the logical occupying force, and as early as 1943 the Navy Department began recruiting scholars at Yale, and later at Columbia, to accumulate and collate all the available material on Micronesia. Unlike Okinawa and the other Ryukyu Islands, which belonged to Japan, the Micronesian islands were merely mandated. They could thus hardly be considered legitimate spoils of war. What was more, the United States had no wish to take actual possession of them; at the end of the war, we wanted neutral areas to regard us as liberators, not conquerors. On the other hand, we wanted to exercise some kind of control over so broad an expanse of the Pacific; otherwise our national security might again be imperiled.

Casting about for a workable solution to this problem, the White House asked all interested government agencies, early in 1945, to submit their suggestions. The United Nations was then in a formative stage. Under its charter, areas whose status was cloudy were to be designated as trusteeships, and to be administered by U.N. members responsible to a Trusteeship Council under the General Assembly. The charter also provided for a special category of trusteeships designated as strategic, which would come under the Security Council. The principal difference between the two kinds of trusteeships was that in the General Assembly nations with security interests had no recourse to a veto when their administration was challenged, whereas in the Security Council the veto was available.

The State Department recommended to President Roosevelt that Micronesia become a U.N. strategic trusteeship, with the United States as the administering authority. The president received this proposal while he was at Warm Springs, Georgia, trying to get back his strength after the Yalta Conference. He approved it, in principle, on April 10th, two days before he died. President Truman, on assuming office, saw no reason not to go along with his predecessor's way of thinking. With the concurrence of the United States Congress, Micronesia accordingly became one of eleven U.N. Trust Territories—and the only strategic Trust Territory. The arrangement was formally ratified in July, 1947, and President Truman turned over the actual administration of the thereupon christened Trust Territory of the Pacific Islands to the Navy Department, which had been supervising the area all along anyway but without official international sanction.

In line with what was then the American policy toward Micronesia, the Naval administrators assigned to the area did relatively little at first to change the natives' old-fashioned ways—or the ways, at any rate, that remained after the three previous foreign occupations. The idea was that we should try not to alter the age-old pattern of native life, and that Micronesians would fare best if they were left to their own devices and kept apart from Western customs—the "zoo theory" of administration, as anthropologists sometimes call it. One zoophilic Navy admiral who got to know the natives well declared in 1947, ". . . for mercy's sake let them alone in their happiness!" But no one could be certain what the Micronesians considered happiness. The more sophisticated among them—those who lived at or who frequently visited the various district centers—had by then acquired a good many non-indigenous appetites and ambitions.

The zoo theorists thought the Micronesians could subsist quite satisfactorily on the bounty of their soil and of their seas. But many Micronesians thought otherwise. Few of them grow tobacco, yet cigarettes had long made many of them happy. A subsistence economy might keep them detached from the rest of the world, and in admirals' eyes, quaint, picturesque, and unspoiled; but a cash economy, such as had flourished in the district centers at least during The Japanese Period, was more appealing to many of the natives who, however any foreigners might feel about Micronesia, had to live there.

The Navy stood watch until January, 1951, when President Truman issued an executive order turning over the administration of the Trust Territory to the Department of the Interior, which has been in charge ever since and has committed itself, according to a recent statement of policy, "to develop the peoples of the Trust Territory so that they can assume the responsibilities of self-government, to stimulate them to become as nearly economically self-sufficient as possible, and to encourage them to foster respect for their culture while affording them an opportunity to take on those aspects of western life which will enable them to lead richer lives."

It is sometimes thought odd that Interior, of all federal departments, should be in charge of territories notable for their extraterritoriality. The explanation is simple enough. In the 1870's, much of the continental United States comprised land owned by

990
Oceanica

o U.I cab
(ISL = 919.65)

818.52
K122 Kahn, Ely Jacques, 1916-
A reporter in Micronesia. N.Y.
Norton, 1966.
313p. illus. plates, maps (on lining papers)

bklst
BRD Jan. 67

1. Micronesia - Description 2. Islands of the Pacific

Kahn, Ely Jacques.

A reporter in Micronesia.

Norton, 1966.

313p. illus.

1.Micronesia

✓ Polynesia

✓ Micronesia

Melanesia

Oceanica

the government but not within the borders of any state. The management of public lands was the responsibility of Interior, and in the administration of these territories there was nothing more important than land usage. So jurisdiction over them was logically invested in that department. As the nation acquired outlying territories—Hawaii, Guam, Alaska, and so forth—it was convenient to turn them over to the department that already had the supervisory experience.

A strategic Trust Territory, however, is a more complicated dependency than an ordinary territory. While Japan was specifically enjoined by the League of Nations from fortifying Micronesia, the United States has equally specific authorization from the United Nations to do just that. Except for a few dozen Coast Guard men at two transmitting stations for navigational radio signals, however, we have no garrisons within the Trust Territory. But because our Army has a missile-testing center at Kwajalein, radio stations at Ponape and Palau, and a satellite-tracking station at Truk, and because the Trust Territory envelops Guam, where we have a Strategic Air Command base and a Polaris submarine base, the Defense Department is naturally concerned about what goes on in Micronesia. Because we do not own the Trust Territory but in theory run it on behalf of the United Nations, the State Department is concerned, for it is through State that all United States relationships with the U.N. are supposed to be funneled. It is State, not Interior, that puts its seal on the report that the United States annually submits on its stewardship to the United Nations.

The State Department also has the ticklish task of acting as a bargaining agent for those Micronesians who have been arguing for twenty years, not unreasonably, that Japan ought to reimburse them for the devastation wreaked on their land during the war. Some Micronesians think they have justifiable war-damage claims, moreover, against the United States, but our position has been that we didn't start the fighting and could hardly have been expected not to try to evict an enemy from wherever he chose to entrench himself. The logic of that argument does not overwhelm all Micronesians. Many of them are not unaware that in October, 1965, President Johnson signed a bill authorizing the payment of twenty-two million dollars to Okinawans for damages inflicted on their property by Americans *after* the war—reparations which, the United States declared, it was under no legal obligation to make but was making anyway on moral grounds.

Periodically, one of the Micronesian districts will draw up a petition requesting indemnity for wartime losses. Some of the demands have been substantial. The Yap district, where there was no ground fighting during the war, and where the total population is now slightly over six thousand, once asked for over twelve million dollars from Japan, or about two thousand dollars per person—and this in a district where the annual per-capita cash income, on some of the remoter islands, is eighty-three cents. The United States, without committing itself on amounts due, has assured the U.N. that the Micronesians' claims against Japan are "valid and just," and whenever the subject is raised the State Department proclaims that it is negotiating with the Japanese government. In 1961, the United States formally told the U.N. that the matter had the "highest priority." In 1965, a year in which Secretary General U Thant called for "prompt and definite" settlement of the Micronesians' claims, a responsible State Department official, when asked informally how the negotiations with Japan were coming along, replied that they hadn't got anywhere at all and added, "Realistically, there have been other areas of U.S.-Japan relations with higher priorities." To get higher than highest is easy for the most perfect government on earth.

Interior keeps in touch with Micronesia through a departmental branch called the Office of Territories. (Considering the physical makeup of Micronesia, a case could probably be made for switching the handling of its affairs to another branch of Interior called the Office of Saline Water.) For a federal agency, the Office of Territories is astonishingly small. It is manned by only thirty people, including messengers and clerks. Presiding over this microbureaucracy is an energetic young lawyer, Mrs. Ruth

G. Van Cleve, a Minnesotan whose husband is also a government attorney.

Mrs. Van Cleve's predecessor in charge of territories was Richard F. Taitano, a native of Guam, who moved on to become deputy high commissioner of the Trust Territory. Taitano is a slim and soft-spoken man, born in 1921, whose father was an American Navy employee on Guam for thirty-three years. When Richard, the oldest of seven children, was thirteen, his father went blind; at sixteen, Richard was teaching school every morning, and attending classes himself in the afternoon to learn enough to keep ahead of his pupils. In the evening, when not helping his burdened mother with the family livestock, he had his choice of doing his own homework or correcting his students'. After the war, he got a scholarship at Berea College, in Kentucky, and he later did graduate work in government administration at the University of Pennsylvania. He was the first territorial native to be director of the Office of Territories.

Mrs. Van Cleve was one of the fifty women whom President Johnson appointed to reasonably high federal posts soon after he took office. Her office, which comes under Interior's Assistant Secretary for Public Land Management, is the Department's liaison with the Virgin Islands, Guam, American Samoa, the Trust Territory, and what she sometimes calls "the funny places"—among them Canton and Enderbury Islands, two Pacific dots that we administer jointly with the British; Holland, Baker, and Jarvis Islands, three more Pacific specks that we administer alone, but which take up little time since all are uninhabited; and Wake Island, which is mainly an airport and the day-to-day supervision of which Interior has gladly ceded to the Federal Aviation Agency. (The Office of Territories does *not* have jurisdiction over Puerto Rico, which is a commonwealth; or over Okinawa and the rest of the Ryukyu Islands, which—like the Bonin Islands, Midway and Johnston Islands, and the Panama Canal Zone —are subordinate to the Department of Defense.) The funniest place of them all, probably, is Palmyra Island, a thousand miles south of Honolulu, which actually consists of fifty islets totaling about a thousand acres. Palmyra, which is also uninhabited, would be part of Hawaii except that it is privately owned by a Honolulu family that bought it from King Kamehameha IV in 1862 and that later incurred the wrath of a United States senator. So when Congress passed the act that made Hawaii a state, Palmyra was excluded, the senator not wishing the family to benefit from the privileges of statehood.

The Trust Territory has always had a High Commissioner, a rank rare in United States history, though not uncommon in colonial affairs. Under the Navy regime, the High Commissioner was non-resident, the title being invested in the Commander-in-Chief of the Pacific Fleet, who made his headquarters at Pearl Harbor and governed Micronesia through deputies. The only other United States High Commissioner still functioning is a similar two-hat-wearing operative, the general commanding our armed forces in the Ryukyus.

Since 1951, the Trust Territory's High Commissioner has been appointed by the president. The incumbent, William R. Norwood, who took his oath of office in May, 1966, is a former reporter and public-relations man who came to Micronesia from Hawaii, where he was the governor's chief administrator. The job has a Civil Service rating of GS-18, which means that the High Commissioner's base pay is $25,382 (Micronesia being rated a hardship area, like all civil servants working there he also gets a 20 percent bonus and a housing allowance), and that he belongs to the highest category of government officials who don't have to be confirmed by the Senate. He is more powerful within his three-million-square-mile realm than the President of the United States is within *his*. The High Commissioner is not only the supreme executive but also the supreme legislative authority; he falls short of being omnipotent by virtue of the supreme judicial authority reposing in a chief justice who is also designated by and responsible directly to the Secretary of the Interior. The High Commissioner has his own flag (on it is displayed the Trust Territory seal, which features a coconut palm), and he has been accorded by the State Department's Office of Protocol a status equivalent to that of an ambassador.

The first civilian appointee to this post of exalted isolation was Elbert D. Thomas, a Utah Democrat who was chosen in 1951 after failing to be reelected to the Senate, and who seemed especially qualified because as a young man he had been a Mormon missionary in Japan. Thomas died in 1953, and was succeeded by Frank E. Midkiff, a Honolulu civic leader. Trust Territory headquarters were still in Hawaii then, twenty-seven hundred miles east of the center of Micronesia. In 1954, Interior moved the headquarters to Guam, which was, as it still is, the main port of access to the Trust Territory. Midkiff resigned, preferring to stay in Hawaii, and he was followed by Delmas H. Nucker, a government career man from Pennsylvania who had been executive officer of the Office of Territories.

Nucker presided over Micronesia for six and a half years, during most of the Eisenhower administration, and attained the reputation of a man who liked to stay within his budget. Since the most money ever allocated to the Trust Territory by Congress during that period was just over a million dollars a year, and since a good deal of that had to go into subsidizing transportation, making ends meet was not easy. But it was still American policy then to move slowly in Micronesia, and everything just sort of limped along. Most of the money that was spent was spent on facilities for the Americans who were out there to spend the money. The Nucker administration did try, though, to indoctrinate Micronesians, who have feet so tough they can walk barefoot on coral that would lacerate most soles, into the habit of wearing shoes. One result was a minor outbreak of podiatric ailments.

Nucker stayed on until early 1961, when the Kennedy administration assumed power and began reassigning jobs that, like the High Commissioner's, were rated as patronage plums. The Trust Territory was given to M. Wilfred Goding, who administered the region for the ensuing five years. Under the first four years of his direction, the area is generally considered to have made more headway than during the entire sixteen previous years of The American Period. Goding's surname is pronounced as if it were spelled "Godding," and it became a Trust Territory quip to say "In Goding we trust." A tall, gruff, grizzled, hearty man, born in 1912, Goding had a background that seemed almost tailor-made for his High Commissionership. He came from Skagway, Alaska, and Alaska, with a very few people scattered over a very large space, has long been vexed with administrative problems comparable to those in Micronesia. The only basic difference, aside from the temperature, is that the untracked wastes of Alaska are solid and those of Micronesia liquid. One of Goding's assistant commissioners, James Hawkins, was posted to Micronesia in 1964 following many years of service for the federal government in Alaska. After a few weeks on the new job, Hawkins said, "It's almost like coming home."

As a young man, moreover, Goding had taught school to Eskimos, and to educate one group of non-English-speaking American wards is not very different from educating another. He had worked for Interior as far back as 1944, for ten years of that time in the Office of Territories, as assistant director for Alaskan affairs, so he was acquainted with the problems involved in the evolution of the political status of a territorial region. When Alaska and Hawaii were on the edge of statehood, he had a good deal to do with working out the mechanics of their changeovers with congressional committees, so he knew his way around Capitol Hill—a useful experience for an administrator who has to present budgets for legislative scrutiny and action. He was also on good terms with Alaska's two senators; a sister of Goding's was one of Senator E. L. Bartlett's administrative assistants. Upon acceding to the High Commissionership, one of Goding's very first accomplishments was to persuade Congress to raise the annual budgetary ceiling for the Trust Territory from seven and a half to seventeen and a half million dollars—a feat for which one of his American subordinates in Micronesia hailed him as "the greatest money-getter in Trust Territory history."

The High Commissioner's headquarters are now in a handsome complex of buildings, called Capitol Hill, on Saipan, the main island of the Marianas. By Micronesian standards, Saipan life is plush. The island has dial telephones and a bowling alley, and is only a hundred and twenty miles from Agaña, the capital of Guam—which, though no great shakes compared to Hong Kong, Paris, or New York, is to many Micronesians a metropolis of breathtaking glitter. Like Guam, moreover, Saipan, alone of Micronesian metropolises, is hospitable to the sport of cockfighting.

It is common in any bureaucratic society for individuals far from the seat of power to be envious and resentful of the higher-ups, and the Trust Territory is no exception. Its employees who are hundreds or thousands of miles from Saipan are forever grumbling that the administrators there don't understand conditions in the field, and that they try to exercise too firm a grip on the routine activities of their outlying representatives. (The headquarters does in fact exercise tight control. It even specifies the color schemes for houses built for Americans in distant districts: ceilings must be light ivory except when blue is used on walls, in which case white is permissible.) The district men like to tease the headquarters men. Among Saipan's other splendors is the only golf course in Micronesia. It is called the Whispering Palm Country Club. When some Americans in Koror converted a vacant field into a crude pitch-and-putt course, they called it Whispering Boondocks. When the chief public-information man at Saipan sent a contribution to the Truk district's weekly paper, its American editors identified him as a foreign correspondent.

The comparative opulence of the Saipan headquarters installation is the result of the Trust Territory's having inherited its Capitol Hill from the Central Intelligence Agency, which built itself a postwar enclave there at a cost of some twenty-eight million dollars and occupied it between 1949 and 1962. Purportedly a "Navy Technical Training Unit," the place was actually a training area for Chinese Nationalists who, with C.I.A. backing, were contemplating an assault upon the Chinese mainland. (Why the United States, strategic trust or no strategic trust, elected to establish an installation of that sort on alien soil has never been clearly explained.) The whole operation was very hush-hush. Nowadays, nearly every old-timer in the Trust Territory administration says that *he* knew what was happening furtively on Saipan all that time, but that nobody else knew about it.

During the thirteen C.I.A. years, the Navy had administrative control over Saipan, and Trust Territory officials had hardly any access to the island. This awkward state of affairs provoked embarrassment whenever a United Nations mission would go to Micronesia, and its members, who knew that Saipan was one of the area's principal islands, would ask to be shown around it. The Navy and a few Trust Territory men who were in on the secret would arrange an itinerary calculated to disclose as little as possible and at the same time to avert idle speculation. They would fly the U.N. visitors from Guam to Tinian, three miles west of Saipan, in the morning, and would dawdle around there pointing out the air strips from which the B-29's departed to drop atomic bombs on Hiroshima and Nagasaki, and inspecting Tinian's ancient ruins—sixteen-foot-high stone pillars that back in A.D. 800 or thereabouts supported the house of a Bunyanesque chieftain named Taga.

The escorts would recount in detail the saga of Taga: how he jumped sixty miles from Guam to the island of Rota, where he fought and killed its chief; how he then jumped another sixty miles to Tinian, where he challenged its chief to a coconut-picking contest and won hands down by plucking a tree from the ground and shaking off its nuts; how, when Taga's son performed the same trick, the father felt his own supremacy threatened, and slew the boy; and how, in remorse, Taga then became converted to Christianity. Having exhausted the possibilities of Tinian, the escorts would then take their guests, by slow boat, over to the part of Saipan farthest away from the C.I.A., and would show them the golf course and some old churches and a few fresh-water lakes, and pretty soon it would be time for a long, long lunch, and after that, just about when the visitors began wondering when they were really going to get to see something of Saipan, it would develop that the party's schedule called for it to return to Guam.

The frustrations of such transients were nothing compared to those of the resident Saipanese, who were barred from half their home island and became understandably nervous about what was happening in the off-limits area. They are still somewhat edgy about the effect on them of the United States' strategic moves. The Saipanese reaction to the escalation in February, 1965, of the war in Vietnam was indicative of their apprehensions. For the three preceding months, as most Saipanese were well aware, the Soviet Union had posted a trawler off Guam, just beyond the three-mile limit. Its mission was presumed to be to obtain whatever information it could, from that sanctuary, about American Polaris-submarine operations. When the Saipanese heard that American planes had begun dropping bombs in North Vietnam, there was a wild exchange of frightening rumors. The most widely circulated one, for which there was no shred of evidence, was that the Soviet trawler had steamed north from Guam and was lying off Saipan, ready to launch an invasion force. Before the day was out, every pound of rice in every store on Saipan had been bought up by panicky natives who thought the Third World War was under way.

Like many proud peoples, Micronesians are sensitive. Their morale, like a taro patch, needs constant tending. Shortly after Goding became High Commissioner, he gave local spirits a boost by authorizing (his authorization was tantamount to law) the adoption of an official Trust Territory flag. A Territory-wide contest was held to pick a design. The first prize of five hundred dollars went to a radio operator on Saipan; a consolation prize of two hundred dollars was awarded to a Marshallese schoolboy whose entry was nearly identical. The winning design consisted of six white stars, arranged in a circle, on a blue field, the white standing for purity, as well as for the six districts; the blue for loyalty, as well as for the sea. Not long ago a fourth-grade Yapese girl, writing a poem about her flag, referred to the stars as the six sisters; at the same time she referred to the United States, which as any Micronesian knows has the most stellar flag anywhere, as

Uncle Fifty. The Trust Territory flag looks like an American admiral's flag, except bigger and better. The Navy has never had a flag officer who rated six stars. It is just possible that the judges of the flag-design contest, when they made their selection, chose something that was a cut above, or a star above, the best that could be paraded by the Navy that had once been their overlord. At any event, the Navy has learned good-naturedly to live with the new flag that may be a joke at its expense, and since the Trust Territory colors were first unfurled—on United Nations Day in the fall of 1962—a few three- and four-star sailors have reportedly ordered desk-size replicas to display in admirals' country and confound visitors to it.

To the regret of many Micronesians, their flag was not on exhibit at the first important ceremony where it might have fluttered before the eyes of the whole world—President Johnson's 1965 Inauguration. As a United States High Commissioner of high protocolary standing, Goding was invited to ride in the procession of governors and others that followed Johnson's swearing-in. There was some question of whether he should be in the parade at all, inasmuch as every other participating official represented one kind or another of unarguably American soil, whereas the Trust Territory was just as unarguably alien territory. Finally the State Department decided that he could ride in the very last car, and that while the other cars could fly regional flags, he would have to settle for the Stars and Stripes. Micronesians were sorry that their flag got left out, but they realized that practically nobody watching the parade in person or on television would have known what it was anyway. And it did not surprise them that their High Commissioner was bringing up the rear of the serpentine cavalcade, for they have become reconciled, no matter what the circumstances, to being way out on the end of the line.

In his first four years of office, Goding made thirty-eight trips back to the continental United States. He had to present himself, in a fund-raising capacity, before congressional committees or the Bureau of the Budget, two groups that in Trust Territory eyes have the same constructive potential as a good coconut crop, and the same destructive potential as a typhoon. There was an annual spring pilgrimage to be made, too, to the United Nations. By 1962, eight of eleven original U.N. trust territories had become independent nations. The remaining three were Micronesia; Papuan New Guinea, which is administered by Australia; and the small south Pacific island of Nauru, which though it has only forty-eight hundred inhabitants has three administrators—Australia, New Zealand, and the United Kingdom. Each spring, the Trusteeship Council holds a session at which the administering authorities report on the progress they've been making toward achieving the U.N.'s long-range goals for their territories: self-sufficiency and self-government.

According to the Charter of the United Nations, the Trusteeship Council is made up of a representative of each of that body's founding members—the United States, the United Kingdom, the Soviet Union, France, and China; a representative of each administering nation (if it is not one of the big five); and a representative of enough other nations to make a like number of administrators and non-administrators. Now, with four administering nations and three founding nations automatically on the Council, there is room for only one outsider; Liberia currently holds that seat.

The Soviet Union considers the Trusteeship Council "a bastion of the colonialist powers" and would like to do away with the Council entirely, or else make it subservient to the General Assembly's whoppingly named Special Committee of Twenty-four [mostly African and Asian nations chummier with the Russians] on the Implementation of the Declaration on the Granting of Independence to Colonial Countries and Peoples—a committee that wants every place on earth to be independent, whether it's ready or not or whether it likes it or not.

The Trusteeship Council session usually lasts about a month. Its deliberations are open to the public, but hardly anyone bothers to attend, and the press rarely prints a word about them. The Russians do most of the talking. When they are not complaining that in all the years of the Council's existence nobody has yet furnished them with a translation into Russian of the original trusteeship agreement for Micronesia between the United Nations and the United States (as if there were some deep plot to hide the document's meaning from them), they are challenging the motives and the actions of the administering powers. But the Soviet denunciations don't seem to have much zing to them; the Russian spokesmen at these sessions give the impression that they are merely speaking for the record, which by now they have contrived to make a bulky one.

The High Commissioner is usually accompanied by at least one Micronesian, who usually arouses curiosity, inasmuch as not more than a few dozen Micronesians have ever been to the continental United States. (Considerably more of them have visited Hawaii.) Those who have been here have had mixed experiences. One distinguished elderly Marshallese hasn't yet entirely recovered from learning that sometimes when you want to use a toilet in America you have to pay ten cents, and two nickels won't do, for what is laughingly called a public convenience. A young Trukese, in Washington last year, astounded the staff of a supermarket he wandered into by asking where the fifty-pound sacks of rice were kept. He wanted two. Returning to Truk, he astounded his American friends there even more by blurting out, when they asked him how he'd enjoyed his trip, "You don't like me because my skin is black."

Another Trukese, who went to the annual session of the Trusteeship Council, was received with special warmth, and he soon learned why. Some U.N. delegates had been to the Trust Territory a few years earlier, and the hospitable, generous islanders had given them hand-carved model canoes, but the U.N. men had never been able to rig the sails. They asked the Trukese to help them out. He was glad to be of service, though he confessed when he returned home that, being from Ta Island, in the Satawal atoll, and the canoes being from Kapingamarangi, he'd had no idea exactly how the sails went on and had probably botched the job. (Most Micronesian sailors change direction not by tacking but by switching the mast of their single sail—this formerly made of woven straw but now more often of store-bought cloth—from one end of a canoe to the other.)

Every three years, the Trusteeship Council sends a delegation from its ranks to inspect the Trust Territory. (No country unfriendly to the United States has ever been represented on one of these missions, but even so some of the reports, considering the diplomatic language all such documents are couched in, have been highly critical.) Micronesians are always glad to have outsiders drop in, and usually welcome them with flowered leis and splendid feasts. But while delighted to welcome the United Nations folk, Micronesians try not to let themselves be deluded about the permanency of the visitors' interest in their welfare.

Not long after the 1964 mission departed, leaving behind all sorts of pledges of what was going to be done to help Micronesia, one Ponapean leader got to thinking about these inspection trips. He was Leo A. Falcam, a thirty-year-old graduate of the University of Hawaii, who is married to an American and who was the first Micronesian—there are now six others—to be made an assistant district administrator in the Trust Territory hierarchy. (Falcam was later granted a Parvin fellowship to study public administration for a year at the Woodrow Wilson School of Public and International Affairs at Princeton—the first Micronesian, Trust Territory headquarters proudly announced, ever to receive a Parvin.) Reflecting that absence, while perhaps making the heart grow fonder, does not always make the head think faster, Falcam advised his fellow Micronesians that other U.N. missions would be turning up in the future, and added, ". . . let us not forget that they will also come and go, but we are here to stay and work." He got ahead nicely in his own work; he became Acting Dictrict Administrator of Ponape.

4.

Their President, Too

WHEN JOHN F. KENNEDY WAS PRESIDENT, HE expressed the hope that Micronesians would eventually "participate fully in the world of today." Some Micronesians still consider him their best American friend in this or any other world. In the Yap jail, the only pictures that the prisoners have on display are of saints and of Kennedy. The president was genuinely concerned about the islanders' affairs, though he naturally could not devote too much of his time to so small, untroublesome, and undemanding a group; as a sailing man, he was also genuinely pleased when some Micronesians sent him a model outrigger canoe. He was beguiled with its reversible sail, and put it in the Fish Room of the White House.

When the president was assassinated, the only American living on one outlying Trust Territory island, who had the only radio there, hesitated at first to pass along the news. To many of the natives, a government is inseparable from the man who presides over it; to them, Kennedy *was* the United States. In their view, the Trust Territory existed solely through his special grace and dispensation, and the funds to subsidize it came out of his own pocket. The American with the radio accordingly thought it prudent to preface his disclosure of the sad information with a brief reassuring lecture on the continuity of American policy.

On the first anniversary of Kennedy's death, a sculpture of his head, commissioned in Japan, was unveiled in front of Our Lady of Mount Carmel Church, the principal Catholic cathedral on Saipan. (A Spanish priest said the first mass on that island four hundred years ago.) The Saipanese rather hoped that some member of the Kennedy family might attend the ceremonies. No one did, but the hosts saved face, having refrained from sending out any invitations until four days ahead, when there would hardly have been time for an acceptance and appearance. (It was a memorable day on Saipan, for that same night, in the main square of the Spanish-looking, white-washed-stucco village of Chalan Kanoa, the drawings were held in a raffle for the benefit of a municipal scholarship fund. The chances cost a dollar apiece, and the promoters of the raffle were so lavish with prizes that although they took in over thirty-five hundred dollars, they netted only four hundred. First prize was a pickup truck and second prize a refrigerator. Both were won, to the dismay of a few Saipanese, by itinerant Filipino construction workers, who late that night hoisted Prize No. 2 onto the back of Prize No. 1 and drove whoopingly away.) Before the head of President Kennedy was unveiled, it was on display in the office of the mayor of Chalan Kanoa. An old Saipanese woman walked in—she had certainly been alive as far back as The German Period, and very probably had known The Spanish Period, too—and looked at the sculpture. She burst into tears and said, "This was my president."

Her sense of identification with Kennedy was shared by many Micronesians in all the districts. At Koror, Palau, there is a T-shaped dock, which the Japanese built as a recreation area. It has two swimming pools and a ramp for pleasure boats, and the Palauans have long called the place the T Dock. A new American administrator was assigned to the Palau district a few weeks after the Dallas assassination. He was an officious man. He at once proposed that, to banish from their lives all vestiges of their downtrodden past, the natives should change the name of their overwater latrines from the Japanese word *benjo*, which they'd long been using, to a new name, whereupon the natives shrugged and switched to *his* name. He also thought that the old T Dock should have a name more contemporary in spirit. So he had a big sign painted up and posted on the scene, identifying the area as the "Koror Marina." That was too much for the Palauans. Within a few hours they had covered the second of the two words with a thick coat of black paint. Loving Kennedy as they did, they were damned if they were going to let anybody put on public display the name of Lee Harvey Oswald's wife. The testimonially defaced sign remains that way today.

A few months before he died, President Kennedy set up a small mission of his own to visit Micronesia and make recommendations on what the United States could or should do to speed up its progress toward wherever it might be going. The head of the inspection team was Anthony M. Solomon, who later became Assistant Secretary of State for Economic Affairs and at that time —following a business career in Mexico and a wartime stint as economic director of southwest Iran—was a lecturer on international economic relations at the Harvard Business School.

Solomon had already led a somewhat similar mission to Colombia, for the Bureau of the Budget, but he was unacquainted with Micronesia. (When the White House telephoned news of his appointment, he was entertaining dinner guests. Returning to the table, he asked if anybody in the room knew where the Trust Territory of the Pacific Islands was. One man said he thought it had something to do with the Solomon Islands, and until Solomon got to an atlas, he was pleased at the prospect of touring so aptly named a region.) The Solomon Committee, as the group became known, spent several weeks in the Trust Territory. On its return, it drew up a five-hundred-page report, which contained sweeping recommendations for altering the structure of the American administration. The committee, for one thing, advocated a six-year capital improvement program that would have required an increase in annual Trust Territory appropriations from a maximum of seventeen and a half million dollars to an average of about twenty-six million.

While the Trust Territory administration was not displeased at this prospect, it was less enthusiastic about some of Solomon's other proposals. He thought, for instance, that it would be practical for a good many of the services the United States provides out there to be handled not on an individual hiring basis, as had been done all along, but through contracts with outside organizations. All American teachers in the Trust Territory would be recruited, according to this plan, through the relatively nearby Hawaii public-school system; all American doctors through the international organization MEDICO-CARE; the contract for a fisheries-development program would be let to some place like the Scripps Oceanographic Institution, at La Jolla, California. Any such arrangements would, of course, have diminished the authority of the High Commissioner and his staff.

What was more, the Solomon Committee felt that, except in special circumstances, no American should spend more than four years on Micronesian duty. On these cloistered islands, a man's viewpoint and efficiency can easily be affected by the torpid environment. If any such scheme had been adopted, the administration would have had to be radically changed, for there are quite a few old hands around with more than a dozen years' service, and there are a few who have been in Micronesia since 1946. Solomon also urged upon both President Kennedy and Sargent Shriver that some Peace Corps volunteers be sent out that way. In 1961, the High Commissioner had put in a request for some. Five years later, the closest the Trust Territory had come to getting any was to hire a Hawaiian agriculturist who was trained for Peace Corps work in Ecuador, but then learned he had a red-cell blood count that made service in a high-altitude area inadvisable. He ended up in Majuro, in the Marshalls, where the elevation nowhere exceeds eight feet. In the spring of 1966, however, to the delight and astonishment of nearly everybody who cares about Micronesia, Washington disclosed that a Peace Corps corps three hundred and fifty strong—nearly equalling all the Americans in the Trust Territory in any capacity—was being recruited to serve out there, and that within a couple of years the Peace Corps contingent might number a whopping eight hundred.

President Kennedy liked most of the Solomon Committee's ideas, and was on the point of implementing them when he was killed. In the ensuing two and a half years, a few of Solomon's recommendations, or modifications of them, were adopted, but many were not, and his report has never been made public—principally, one suspects, to deprive the Russians of any further critical comments about Micronesia they could berate us with at U.N. meetings. On May 13, 1966, however, the Secretary of the Interior submitted a blockbuster of a proposal to Congress, which went beyond anything the Solomon Committee had contemplated. Interior, as if suddenly jolted awake from a twenty-year reverie, asked Congress to raise the annual appropriation ceiling for the Territory to twenty-two million dollars in 1967 and to thirty-eight million by 1971; what's more, Interior concurrently requested a five-year capital-funds outlay of one hundred and seventy-two million additional dollars, which was more than the United States had spent in Micronesia since 1946.

Whatever anyone may propose about Micronesia, it is the United States Congress that disposes. Congress is always jealous of its prerogatives, and in the case of outlying lands over which America has some kind of jurisdiction Congress has the Constitution to back it up, for its authority derives directly from Article IV, Section 3 of that document: "The Congress shall have power to dispose of and make all needful rules and regulations respecting the territory or other property belonging to the United States . . ." True, Micronesia doesn't belong to us, but while we're footing its bills the distinction makes little difference to Congress, which, as the head of the U.N.'s 1964 mission to Micronesia declared, "has immense power for good or ill over the evolution of Micronesia in the period immediately ahead."

But of the men who hold this power, probably fewer than one tenth have ever heard of the Trust Territory, and those congressmen who are ignorant of it have been pretty much content to leave its fate in the hands of the Senate and House Committees on Interior and Insular Affairs. Inasmuch as appropriation bills originate in the House, its committee is the key one to reckon with. Its chairman, since 1961, has been Wayne N. Aspinall, of Colorado, and in general what he says about Micronesia goes. Representative Aspinall thinks we have treated Micronesians fairly and squarely and that we might be doing them more harm than good if we poured a lot of funds in there that they weren't equipped to cope with. "If you spend money before they can appreciate it or before they can absorb it into their culture, you destroy the very thing you're trying to develop," he says. "We've never been niggardly. We must not only do our best to give these people whatever advantages they want; we must always also see that we don't impose western culture on them that they don't want. We must challenge them to see for themselves what it is they actually do want. If we throw things at them that they can't absorb, it's going down a rathole."

Mr. Aspinall has been to Micronesia four times. (His committee's staff expert on territories, Dr. John B. Taylor, also knows the area; he was in the first American wave that landed on Saipan in 1944.) Congressional junkets rarely last longer than two weeks, but Aspinall and some of his fellow committee members once devoted six weeks to a comprehensive tour that included not only the Trust Territory but also Hawaii, Guam, and American Samoa. Some members of the committee try conscientiously to get to Micronesia once every year or two, but it is a long way off. And when they get there they do not all always exhibit as sensitive an understanding of Micronesia's problems and customs as does their chairman. Micronesians are proud of being under the United Nations, and they display the U.N. flag all over the place. At one district headquarters, the chief American administrator apologized to one congressman because the U.N. flag flying over their heads was a bit tattered; a replacement was on order, the administrator said, but it hadn't arrived, so they had to fly the old worn one. "I don't care if you never fly it at all," said the congressman, within the hearing of a number of Micronesians, who were shocked.

Another congressman asked, while in the Yap district, to be excused from some of the formal receptions and to go to a really primitive area. He was escorted to a remote, normally unvisited island whose elderly chief, who had never had so eminent a guest, presented him with a delicately carved model canoe that the chief had made with his own hands. The congressman examined it admiringly and then told the chief that it was a fine piece of work and that if he'd make fifty more like it he, the congressman, was certain he could get them all sold in thirty days in the States, at a nice profit. Without a word, the chief took back the model and, a tear rolling down each cheek, smashed it over his knee.

5.

Launching a Leading Canoe

WHAT MAY PROVE TO BE THE BIGGEST FORWARD STEP yet in the political evolution of the Trust Territory occurred in the summer of 1965, when the first session of the Congress of Micronesia met at Saipan. High Commissioner Goding delivered an appropriate State of the Territory speech, and a message signed by President Johnson acclaimed the event as "a momentous occasion" and characterized the Congress as "a remarkable experiment in progressive self-government."

Patterned after its United States big brother, the Congress, the establishment of which had been authorized the year before by Secretary of the Interior Udall, has an upper chamber, the House of Delegates, with two members from each of the six districts, and a lower chamber, the General Assembly, with twenty-one members, each district being represented according to its population. Truk has five members, the Marshalls and Ponape four each, Palau and the Marianas three each, and Yap two. This apportionment was not arrived at without rancor. Saipanese are much given to theatrics—on hearing a rumor that there was some doubt about the eligibility of a congressional candidate they favored, some women there marched to the Marianas district administrator's office armed with machetes and seemingly bent on using them if anybody stood in their man's way—and when they first learned that their district was to be outnumbered by three others just because of some prosaic old census figures, they threatened to blow up the High Commissioner's residence.

To avoid possible conflicts of interest, it was at first decreed that Micronesians employed by the Trust Territory administration couldn't run for Congress. But then it became apparent that if this policy were adopted there simply wouldn't be enough capable Micronesians to go around. So a compromise was worked out: For the first four years of Congress, men who held major government jobs could serve in it. After that, they would have to choose between being civil servants and politicians.

The Congress of Micronesia has limited legislative powers. It has nothing to say about the Trust Territory budget; that is up to the United States Congress. (Toward the junior Congress' own annual operating budget of $145,000, the senior Congress graciously advanced $50,000.) It can pass laws, but the High Commissioner can veto them, though if he twice vetoes a law that the Congress of Micronesia nonetheless thinks desirable, the legislators may go over his head and appeal to the Secretary of the Interior. (One of the first resolutions adopted by the new body, which the High Commissioner at once endorsed, was the designation of July 12th, when the Congress first sat, as a regional holiday known as Micronesia Day.) Circumscribed, thus, as is the authority of the new legislature, it is still the nearest thing Micronesia has ever had to an indigenous, territory-wide, law-making body, and its institution has caused a stir both on the islands and beyond them. For the chairman of the last U.N. visiting mission to the area, Frank Corner of New Zealand, a single metaphor has been inadequate to acclaim the new institution. He has hailed it as "the roof-tree under which all the people of Micronesia will be gathered," as "the big leading canoe which will explore the seas and chart the course on which your six canoes will sail together," and as one of Micronesia's great watersheds.

The report of his mission had some further collective thoughts about the new Congress and the United States Congress' attitude toward its fledgling dependent counterpart. The older Congress, the report said, "has before it a challenge. It is being challenged to create a political consciousness in Micronesia—a consciousness which can only develop in such a small territory if the United States Congress is willing to restrain the otherwise crushing weight of its own powers. Congress' experience of its own past and its imagination can point the way to helping another legislature to maturity. So also can enlightened self-interest. If the Territory is to come alive, to begin the self-directed progress which alone offers any hope of a halt to steadily rising United States subsidies, the Congress will have to begin to limit and share its authority over Micronesia. The alternative—to retain an unyielding control over these grants—will be to leave the Territory an inert and politically lifeless burden on its pocket and on its conscience."

Every Micronesian over eighteen, male or female, was eligible to vote for Congress. The first Election Day was January 19, 1965, but on some of the remoter islands the balloting was conducted a month or more before that, so that boats could deliver these votes to district centers by counting time. In Palau, high seas made it impossible for a ship to pick up the ballots at one island, but since there were only fourteen voters there, and since no race was decided by that narrow a margin, that particular forfeiture of suffrage was dismissed as irrelevant.

The extent, and the intensity, of pre-election campaigning varied according to district customs. One Yapese candidate, who lived and worked at Trust Territory headquarters on Saipan, made the thousand-mile trip home and spent several weeks beseeching votes and chewing betelnut with the electorate, though while in Saipan he hardly ever touched the stuff. He won, barely beating out a full-time resident opponent whom the American colony on Yap expected to come out on top because, alone of all candidates, he had an Abraham Lincoln-type beard. "I don't think I campaigned hard enough," the loser said afterward. The principal Palauan candidate, who was generally considered a shoo-in for office, didn't campaign at all. He was at a conference at Saipan and stayed there during the last two weeks before election. He lost.

In the Marshalls, there was little conventional politicking, because no Marshallese would ever dream of praising himself. (Candidates there, moreover, found it less effective to be seen kissing babies than to pose for photographs with nonagenarian matriarchs.) In Ponape, candidates went even further and belittled themselves. In Truk, free radio time was offered to any office-seeker who wanted to make use of the government station's facilities. Nobody availed himself of the opportunity—not even one candidate who was employed at the station.

Only in Palau and in the Marianas, where outspokenness and dissension are more acceptable than in the rest of Micronesia, were there organized political parties. Palau's date back to 1963, when several community leaders in Koror decided that if they were ever going to move into the modern democratic world they had better start by adopting a two-party system. So they divided themselves up into Liberals and Progressives, though there were no issues of real consequence separating them at the time. (When a Catholic missionary in Koror happened to refer to John F. Kennedy one time as "progressive," the stock of the Progressive Party rose sharply.) The Progressive Party came to have a Catholic orientation, and the Liberal Party to reflect the viewpoint of the Seventh Day Adventists, who are well-established in Koror. Some Palauans contend that the only other present distinction between their two parties is that the Progressives want to continue to receive American subsidies but want the United States to clear out of Micronesia soon, whereas the Liberals want the money, too, but want us to clear out immediately.

Before the Congressional elections, both parties had campaign posters printed to boost their tickets, and the Liberals even drew up a platform, which they circulated in Palauan and English. So markedly different was the campaigning in that district from the diffidence displayed in all the others, save the Marianas, that one Palauan candidate actually attacked another, by name, over the local radio station, and another concluded a broadcast on his own behalf by singing "My Country 'Tis of Thee," with the words translated into Palauan.

On Election Day, the Palauan candidates were bustling around when the polls opened at 7 A.M., escorting voters to the polls—mostly schools and municipal offices—in jeeps and pickup trucks, and hanging around to try to convert waverers at the last minute. The ballots were mimeographed, and because even after twenty years of American occupation many Palauans continue to cling to habits they formed long ago, the names of the candidates appeared in English letters and also in Japanese characters.

Most Palauans, except for a few unbendingly partisan party functionaries, found the results of the election a gratifying testimonial to their adoption of democratic ways. Of the five positions contested for in both congressional houses, two were won by Progressives, two by Liberals, and the remaining one by an independent—a forty-year-old school administrator who made a door-to-door canvas of quite a few rural villages and whose diligence and footwork paid off. Throughout Micronesia, something over eighty percent of all registered voters cast ballots, and this splendid turnout brought smiles even to the faces of some of the losers.

The outcome of many of the Trust Territory congressional races was predictable (nobody in Truk, for instance, ever doubted that the powerful Petrus Mailo, chief of the main island, Moen, could win; the only question was whether he would deign to run), but there were several surprises, too. One that occurred in the Marianas District was particularly unsettling to the American administrators. This was the election to the House of Delegates of José R. Cruz, a goldsmith, a former parliamentarian for the district legislature, and the publisher, editor, and sole writer of a gadfly newspaper that would appear whenever he felt like putting out an issue. It was the only publication in Micronesia, not counting a few high-school newspapers, that was not editorially controlled by the American administration. (One of the school papers, produced by Xavier High School, runs fiction along with news. A characteristically Micronesian tale that it printed had to do with a rebellious daughter who, among other unfilial acts, refused to pick lice out of her mother's hair; both mother and daughter were ultimately devoured by coconut crabs.)

When Cruz made his journalistic debut, in the fall of 1963, he called his paper the *Free Press* and said its objective was "to free the soul and pulse of things which affect Saipan." In the spring of 1964, he began calling it the *Free Press of Micronesia* and said its objective was "to free the soul and pulse of things which affect Micronesia." Cruz would sometimes refer to himself as a "Small Potatoe" and to the High Commissioner's staff—the capitals were his—as a "GANG." Sometimes he had a kind word for the High Commissioner himself. "High Commissioner M. W. Goding is doing a great deal of benefit for Micronesia," Cruz wrote once, "but unfortunately he is the HiCom and is the TARGET for CRITICISM." Goding was also twice the TARGET for LAW SUITS brought by José Cruz. Both were technical cases involving the licensing of outside companies operating on Saipan; both were thrown out of court at the plea of the High Commissioner's Attorney General.

A freeswinging journalist, Cruz, who when other Micronesians were considering what might be an appropriate motto for the Trust Territory suggested "Insufficient Funds," has had no qualms about calling some people lunatics and identifying others, by name, as adulterers. (This sort of thing goes on elsewhere in Saipan, too, where vitriolic broadsides filled with personal abuse are periodically circulated and signed "The Avengers" or "The Vindicators"; but Cruz put his stuff out over his own name.) Because of Cruz's lack of respect for the administration—"A well educated Micronesian is nothing but a Micronesian who thinks and does things the American way," he has scornfully written—his candidacy for Congress distressed some of his targets, and his victory distressed them even more. On the eve of the Congress' inaugural session, an attempt was made by some fellow Micronesians to deny Cruz his seat, because of "a number of serious lapses of character in the past," but the credentials committee to which the matter was referred ruled in his favor. Cruz, who had been in some bad-check trouble in the United States and is *persona non grata* to American immigration authorities, thereupon was elected by his fellow members of the House of Delegates chairman of its Judiciary and Governmental Relations Committee.

One of Cruz's first post-election gestures was to make a trip to Yap, whence he said he hoped to bring back a ton of betelnut for Saipanese fanciers of that chewy delicacy who had had difficulty obtaining it. Because of agricultural-quarantine restrictions, he was able to take home only a bagful. Some of the Americans in Micronesia thought this was poetic justice, for not long before the *Free Press* had roundly dressed down the High Commissioner for allegedly violating quarantine by having a Christmas tree shipped to Saipan. The *Free Press* was mimeographed and cost a nickel. In line with his enhanced stature as a member of the House of Delegates, Cruz abandoned that paper in favor of a ten-cent printed weekly, somewhat milder and more statesmanlike in tone, called the *Micronesia Times*. It was printed—until it, too, went out of business—on Guam; the Trust Territory's only printing facilities belong to the administration.

Most Micronesian publications are quite tame. The principal one is a magazine, the *Micronesian Reporter*, which is theoretically put out seven times a year by the High Commissioner's headquarters but has fallen as much as five months behind its scheduled publication dates. The six districts have, from time to time, had weekly newspapers of their own. The liveliest is Yap's, entitled the *Rai News*—*rai* being Yapese for the famous stone money peculiar to that area. For a while, the Americans who ran this paper called it the *Yapper*, but the name was changed by an incoming district administrator who felt that it reflected unfairly on the Yapese, who hardly ever yap.

Yap is the most primitive and most conservative of all Trust Territory districts, but the *Rai News* revealed not long ago how its traditional ways are being altered by the encroachments of Western civilization. The paper covered a play about modern Yapese life put on in connection with some school commencement ceremonies. Among the dramatis personae were a woman and her three children, who dined meagerly on coconut crabs and taro. Then the paterfamilias came in, drunk, with a bottle of gin in his hand. He spat on the floor and loudly demanded his dinner—and he wanted a good one. When that was not immediately forthcoming, he beat up his wife and kids, and was sentenced to twenty years in jail. Another offering on the commencement program stressed a similar theme: it was a song-and-dance number entitled "No Money on Pay Day." An indigenous correspondent of the *Rai News* concluded his report on the proceedings by commenting, "These offenses did not seem so bad because they were put on the stage and that made them somewhat impersonal. . . . The song and the play contain many very good lessons, especially for some of the husbands here in Yap, and perhaps some of the husbands throughout the world as well. . . ."

Micronesia is so remote that many Americans who've been out there for a while all but stop caring about what is going on throughout the other world. An heroic exception is a school teacher from Pennsylvania, assigned to Koror, who subscribes by airmail to the daily and Sunday editions of *The New York Times*. It sets him back $606.20 annually. Some of his colleagues think him daft for the indulgence; he considers the investment well worth it. What little news the district weeklies publish is mostly gleaned from short-wave radio broadcasts monitored by other American teachers. A paucity of information about world affairs has long plagued Micronesia. In 1965, Trust Territory headquarters filled the void somewhat by receiving from the Manila office of United Press International, and transmitting on to each district center, two five-minute news summaries every day. These were then rebroadcast over intradistrict frequences, interspersed with local announcements about ship arrivals, airplane passenger lists, scooter accidents, and PTA meetings; as well as taped features that the Trust Territory got from the United Nations and the Voice of America—"Science in the News," "Life on the Planets," and a three-installment biography of Samuel Gompers. To date, there are no trade unions in Micronesia.

Until recently, communications were spotty in the Trust Territory. Now, each district center can hold two-way conversations with Saipan, and with the other district centers, by means of a radio-telephone hookup. Since the opening, in May, 1965, of a radio station at Yap, each district has had its own one-way broadcasting facilities to its outer regions, although many of these places often have no way at all of getting in touch with district headquarters except when a ship stops by. For the district radio stations, half the operating funds are provided by headquarters on Saipan; district legislatures provide the other half through taxes—import licenses, liquor and beer licenses, cigarette taxes, boat taxes, and so on. One of the first laws passed by the Congress of Micronesia, and approved by the High Commissioner, was a territorial import tax on tobacco, hard and soft drinks, and a few other items. Only in the Marshall Islands district is there a personal income tax: one percent of the salaries and wages of all resident Micronesians. (Some sub-district municipalities have their own local taxes, principal among these a head tax, which varies from a dollar and fifteen cents to thirteen dollars and forty cents but is as often ignored as it is paid. The island of Rota, in the Marianas, imposes a twenty-five-cent tax on every chicken exported.)

For a while, an enterprising American weather bureau employee ran a small commercial radio station of his own at Moen, the administrative center of the Truk district. The station did quite well. It had a Micronesian disc jockey who played records for boy friends and sweethearts on request. (One time, the disc jockey announced that he was going to dedicate his next number,

"I Got Heaven in My View, Hallelujah," to all the missionaries within earshot.) It had sponsors, including the Budweiser distributor on Guam. It had a wide and faithful audience; when, for instance, a bargain price for canned corned beef at a Moen store was proclaimed, canoes would come darting in from all over the Truk lagoon. But Saipan said the proprietor of the station was darting all over the frequency band, and made him shut down. Some five thousand Micronesians now own radio sets, and they are looking forward to television, which, as they are aware, has already reached American Samoa. Micronesians can hardly wait until they are similarly blessed, and they may not have to wait too long; the Interior Department has been studying the practicability of speeding up the pace of education by means of television.

6.

Nikes and Iroij

It is a characteristic paradox of Micronesia that the only daily newspaper published within the Trust Territory appears in a part of it that is off-limits to most of the rest of it. The paper is the *Hourglass*, printed at Kwajalein, in the Marshall Islands. The name of the paper derives from the shoulder patch of the celebrated American Seventh Infantry Division, which in February, 1944, invaded Kwajalein, the largest of the ninety-seven islands that form the Kwajalein atoll, the biggest atoll in the world. The islands altogether measure six square miles. The lagoon they embrace measures eight hundred and thirty-nine square miles. At the time the Seventh Division landed, the main island had no vegetation on it other than a few battered coconut trees. Today Kwajalein is a handsomely landscaped oasis, crisscrossed by smooth paved roads, where three thousand Americans live in air-conditioned splendor. They work for the Kwajalein Test Site, where Nike missiles are regularly fired to intercept intercontinental missiles launched from California. The United States has spent nearly a billion dollars building and equipping installations at Kwajalein. Up to July, 1964, the site was under Navy jurisdiction and was called the Pacific Missile Range Facility. Now it is under the Army, subordinate to the Redstone Arsenal, at Huntsville, Alabama. The Test Site, though on the Asian side of the International Date Line, operates on a continental United States calendar; this makes the people on Kwajalein feel closer to Huntsville. Thus it is always one day later in Kwajalein than in the rest of the Marshalls. This state of affairs can lead to trouble. In the Marshalls, nominations for the congressional elections closed at midnight on December 31, 1964. Twenty-four hours after all the candidates' names were supposed to be in, the Marshallese living on the Kwajalein atoll came up with a couple of last-minute entries. On being told they were too late, they argued that nobody had specified *which* December 31st was the deadline. They won their point. It is possible, for anyone who cares enough and can make the right plane connections, to celebrate New Year's Eve twice in Micronesia.

The *Hourglass* is circulated throughout the Trust Territory, and anyone who cared enough what went on at Kwajalein could read in the paper, several months back, that as part of a Nike-X Anti-Missile System an old Zeus Acquisition Radar, or ZAR, was being phased out, and a new Multi-Function Array Radar, or MAR, was being phased in. The story was illustrated with an aerial photograph of Kwajalein. Nonetheless, the military administrators of the place are security-conscious to the point of absurdity. In theory no one may even pass through Kwajalein in transit to another destination unless he is on official business. This regulation is awkward for the Trust Territory administration, because as Guam is the transportation and communications hub of the western part of Micronesia, so is Kwajalein the hub of its east. In fact, the only way one can normally get to the rest of the Marshall Islands from any spot on earth is via Kwajalein. Through its portals, accordingly—although it is the policy of the Department of Defense to exclude American correspondents accredited to the

Department of Defense—alien Filipino construction workers may freely pass en route to jobs in the Marshalls.

American school teachers and their families employed by the Trust Territory in the Marshalls, or Ponape, or Truk—half of Micronesia—are *required* to travel through Kwajalein to and from the United States if they want the government to pay their fare. Such transients are treated to guided tours of some of the installations, and are presented with an illustrated souvenir brochure about the place issued by the Army officer in charge. The booklet, a non-classified document, bubbles with information about ZAR's and MAR's, and says chauvinistically that "Kwajalein is the only place" where "ZEUS missiles . . . have successfully intercepted target nose cones fired over the Pacific by ICBM boosters launched from California." The nose cones, according to what the Army hands out to its guided tours, are fired from Vandenberg Air Force Base, and they travel at a speed of four thousand miles an hour. Visitors to Kwajalein may also buy souvenir shirts for their children, with maps of the Test Site imprinted on them.

The children who live on Kwajalein sometimes seem to be the only individuals other than reporters who are affected by security. Not long ago a ten-year-old American boy there, after school had been closed down one day because an anti-missile missile was scheduled to be fired (there is apparently a good deal of debris flying around at such times), asked his father why there had to be those old test shots anyway. "Why, that's the whole idea of the place," the father said.

"But what do we need missiles for?" the boy went on.

"To shoot down other missiles," said the father.

"But why do we need *those* missiles?"

"It's high time you were taught the facts of life," the father said.

The veil of secrecy with which the Defense Department has sought to surround the facts of Kwajalein is sometimes thought by Americans in other sections of the Trust Territory to be attributable to the Army's desire not to let it become too widely known how comparatively well off are the Americans—mostly civilians under contract to private industries—who occupy the island. (Among the Army personnel there, the officers outnumber the enlisted men by ten to one. That makes it tough on the officers, who not only have to work under wraps but without the counsel they usually have available on other assignments.) There are only six motion-picture theaters in all the Marshall Islands. Five of them are on Kwajalein. (The *Hourglass* gives the films on display acceptability ratings.) Kwajalein has a Teen Club, two swimming pools, four tennis courts (two of them lighted, for night playing); a fleet of taxicabs that look like armored cars, and for all any outsider knows may be; a ferris wheel for the younger sporting set; a high school that is completely air-conditioned; and a salary rate so juicy that even the Catholic priest hired by an American company that handles the logistics of the place gets ten thousand dollars a year. (He gives most of it to Bishop Kennally, in Truk.) Kwajalein has a big department store (cutely called Macy's), a branch of the Bank of Hawaii (called Bankoh), and bowling alleys with automatic pinsetters (called Kwajalanes); and it receives so many cargo flights from Hawaii and points east that the commissary usually has a wide selection of fresh fruits and the resident housewives complain if a head of lettuce has a wilted leaf. There is little fresh lettuce in the rest of the Trust Territory. When High Commissioner Goding returned to Saipan from President Johnson's Inauguration, he was considered a very fortunate man because, during a stopover at Hawaii, he had had a chance to pick up a couple of heads of lettuce.

The Trust Territory government has practically nothing to say about what goes on at Kwajalein, though it keeps a liaison officer stationed there, to smooth the passage of its transients. Micronesians, however, have derived a good many economic benefits from the existence of the missile center. Next to the Trust Territory administration itself, the Test Site is the largest single employer of native labor. It has nearly seven hundred Micronesians on its payroll, and they receive annually something over three quarters of a million dollars in wages. The figure is closer to a million if one adds the pay of the Marshallese women who work as domestics for the Americans. They used to get a dollar a day but, the laws of supply and demand having begun to operate, some of them have lately been asking, and getting, seven dollars a day—which makes them mighty rich Micronesians.

None of the Marshallese who work on the test-site island, however, are allowed to live there. They live on Ebeye, a neighboring island of the Kwajalein atoll, and are ferried to and from their jobs by boat. Until very recently, Ebeye was a slum—a dingy agglomeration of shanties, with a few rundown stores scattered among them. (One of these began, elementally enough, when the proprietor scrounged a single can of ice-cream mix from the Navy. He peddled the ice cream he made from it at a Marshallese dance, and with the proceeds set up shop.) As the armed forces have felt compelled to evacuate natives from parts of the Kwajalein atoll that they coveted for building sites or that they feared might be struck by debris, Ebeye has become increasingly crowded. At the end of the war it had three hundred inhabitants. Now it has more than thirty-four hundred, making it the fourth most populous community anywhere in the entire Trust Territory. From the start of its postwar status as a dormitory for Kwajalein employees, it has had poor sanitation and water supply, and in the last four years it has thrice been hit by epidemics. There was one of gastroenteritis, and one of influenza, and the worst of all was one of poliomyelitis that struck early in 1963. Before it had run its crippling course, the epidemic had spread from Ebeye throughout the Marshalls, afflicting one hundred and ninety-six people. There were eleven deaths.

President Kennedy, who kept remarkably well-informed on Micronesian affairs, heard about this and, boiling mad, called in Secretary Udall. The President wanted to know why people under the aegis of the American eagle had to live so meanly, and whether the Interior Department condoned a double standard for Americans and non-Americans. It had been Interior's policy from the start that, however much it subsidized the Micronesian economy, it was not responsible for providing housing for natives in their own habitat. Here, however, was a different situation, where indigenes had been shunted from their own part of an atoll to another part.

When, soon after the polio outbreak, Defense wanted to relocate still another three hundred and seventy-two Marshallese to Ebeye, Interior, which had already absorbed a good many cutting remarks about the slum from United Nations critics, balked. It declared that no more natives could be moved there until some decent shelter could be provided, and it added that its appropriations for the Trust Territory didn't allow for housing funds. Defense said the Marshallese *had* to move, or it couldn't conduct some missile tests it had coming up. Interior reported that in that case Defense could foot the bill for some suitable accommodations. Defense accused Interior of blackmail. Interior stood firm. Defense capitulated, and asked Congress (Defense can usually ask Congress for things that Interior feels it can't) to augment its annual budget by one hundredth of one percent and give it an additional five million dollars. Congress was agreeable.

Now Ebeye has some new facilities—community sewers and toilets, and some apartment buildings, each containing four twenty-by-thirty-foot homes (designed to house ten people), with concrete floors, partitions, and electrical outlets. Even so, one of High Commissioner Goding's last executive orders, issued late in March, 1966, was to the effect that no more permanent residents were to be admitted to Ebeye, since the place had become intolerably overcrowded. There has been no further outbreak of polio, and the Trust Territory has a full-time physical therapist on its staff—her salary comes to one twentieth of one percent of *its* budget—who is trying to rehabilitate the Marshallese children, most of them originally from Ebeye, who are maimed from the disease.

The Kwajalein atoll belongs to one of two more or less parallel chains of islands, running more or less north and south, that constitute the Marshalls. The western chain is known as Ralik, the Marshallese word for sunset, and the eastern chain as Ratak, Marshallese for sunrise. In Ralik and Ratak together there are eleven hundred islands, but *they* all together amount to just seventy-four square miles of land, scattered over one hundred and eighty thousand square miles of water. A school administrator in the Marshalls estimated recently that if he wanted to make an inspection of every educational installation in that sprawling district, and if he stuck to the regular transportation schedule of the boats that link these fragments of coral to one another, it would take him seven years.

The Marshall Islands sometimes seem disconcertingly small to a visitor. Some of the larger ones are no more than fifty yards wide, with a broad lagoon on one side and the boundless ocean on the other. Marshallese are, by and large, unargumentative, though they have occasional flare-ups; they have learned over hundreds of years that people living in confined areas can best get along with their neighbors if they talk out their problems. Moreover, they are fond of talking per se. They love to prolong debates. To terminate one would be to abandon the delightful uncertainty of irresolution. When a controversy arises, they will fondle and pinch both sides of an argument endlessly, like a woman shopping for papayas. (The only thing they are in a hurry about are funerals. Many of them believe that if a grave that has been dug remains unoccupied after nightfall, the empty grave will reach out and grab a passerby to fill it. There was consternation not long ago when some Americans tried to defer the burial of a man who'd been run over while sleeping on a road, and for whom funeral arrangements were well under way, because his wife was in a hospital and couldn't be released before morning. Fortunately, another Marshallese died, of natural causes, in time for the grave to be used before dark.) Most low-islanders in Micronesia talk loudly, to outshout the noise of the surf that constantly pounds at their nearby shores. Most Marshallese, contrarily, speak softly; they are sometimes said to undershout the waves. Courtesy and patience rank high among their virtues, along with hardiness, shrewdness, and independence of spirit.

In attending to their internal affairs, Marshallese, like most other Micronesians, rely heavily on the counsel of their hereditary chiefs, the majority of whom accede to power through matrilineal relationships. If a chief's son wants to succeed his father, he must marry his father's oldest sister's oldest daughter. Land is matrilineally inherited, except on a couple of atolls, where patrilineal connections are what count, as they do in the Yap district and certain parts of Ponape. If a Marshallese from the patrilineal atoll of Likiep marries a girl from the matrilineal atoll of Ailinglapalap, both the bridegroom and bride can expect to become landowners; a Likiep girl, on the other hand, who marries outside her atoll has slim prospects. A Marshallese chief is called an *iroij*, and *iroij* are abundant. One atoll with a population of six hundred and twelve has five of them. Since the Second World War, the *iroij* have sometimes been known, in English-speaking circles, as "kings." The American Navy began calling them that; it sounded good and made the Marshalls seem more romantic. Some *iroij* began to claim regal prerogatives, inasmuch as white men had invested them with royal rank and as white men always know best.

The administrative center for the Marshall Islands district is in the Ratak chain of islands, on the atoll of Majuro, which Robert Louis Stevenson described as "the pearl of the Pacific." Compared to Kwajalein, Majuro is a puny pearl; it consists of a mere sixty islets, and the lagoon that these encircle covers only one hundred and fourteen square miles of water. Until he was transferred recently to the Mariana Islands, the district administrator for the Marshalls was a Polynesian-American, Peter T. Coleman. He was born in 1919 at Pago Pago, the capital of Samoa; his mother was a Samoan and his father an Irish-American sailor who settled there. Marshallese, like other Micronesians, go in for large families and aspire to higher education. Coleman was their kind of man. Not only was he an authentic Pacific islander, but he had thirteen children, twelve of whom were living, and he was the first Samoan who ever earned a law degree. He got it from Georgetown University, in Washington, D.C. He helped pay his way through law school by working a night shift as a Capitol Hill policeman. Later he became the first native-born governor of American Samoa, a job he held until he was assigned in 1961 to Majuro.

In Samoa, Coleman became celebrated for initiating a plan that brought that area an airport capable of handling jets. At Majuro, he built a road. In the Japanese Period, Micronesia had a lot of paved roads, but most of these have badly deteriorated. Americans who never get seasick or airsick have felt queasy riding over a main road of the Truk district center. (Three years ago, in a report about that district to Trust Territory headquarters, the Truk administrator said, "Road plans for Dublon, Fefan, Uman, Tol, Udot, and other large islands are presently in the planning stages." The plans are still being planned; if Interior's latest plan is approved as presented, more than ten million dollars will be spent by 1972 on road improvements.) An American who returned to Koror after a five-year absence was saddened to perceive that road conditions there had not materially improved. "I drove down a back road and at a certain point I knew a bad hole would be there," he said, "and I slowed down and it was."

Saipan has some fairly decent roads, but they are a wartime legacy and, the story goes, an accidental one at that. Old Micronesian hands assert that in 1944, when the United States was constructing air strips on Saipan, a good deal more surfacing material arrived than was necessary, owing to someone's inadvertently having added an extra zero to a figure on a requisition. In an effort to use up some of the tenfold surplus, paved highways were built all over the island.

Shortly after Coleman arrived in the Marshalls, he became aware that the residents of an island called Laura, the most outlying one of the Majuro atoll group, and an island of uncommon fertility, were morose. They were having trouble getting their copra and other produce by boat to the district center, where they could sell it, because of the high winds that roiled the lagoon waters. By putting in a few causeways, Coleman reckoned, he could connect Laura to the district center by a curving road, thirty-two miles long. It was a bold concept, for some of the stretches of reef the road would have to traverse were so narrow the highway would have to be practically in the ocean. On an exploratory survey of one stretch of the proposed route, where a causeway nearly two miles long was required, Coleman and several strong-backed Micronesians bounced out along a reef in a pickup truck. When the tide came in unexpectedly fast, and the truck could no longer carry them, they picked it up and carried it.

The road was begun in October, 1961, and was finished in seven months, with the enthusiastic cooperation of the local Marshallese, who provided most of the necessary funds and all of the manual labor. Some of the residents of Laura said afterward that the new road was the first practical thing they'd received during the American Period. Almost at once their spirits perked up, and so did their copra production. Coleman was so pleased with this combination road-and-morale-building operation that he subsequently had an eighteen-mile road put in for the inhabitants of the island of Jaluit, who had been down in the dumps ever since they were devastatingly struck by a typhoon in 1958.

When Coleman first went to Majuro, his car was the only one at district headquarters. By the end of 1964, there were so many cars around that he had to institute a reserved-parking system so he could be sure of finding a place to put his vehicle. Majuro has a population of less than four thousand, but it already has more than two hundred cars. Most of them are Datsuns, the Japanese counterpart of the Volkswagen. The Marshall Islands Import-Export Company, called Mieco for short, once sold thirty-nine of these during a two-and-a-half-month period, even though there was then not a single service station in the area. (Owners got their gas and had their flats fixed at the public-works garage.) All Micronesians are becoming car-conscious. The principal native chief on Yap has a car and a chauffeur, not so much for prestige as because the chief couldn't pass a driving test. Yap now has a service station, a high testimonial to the rate of progress in that district—of a certain kind, for as late as the fall of 1964, when an American woman asked two Yapese employees of the public-works department there to do a grease job on her car while she was shopping, she found, on returning, that they had industriously smeared grease over its entire exterior.

7.

Wards vs. Guardians

To PROTECT MICRONESIANS AGAINST THE POSSIBILITY of losing their most permanent and most precious asset—their land—the United States decreed from the start that non-Micronesians could not own property within the Trust Territory. The United States government, which was aware that it might have to acquire land for its administrative and strategic installations within the area, did so by long-term leases. Back in the Navy era, the American Congress appropriated over a million and a half dollars for obtaining suitable land. Some of the negotiations that ensued were exceedingly complicated, because the owners would sometimes turn out to be not individuals but whole clans or villages.

In 1960, for instance, the United States needed some sixty acres for a Coast Guard station in the Ulithi atoll of the Yap district. The Trust Territory administration was to lease the land on an indefinite-use basis and sublet it to the Coast Guard. One hundred and sixty-nine separate parcels of property were involved. The owners insisted on being paid in cash, and they stipulated further that they wanted several hundred dollars in coins and the rest in bills of no denomination larger than twenty dollars. There are no banks on Ulithi, or, for that matter, anywhere in the Yap district. So during four days of haggling over details the Trust Territory's negotiator, Attorney General Robert K. Shoecraft, a Negro lawyer from Xenia, Ohio, walked around with a suitcase containing $19,939.28. At night he used it for a pillow.

The ownership and occupancy of land is of paramount concern to all Micronesians. For the last couple of years there has been considerable grumbling in Palau as to just who has rights to just what. The confusion can be traced back to the mid-nineteen-twenties, when the Japanese civilian administration superseded the Japanese Navy. The civilians undertook a survey of all Palauan property, but the Palauans didn't take it seriously, because there was plenty of land to go around. When the Japanese gave them concrete markers to set out at boundary lines, the Palauans didn't feel like carrying them far, because they were heavy. So they merely dropped them helter-skelter.

In 1938, the Japanese began another survey, which the United States has since taken seriously, and has in fact accepted as the principal authority on landholdings. That survey took three years to finish, but then the war came along, and nearly all the pertinent records were lost or destroyed. One consequence has been that some two-thirds of the land in Koror is now judged to be public land, and to be available for homesteading. The Palauans who insist that that land belongs to them were given a chance to prove their ownership, and the principal chief of Koror made two trips to Japan, in 1963, vainly hoping he could find some records there. He returned empty-handed.

Some of the property in dispute contains rocks and platforms denoting burial plots. These are sacred spots to many Palauans, especially the older women, who are determined not to yield them up. A few dowagers who could scarcely walk have hobbled on canes to the district administrator's office to let him know their feelings, and some of them have announced that although the time has long since passed when they should have died, they haven't the slightest intention of departing this earth until they obtain redress of their grievances and assurance that their great-grandchildren can continue to live where their ancestors are interred. The Palauan women, and the more articulate of their menfolk, have been so militant that the American authorities have for the time being prudently stopped talking about homesteading in Koror.

The Marshallese, not having much land, are all the more possessive of what they do have. They have a complex system of ownership, with as many as four strata of titleholders—from the loftiest *iroij* down to the lowliest commoner—sharing in a single lot, this being a *wato*, a slice of land one to five acres in size that usually runs from the lagoon side of an island to the ocean side. Most Marshallese chiefs do not rule over groups of people but over groups of *watos*. Each *wato* has a distinctive name, which the land bears no matter who owns it. Marshallese who possess several *watos* may be subservient to several chiefs. And a man who is a chief in one region may be a commoner on another chief's land. Although the Marshallese will now give away land freely for some such community purpose as a school, in the not too distant past they would often fight for land and kill for it. They do not ordinarily abandon it without the stiffest resistance, but when the United States took over Micronesia it found them compliant, if not exactly enthusiastic, about its determination to evacuate a couple of atolls for nuclear tests.

These were Bikini and Eniwetok, at the northern end of the Ralik chain. From an American viewpoint, their selection was sensible. There were not very many places on earth available to us with a minimum of inhabitants in a maximum of space, and Bikini and Eniwetok together had a population of only three hundred and twelve. The natives were promised new lands to live on, and were reimbursed for their home islands at what seemed a reasonable enough price. The one hundred and sixty-six Bikinians got twenty-five thousand dollars in cash and a three-hundred-thousand-dollar trust fund. The one hundred and forty-six Eniwetokese, who had less land, got the same lump sum and a one-hundred-and-fifty-thousand-dollar trust fund. The Eniwetokese were moved in 1947 to an atoll called Ujelang, where they have remained ever since. Now there are more than three hundred of them, and altogether they have an income of five thousand dollars a year from their trust fund, which, like all Trust Territory trust funds, is administered for them by the High Commissioner, who receives no extra pay for this fiduciary task.

The Bikinians made more money on the deal, but they also encountered far more trouble. They migrated at first to the atoll of Rongerik, which was not far away and was uninhabited. Rongerik had been shunned because many Marshallese have long believed it to be accursed. It has undesirable historical associations with a certain Libokra, a bygone witch who, as legend has it, stole Rongerik from its original location and hid it at its present site. (All Micronesian islands being comparatively small, there are many yarns in the region about supernatural beings who are supposed to have shifted islands from place to place. Some of these stories may have been originated by embarrassed navigators who couldn't find islands they were seeking in the hugeness of the ocean.) Libokra was said to have had a fancy for poisons, too. She allegedly stunted the Rongerik coconut trees, rendered the fruits of many of its pandanus trees inedible, and contaminated the reef fish in its lagoon. At her death, her body was thrown to those fish, who ate her and became all the more unsavory themselves. It was no surprise to the exiles from Bikini, accordingly, that upon trying to settle at Rongerik and to live off the produce of its blighted land and waters, they nearly starved to death.

They stuck it out for a few months, and then asked to be resettled. For a while they occupied a makeshift tent camp at Kwajalein. Thence they were moved to Kili, an unpopulated island in the southern Marshalls. For atoll people, it was an environmental wrench. At Bikini, they had had thirty-six islands with a total area of 2.32 square miles, and what was equally important, a lagoon of 229.4 square miles. Kili is a single island in the middle of the ocean. Lagoonless, it measures only .36 of a square mile. To help the exiles get to the nearest populated place, Jaluit, thirty-five miles away, the Navy gave them a forty-foot motor launch, but this shortly capsized and was wrecked.

Now there are nearly three hundred Bikini people on Kili, and for at least four months out of every year, when the trade winds blow strong, and the waves rise high, they are inaccessible to the rest of the world. They have enough money—in addition to the nearly ten thousand dollars they get from their trust fund, they made nearly three thousand dollars in 1964 from copra sales and another six hundred and twenty-five from sales of handicrafts—and they have enough food, but they still yearn to return to Bikini. That atoll is no longer oppressively radioactive, and the Trust Territory administration has lately been sending crews in to dismantle some of the buildings there and at Eniwetok and has been using the materials for schools and other structures, among them a rehabilitation center at Majuro for victims of the 1963 polio outbreak. But the shellfish and reef fish off Bikini are still radioactive, and the vegetation has not yet been given a completely clean bill of health.

Nonetheless, the Bikini people—including some who were born after the evacuation—want to go back to their homeland. They feel uneasy and lonely at Kili, and have shown their disaffection in a fashion quite uncommon for the usually mild-mannered Marshallese. Not long ago, when the trade winds themselves were mild, a field-trip ship dropped anchor off Kili, to take on copra the islanders had made and to sell them rice, sugar, dried milk, and other staples they couldn't grow. But then, with the loading and unloading still incomplete, the weather turned nasty, and the captain of the big boat had to decide whether to endanger it by staying near shore overnight or to pull away. He decided, reluctantly, to leave. When the Bikini folk heard of this, some of them paddled out, climbed aboard, and refused to budge. It was Micronesia's first sit-in, and it was successful. The ship stayed until all the trading was finished.

When it came to reimbursing the Marshallese who owned six

hundred and eighty-two acres on Kwajalein that had been taken over for the missile test site, as well as sixty-eight acres that the Trust Territory government was using on Majuro, mostly for an air strip, headquarters officials on Saipan found themselves at an impasse. The natives had meekly enough yielded up their land, but they had strong views about how much they should be paid for this dislocation, and in customary unhurried Marshallese fashion were quite willing to discuss the matter for years rather than accept a quick cash settlement.

The principal landowner on Kwajalein was an *iroij laplap* (the most eminent kind of *iroij*), now seventy-three, named Lejolan Kabua. He can trace his regental ancestry back, in all-important matrilineal fashion, to a sister of Larkelon of Wotje, a famous Marshallese mariner and warrior whose armada of canoes conquered Bikini in the early nineteenth century. In the negotiations with the American authorities over the value of these seven hundred and fifty acres, the principal Marshallese spokesman was Lejolan Kabua's son Amata, a Majuro businessman and politician, born in 1928, who in a society where a small new Datsun cheaply imported from Japan is a status symbol, drives a largish new Rambler expensively imported from the States. Amata Kabua is, among other things, chairman of the Ways and Means Committee of the upper house of the Congress of Micronesia and president of the Marshall Islands Import-Export Company, one of the most thriving enterprises owned and operated by Micronesians. He has chiefly blood on both sides of his family; his mother was a *leroij*, the female equivalent of an *iroij*. A rival businessman once struck Amata Kabua with his fist; the rival was finished commercially then and there, because in the Marshalls one does not lightly smite a scion of sovereigns.

In December, 1953, when he was twenty-three, Amata Kabua —who is widely traveled, having by now been to Tokyo, New York, and the Gilbert Islands—was in Hawaii, studying for an Associate in Arts degree at a junior college. Eight years had then passed since the conversion of Kwajalein into a test site for missiles—missiles that, reflective Micronesians like Kabua were wont to point out, were not being perfected to protect *them* against anything but to protect the continental United States—and there had been little headway made in agreeing on recompense for the expropriated acreage. Kabua thought the time had come for him and his fellow Marshallese to get outside help. Specifically, they wanted a lawyer, and there was then no indigenous lawyer in all of Micronesia. (Now there is one.)

In Honolulu, Kabua met an attorney named E. E. Wiles, who has since moved to Washington as a legislative assistant to a Congressman from Hawaii, Spark Matsunaga. Trained by the Navy, during the war, as a Japanese-language officer, Wiles was married to a Nisei and felt sympathetic to Micronesians. Wiles agreed to help press the Marshallese cause in Washington. Wiles was subsequently to observe to the Department of the Interior that it seemed a shame that although a war had been fought in the Marshall Islands nobody in Washington had ever proposed a Marshall Plan for the Marshalls.

Wiles was from Macksville, Kansas, and he didn't then have many Washington connections. He happened upon some when another Macksville-born attorney passed through Honolulu. This was Paul C. Aiken, who knew Washington well, having been an assistant postmaster general under President Truman and having later gone into private practice there. Wiles and Aiken—with the help of still another Washington lawyer, Turner Smith—took on the Marshallese case, without any retainer and without any inkling at the start that it might drag on, as it did, for more than ten years. The delay was by no means the fault alone of the United States government. There would be stretches of months, because of the tortoise-like pace at which Marshallese customarily move, before the Washington lawyers would get an answer to an urgent letter they dispatched to their clients in Majuro.

Up to 1953, no Micronesian land had ever been sold for more than three hundred and fifty dollars an acre, and this was an exceptionally high price; the going valuation for desirable land was closer to one hundred dollars an acre. The Trust Territory administration, trying to arrive at fair compensation for the seven hundred and fifty acres in the Marshalls, decided that two hundred and fifty dollars an acre—not for outright purchase but for "indefinite use," which the Navy insisted on as far as Kwajalein was concerned—was what the land was worth. It then doubled its own figure and offered the Marshallese five hundred an acre.

Amata Kabua countered with a demand for a thousand an acre, plus enough interest for back use to bring the total to fifteen hundred. (His figure was later eclipsed by his lawyers' contention that Marshallese land was worth $6,240 an acre, like parts of Westchester.) Kabua and the other Marshallese didn't like the idea of indefinite use, either. They wanted to be satisfied that their descendants would get their ancestors' land back at some specific time. Neither side would budge. By the spring of 1957, though, the High Commissioner's office thought a cash-on-the-barrelhead approach might clear up the disposition of six hundred of the acres in contention. A meeting of the disputants was arranged at Kwajalein, and a headquarters representative put three hundred thousand dollars in bills on the top of a table. It was a whopping sum for that part of the world, and not bad anywhere, but Amata Kabua and his fellow Marshallese merely looked at it and then walked out of the room.

Back on March 1, 1954, not long after Kabua met Wiles in Honolulu, the United States had set off an experimental thermonuclear weapon at Bikini. Two days later, the eighty-six inhabitants of the Marshallese atoll of Rongelap, nearly one hundred miles east of Bikini, were exposed to radioactive fallout. Some suffered skin burns, some soon lost their hair, some fell prey to intestinal disorders. There were no fatalities, but there was much embarrassment. The Atomic Energy Commission hustled all the Rongelapese off to Kwajalein for extensive medical tests, and the A.E.C. has been reexamining them ever since, and comparing them to a control group of Marshallese who were not exposed. After twelve years, the only discernible differences between the two groups seemed to be that the physical growth rate of Rongelapese boys was a mite slower, and that several Rongelapese girls required surgery for thyroid nodules—all of these, however, turning out to be benign. Thirteen of the afflicted Rongelapese have died since 1954, but there is no reason to believe they have not died from natural causes.

Beyond keeping careful tabs on their health, the United States has tried to make amends to the Rongelapese by giving them building materials, tools, and livestock, but the islanders have nonetheless complained of general malaise. When they learned that the twenty-three-man crew of a Japanese tuna-fishing boat that strayed into the fallout path of an American nuclear test in 1954 had been awarded two million dollars by the United States government for their pains, the Rongelapese thought that *they*, as wards of the United States government, deserved no less substantial reparations, and they sought legal help. Since there were already American lawyers representing Marshallese in the land dispute, it was logical enough that the Rongelapese should engage the same counsel.

The plaintiffs began by filing suit against the United States in the High Court of the Trust Territory, Micronesia's supreme judicial forum. Because the Japanese fishermen had received approximately one hundred thousand dollars apiece, the eighty-six Rongelapese asked for eight and a half million. The Chief Justice of the Trust Territory ruled that the High Court didn't have jurisdiction, on the ground that the United States was immune from suit unless it gave its consent, which it hadn't, or unless Congress passed an act permitting such litigation. Congress, of course, also had the authority to pass an act awarding the Rongelapese reparations, but Congress appeared to feel no sense of urgency in the matter. By 1964, a decade after the fallout, the U.N. delegation that visited Micronesia was reporting, "The Mission realizes that the United States Congress has much business to accomplish but the people of Rongelap, who live on a level of bare subsistence, have been waiting for ten years for justice from the great and rich country which holds the trusteeship for their welfare and caused them (admittedly by mischance) grievous injury. The Mission found that though the people of Rongelap were impatient over the non-settlement of their claim they accepted in generous spirit the assurance of the Administering Authority that Congressional action would soon be completed. It is to be hoped that this generous trust will prove justified."

At the end of its 1964 session, Congress finally passed a bill authorizing the payment to the aggrieved people of Rongelap of nine hundred and fifty thousand dollars, and the following April it actually appropriated the money—just before a U.N. Trusteeship Council meeting at which there would undoubtedly have been questions asked of the American delegation if Congress had waited any longer. Eight months after that, eighty-six Rongelapese—some of them by that time heirs of the original sufferers—received $10,494 apiece.

Many Marshallese were enraged by the Rongelap incident. (It caused so much flap everywhere, especially in the United Nations, that Adlai Stevenson persuaded President Kennedy to direct, even before the 1962 test-ban treaty was signed, that no further nuclear explosions would be conducted in Micronesia.) One of the most articulate Marshallese who got worked up about it was Dwight Heine. Born in 1919, Heine was considered as long ago as 1949 to be an eminent Micronesian, and in some Trust Territory circles he is currently considered the pre-eminent one. He was one of the first two Micronesians to graduate from a four-year college, in his case the University of Hawaii. He was the first president of the Marshall Islands Congress. He was the first president of the Council of Micronesia. He was elected the first Speaker of the General Assembly of the Congress of Micronesia. He had hardly achieved that high honor when he was obliged to resign from the legislature because an even higher one was conferred on him: he was appointed district administrator for the Marshall Islands—the first Micronesian ever to attain such lofty stature.

Heine is of German-Marshallese descent, and has heard that he is distantly related to the poet. His great-grandfather, a jeweler in Danzig, migrated to California during the 1849 gold rush and then went on to Australia, where he married an English girl.

When his wife was ostracized for making so alien a match, the couple moved to the more tolerant Marshall Islands. Heine's son became a Protestant missionary and a teacher. *His* son—Dwight's father—pursued the same career. Both missionaries, along with Dwight's Marshallese mother, were beheaded by the Japanese during the Second World War for refusing to swear allegiance to Emperor Hirohito.

Dwight Heine escaped; he had been impressed by the Japanese into a labor battalion that was digging phosphate on another island. Toward the end of the war, being one of the few Marshallese who knew English, he became an interpreter for the American Navy. In 1944, with a half-brother, he compiled the first Marshallese-English dictionary. In 1948, when he was twenty-nine and supervisor of elementary schools in the Marshalls, he had a chance to start his own higher education when the Navy gave him a two-year scholarship to the University of Hawaii. He had hoped to go into business or law, but at that time the United States was primarily concerned with teaching Micronesians to teach other Micronesians, so scholarships were granted only in the field of education. Heine was a guinea pig. When he got to Honolulu, a four-star admiral told him that if he failed his courses there would be no more scholarships offered to any Micronesians. Heine met this challenge successfully, and after two years he returned to Majuro. In 1955 he was made educational supervisor for the entire Marshall Islands district. In 1957, he finally got a chance to complete his college studies, returning to Honolulu and getting a B.A. in 1959, when he was forty.

Meanwhile, Heine had started to raise a family. In Micronesian fashion, he has nine children. (Amata Kabua has seven.) He was also the leader of a group of teachers that organized the Marshall Islands Import-Export Company, but he pulled out after his second trip to Hawaii; in Heine's absence—and before Kabua took over Mieco—the directors elected as their store manager an American of such unbalanced benevolence that his payroll for Micronesian help far exceeded his gross receipts.

While Heine was in Hawaii, in 1958, he ran into some Quakers, who, with their pacifistic leanings, were especially disturbed about the Rongelap fallout incident. Heine was disturbed, too, and with some financial assistance from the Quakers, he went to New York and turned up as a spokesman for the Rongelapese at a meeting of the U.N. Trusteeship Council, to the surprise and irritation of the Trust Territory administration. On returning home, Heine was suspended from his education job for nine months. At a Majuro bar one night, an American who had had a hand in his chastisement accosted him and said sarcastically, "I understand you've become a Quaker." Heine nodded. "Say something in Quaker," said the American. Heine's response was the tag line of a familiar old Quaker joke. "Fuck thee," he said. He got his job back not long afterward.

Dwight Heine and Amata Kabua form the most powerful political one-two punch in Micronesia. Both are Marshallese, but when the Trust Territory-wide Council of Micronesia, to which both were elected, met to choose a president in 1961, both were nominated. They tied, and Heine won the vote-off. At home, they vie for supremacy. While Heine was superintendent of elementary schools for a while, Kabua was superintendent of all schools. Heine was the first president of Mieco, but Kabua, the incumbent president, has made the company a success. (The openhanded manager is no longer on the scene.) As Heine made a personal appearance before the U.N. Trusteeship Council in 1958, so did Kabua in 1960, pleading the cause of the Kwajalein landowners. "We would rather be a suffering creditor than to lose our rights as owners of what has been taken away from us," he declared in a statement prepared for the Council.

He may have had some help in drafting it from one of his Kansas lawyers, because he went on, "These tiny islands . . . are just as important to us as a burrow in the ground to a prairie dog." (There are no prairie dogs in Micronesia; no prairies, either.) Kabua was accompanied to New York by another Marshallese, Jalle Bolkeim, an Ebeye storekeeper who had not long before been elected chief magistrate of Kwajalein, and who at one point in the land controversy wrote a beseeching letter to President

Kennedy, saying, "We are hopeless slaves to conditions we do not like." Such are the vagaries of the relationships of Micronesians to Washingtonians that even though one of Bolkeim's lawyers was a former assistant postmaster general there is some doubt whether the letter ever actually got delivered.

On May 4, 1960, with the United States concurring, the Trusteeship Council unanimously resolved that the Marshallese land claims ought to be settled, and settled soon. By that time, the disagreement had taken a number of twisting turns. At one point, the American authorities suggested to Kabua and his associates that they get rid of their lawyers and intimated that those slick Stateside attorneys would probably take most of any settlement for themselves. The lawyers ultimately agreed to accept as their joint fee ten percent of any sum realized beyond the original five-hundred-dollar-an-acre offer. At another point, the House of Representatives in Washington passed a resolution authorizing the Marshallese to sue the United States government in the Court of Claims, but the Senate never got around to acting on the matter.

It was Robert Shoecraft, the Trust Territory Attorney General, who finally broke the impasse. First he persuaded the Navy to back down on its demand for indefinite use of the land at Kwajalein and to accept instead a ninety-nine-year lease, beginning at the date of any agreement that might be signed. Once that concession had been made, the Marshallese were in a mood to resume bargaining, and they finally agreed to the long-term lease on the basis of five hundred dollars an acre for past use and five hundred more for future use—or double what the Americans had at the start considered double what the land was worth.

On February 5, 1964, at a ceremony in the Kwajalein base chapel, Amata Kabua, his father the *iroij laplap*, and fifty other Marshallese accepted a United States government check for $712,500. (The remaining $37,500 was set aside for their lawyers.) The Marshallese had been offered a trust fund, similar to the funds established for the Bikini and Eniwetok people, but they said they were perfectly capable of handling their own financial affairs—indeed, they had shown themselves to be astute—and would prefer cash. In keeping with the Marshallese tradition of paying tribute to respected senior leaders, Lejolan Kabua and three other high-ranking *iroij* in their delegation were each awarded a thousand dollars before the rest of the money was divided among the individual landowners.

One aftermath of this protracted tussle between wards and guardians revealed that information is now much more swiftly exchanged among the various parts of Micronesia than it ever was before the American Period. Not long after the payoff at Kwajalein, the Trust Territory administration decided to put up a new courthouse at Truk. After picking a likely site, it asked the owners how much they wanted for their property. The answer was a flat one thousand dollars an acre. And a bit later, when the American government sought to lease some land on bulging Ebeye, its Marshallese owners unblinkingly demanded a rental that seemed to fix the value of that particular piece of Micronesian soil at fourteen thousand dollars an acre.

8.

Never the Same Again

THE INHABITANTS OF THE BAHAMA ISLANDS IN THE Atlantic Ocean think they have problems, especially in the fields of health and education. Bahamians like to point out that there are only one hundred and thirty thousand of them, scattered among seven hundred islands that cover seventy thousand square miles of the Atlantic Ocean. It is hard, they say, to meet the needs of so few people so thinly spread. To anyone in Micronesia—with its mere ninety thousand people and its more than two thousand islands covering three million square miles of the Pacific—the Bahamian situation is enviable. Moreover, the Pacific islanders do not, unlike their counterparts across the world, share a common language. Linguists are not in agreement as to how many different languages there are in Micronesia, but the generally accepted minimum number is nine, or one for roughly every ten thousand indigenes.

In the Marshalls, Marshallese is spoken, and in the Marianas, Chamorro. From there on, things start to get complicated. Among the languages that contribute to disputes about the total is a rare one used by the eighty-three inhabitants of Sonsorol and the sixty-six of Tobi, two minute island groups in the Palau district but far off the beaten Palauan track. It has been argued that the Sonsorolese and Tobians don't really have a language at all but merely speak a dialect of Palauan, which is that district's major tongue. Yapese is another major one, and a complex one, with thirteen vowel sounds and thirty-two consonants. The Ulithi and Woleai atolls in the Yap district have their own languages, provided one accepts Woleaian as such and not as a dialect of Ulithian. The speech of the three hundred and twenty-one residents of still another Yap district atoll, Satawal, may also be a separate language, though some assert that it is simply a dialect of Trukese, the main language of Truk.

Not counting Satawalese, there are at least ten distinctive dialects of Trukese, among them Puluwatese, Pulapese, Pulusukese, and Mortlockese. (A number of scholars insist that the tongue of the Mortlock Islands, named for an eighteenth-century explorer, is a bona fide separate language.) In the Ponape district, in addition to Ponapean, there is Kusaiean; and because the Ponapean sector of Micronesia contains the two Polynesian atolls, Nukuoro and Kapingamarangi, there is a language that is used in those places—with considerable dialectical variations between the version in the one and that in the other. And, finally, there are linguists who maintain that the languages spoken in still two more Ponapean island groups, Mokil and Pingelap, are not, as other linguists maintain, mere variations of standard Ponapean, but authentic individualistic tongues called Mokilese and Pingelapese.

Some Micronesians have become remarkably versatile linguists. The Trust Territory headquarters recently compiled biographical summaries of three hundred and twenty-four native leaders. One hundred and fifty-nine of them were credited with a command of both Japanese and English, along with as many as half a dozen indigenous tongues. But these are the elite, and they are far outnumbered by Micronesians who have found it difficult to commune—to attain an internal cohesiveness that a United Nations spokesman has called a "self"—because they can't communicate.

In 1963, the American administrators embarked on an all-out, long-range program to achieve universal comprehension by teaching all Micronesians English—as logical a *lingua franca* as any language the Americans knew. Since then, English has been the language of instruction in Trust Territory schools, beginning with the first grade. A good many Micronesians are sorry that this didn't happen sooner. Living in a region where nature has always been bountiful, they have rarely hungered for food, but they have long felt deprived of education. The Japanese didn't believe in giving their colonial underlings more than rudimentary schooling, and spent four times the money on policemen that they spent on teachers. Between the First and Second World Wars, only a handful of Micronesians went beyond the seventh grade.

Now, the generation that had little learning is eager for its children to have a lot; there is wide concurrence with the sentiments expressed recently by a young Yapese who declared that "the building of knowledge . . . is the most precious element in developing and improving our community." Quite a few older Micronesians, moreover, are trying to retrieve lost opportunities; Truk, for instance, had a thirty-two-year-old man in 1964 who was ploddingly going through school and had reached the ninth grade. In the spring of 1965, the first Trukese ever to graduate from a four-year college received his degree. As Micronesian college graduates go, he was comparatively young, having just turned thirty.

From 1945 to 1964, there were a few American teachers in Micronesia, but by and large the natives were expected to provide their own educational facilities and their own faculties. The Micronesians were as anxious then as they are now to build knowledge, but they had neither the resources nor the manpower to do much about it. Many municipalities allocated ninety percent or more of their skimpy budgets for education. Even so, most of the school buildings were dilapidated and most of the teachers, few of whom had had much schooling themselves, were so inept that, as one visiting U.N. observer put it, "the blind were leading the blind."

Considerably less than half of the Micronesian teachers employed in the public-school system today have had better than a ninth-grade education, and that is the equivalent of perhaps a fifth- or sixth-grade education in a run-of-the-mill American public school. The current demand for native teachers is so much greater than the supply that Micronesians sometimes say it is possible for any one of them to get a teaching job provided he can count to ten and doesn't have a criminal record. In one outlying island group of the Truk district, a fifteen-year-old boy teacher is doing his best to cope with a class containing some students nearly twice his age.

At the other end of that particular spectrum are dozens of middle-aged Micronesians who have been teaching school most of their adult lives but are barely educated themselves and could never hope to complete high school, let alone college. They are not yet replaceable in their jobs, and to enable *them* to cope better with their responsibilities the administration has set up a Micronesian Teacher Educational Center. Of the fifty-nine students who were enrolled there in 1965, eighteen held the title of school principal.

The Trust Territory administration is currently spending six million dollars—approximately one third of *its* budget—on education, with most of this going into an Accelerated Elementary School Program. Nearly twenty-five thousand children are enrolled in schools (five and a half thousand of these in mission schools), and although Micronesians, like other tropical folk, are fairly lax about sticking to schedules and keeping appointments, school attendance has been running at about ninety percent of the maximum. Some children, to be sure, prefer school to home, with its attendant chores; and in some districts parents are liable to a ten-dollar fine for each day a child is truant; but even so the record is impressive.

The enthusiasm for education has been contagious. An hour's ride by motorboat from the big island of Ponape, for instance, is a small island called Parem. About one hundred and twenty-five people live there. Until recently they had never had a school of their own, and few of their children had been to a school of any kind. When they heard that education was being accelerated, they sent a delegation to Kolonia, the capital city of Ponape. They said if the district education office would furnish them a teacher, they would build a school. This arrangement was soon carried out. The school is a modest affair: a one-room, open-sided structure, twelve by twenty-four feet, with coconut-log uprights, a thatch roof, and a dirt floor. The education office provided some nails, a blackboard, and a pencil sharpener. There are eight desks, made of used dunnage supplied by a sympathetic ship captain. Twenty-four children are enrolled, between the ages of seven and thirteen. They are all in the first grade. After a look at the rapidly expanding school system of the Trust Territory, the 1964 United Nations visiting mission reported, "Micronesia can never be the same again."

The American attempt to teach English to Mokilese, Woleaians, Pulusukese, and the rest is all the more challenging because most Micronesian children, however diligently they may study the new common language at school, are unlikely to hear it spoken much at home. And they will get little chance to improve their mastery of English through reading. Books are alien to Micronesian culture. There are Micronesians teaching elementary school today who do not know how to turn the pages of a book. A native teacher from an outlying island in the Yap district not long ago visited its district center. Before he went home, an educational supervisor asked if he'd like to take some books back with him. The teacher thanked him but said that wouldn't be necessary. "I have a book," he explained. Even high-school students who were studying English long before the new language program began are at a reading level far below that of their American counterparts. The most popular works of fiction among the 1965 graduating class at the Ponape district high school were "Tom Sawyer" and "Huckleberry Finn," but since Mark Twain's prose was generally considered beyond the seniors' grasp, most of them were reading simplified versions.

It is sometimes difficult for Americans in the islands to explain to their wards just where Micronesians stand in the world today. The Commissioner's staff librarian was pleased last year to hear about a book called "The Story of the Interior," one of a series written for young teenagers about federal departments in Washington. To the Trust Territory librarian this sounded like an ideal volume for older Micronesian high-school students: it would be comprehensible to most of them and it would at the same time, he surmised, enlighten them about the agency that ran their lives and instruct them how the Trust Territory fitted into Interior's scheme of things.

The librarian was all set to order several dozen copies of the book, but thought he'd better have a look at it first, so he had one copy sent by airmail. When it arrived, he was dismayed. In all its one hundred and seventeen pages there was not a single reference to the Trust Territory, nor even to Interior's Office of Territories. The librarian changed his plans, not wishing to import further evidence of what many Micronesians of all ages and degrees of literacy gloomily suspect: that very few people in the rest of the world, including the omnipotent U.S.A., know much or care much about the existence of their peculiar fiduciary region.

9.

With a Baa Baa Here and a Quack Quack There

BECAUSE SO FEW MICRONESIANS ARE QUALIFIED TO teach in any language, the Trust Territory has been recruiting Americans to implement its accelerated program, and because so few Americans have ever heard about Micronesia, recruitment has been a problem, even though the pay is generous (everybody gets the twenty-percent hardship bonus) and the standards are minimal (a B.A. degree will suffice). Some teachers were obtained when the Department of the Interior got access to the Defense Department lists of applicants for jobs in overseas schools for Army and Air Force dependents, and others from a similar list Interior had in its own Bureau of Indian Affairs.

Beyond that, Trust Territory headquarters at Saipan sent packets of literature to nine hundred American colleges and universities. The literature is remarkably candid, and designedly so. The

Trust Territory's director of education, John R. Trace, an Ohioan who before coming to Micronesia spent three years at American Samoa and five on Guam, has said, "Our basic problem is to exclude those who shouldn't come out." To that end, prospective teachers are warned that they should have "a broader and more flexible mental outlook than is normally expected of teachers in more conventional schools," and that "The Micronesian child has no English inner voice to be cultivated. Before he can read or write, such a voice must be created. . . . Here in Micronesia the matter is further complicated by the fact that English is the only language you will have available for communication with the students, and thus all school work will have to be done in this language so new to them. It is as if a teacher from Latin America were to attempt to teach first graders in Kokomo not only Spanish, but also all subjects to them in Spanish, and to teach them to read and write Spanish instead of English. This sounds like a big order, and it is."

Moreover, prospects are urged to address themselves thoughtfully to questions like "Can you stand being around harmless bugs and lizards?" (The literature adds, "You don't have to like them, and we don't care how much you stomp on or spray them, but you must be able to live where they are.") Prospects are further invited to assess carefully their ability, and that also of all members of their families, to "climb into and out of small outboard motorboats and outrigger canoes when in water as much as waist-deep on the reef or in the surf, and ride up to 30 or 40 miles in such boats in major (deep) lagoons in all kinds of weather. . . . We want no teachers to come into the Territory who do not have a full realization of what they are doing," the Trust Territory's appeal concludes after a long recital of other hazards, inconveniences, and challenges.

"They really lay it on thick with the discouragement angle," one American teaching on an island in the major (deep) Truk lagoon said. "Their idea seems to be to make the teachers say, 'It can't be *that* bad.' " That particular teacher had not long been at his post when he was stricken simultaneously with a virus, amoebic dysentery, sunstroke, and worms. His temperature rose to one hundred and six. He had a radio with which he was supposed to call in to district headquarters—where there is a hospital—in just such emergencies, but he couldn't rouse anyone there. Finally some native neighbors carried him to the hospital by motorboat; there was a chilly breeze over the lagoon, which may have saved his life, for it knocked his temperature down to a hundred and four.

At present, there are one hundred and fifty Americans teaching in Micronesia. They have agreed to stay for at least two years; if they don't, they have to pay their own fare home. Less than half the group that arrived in 1963 signed up for another two years—a rate of turnover not too much more discouraging than that in the American public-school system. The Trust Territory looks with favor on married teachers, who tend to adjust better to a strange environment, and with special favor on teachers whose wives also teach—housing is limited. Domestic spats can be awkward in Micronesia. When an American and his wife formally separated several months ago, there was no place for either of them to move out to, so they went on occupying the same quarters, not to mention sharing the same motor scooter.

A husband and wife who both hold teaching jobs can jointly earn from twelve to fourteen thousand dollars a year, and can save a good deal of it. (Nearly every wife of an American in the Trust Territory has some kind of government job.) There is little to spend money on in Micronesia. Some young teachers embarking on married life and looking for a quick nest egg come to Micronesia in reasonable expectation of being able to return home after their two years with five or six thousand dollars tucked away. There have been enough such couples so far for a categorical name to be applied to them. They are called the mercenaries.

But there have been just as many with loftier motivations, and they, in general, have had a better time of it and have proved to be the better teachers. One twenty-three-year-old single girl from the southwest, while somewhat disappointed to discover that there was only one American bachelor in the district to which she was assigned, was pleased to discover how eager and alert her third-grade students were (they ranged in age from eight to twelve), and was flattered when they took to dropping in at her home after school hours for informal chats. "In the States, I never cared to see my students after school," she said. For some Americans, the excitement of being in an area as special and remote as Micronesia never wears off. One woman school teacher at Truk exclaimed, as she was about to renew her contract, "This place is as fascinating today as it was the day I stepped off the plane," and a male teacher there, having occasion to set down some of his impressions for the weekly district newspaper, described Truk unequivocally as "Heaven on Earth."

The working day in Micronesia runs from seven-thirty in the morning until four-thirty in the afternoon, when the bars open. Some Americans out there tend to segregate themselves, after hours, from the native community, and it is somewhat difficult, as a matter of fact, for an American to immerse himself in Micronesian life even if he wants to. Micronesians hardly ever entertain outsiders at their homes. An American teaching in Koror had some Palauans at *his* home, and when he thought a feeling of camaraderie had been attained, asked his guests why it was they never invited him back. There was an embarrassed silence. Finally one Palauan spoke up. He said that he didn't think Americans were really interested in going to Palauans' homes and sitting uncomfortably on the floor. What was more, he went on, it is the Palauan nature to be highly competitive in all social matters; it is important for one man to try to outdo another, and how could a poor Palauan ever hope to outdo a rich American?

The American host was persistent. "What would happen if I just dropped in at your house sometime?" he asked.

"Oh, we'd be busy," the Palauan said.

Most of the elementary-school classrooms over which the mercenaries, and non-mercenaries, preside are cement-block boxes, thirty feet square, usually put up in clusters of seven or eight. The first new school of this type was finished at Kayangel, one of the northernmost of the Palauan islands, which also holds the distinction—a rare and envied one in Micronesia—of never having been hit by a typhoon. Its residents know why: their chief has a sacred paddle, and every time a typhoon draws near, the chief's son circumambulates their island, flourishing the paddle, and scares the storm away.

The Kayangel school was completed nine days after President Kennedy's assassination and was at once named after him. Inasmuch as there are few Micronesians skilled at masonry and carpentry, a good many Filipino contract workers have had to be brought to most of the islands to put up the new schools. Palauans, though, pride themselves not only on their social competitiveness but on their aggressive approach to all aspects of life. They built a good many of their schools without outside help. On one Palauan island, where there seemed to be no suitable spot for a school, two hundred and fifty men, women, and children swiftly contrived one by filling in a swamp with stones that they carried to the spot by hand. The Palauans worked so hard and so briskly on the accelerated construction program that, to keep the residents of other districts from feeling self-conscious about their own comparative pokiness, there was talk in administrative circles of decelerating the acceleration. At the dedication of one of the fastest-finished buildings, the Palauans present tearfully thanked the administration for having done what they in fact had largely done themselves.

Being made of cement blocks, the new schools are termite-proof and typhoon-resistant, but they are aesthetically drab and so austere that in the United States they would be unacceptable. There are no teachers' lounges or offices, and the storerooms were designed—presumably to foil pilferers—without any windows. As a result, books and other equipment locked up in them rapidly succumb to mildew. Each school has a flagpole, but few have electricity. Only one, in Koror, has plumbing. The rest have been built without running water or indoor toilets on the theory that what native children don't enjoy at home they won't miss at school. The Koror establishment attained its special state of hygienic grace because the local American public-works officer had two children enrolled in it.

This school is named after another American once stationed in Koror, George B. Harris, Jr., who was killed in a plane crash in 1960. The reading of his will disclosed that he had left a two-thousand-dollar bequest to the children of Palau. The site of the Harris School used to be occupied by a concrete Japanese pillbox. It was too massive to destroy, so when foundations for the new structure were being dug, a bulldozer clawed a big pit into the ground and the Japanese pillbox was buried beneath the American school. What a field day some future archaeologists may have!

Americans who have brought their families to Micronesia often find it difficult to decide what to do about *their* children's schooling. The older ones usually go to boarding schools in the Philippines, Hawaii, or the continental United States, while the younger ones get bored to death, being far ahead, academically, of their Micronesian peers. In a couple of districts, special schools have been set up for Americans. This has led, inevitably, to charges of segregation. The Ponape district has a school, called the New Frontier, which is attended by American children and a few gifted Micronesians. In 1964, an American who had settled permanently in Micronesia—he ran a bar and is married to a Ponapean—became dissatisfied with a mission school his children were attending and enrolled them in public school. Being American citizens, they were assigned to the New Frontier, where they had a terrible time of it because, having been raised according to their mother's native ways, they spoke no English. If the accelerated program works, these young Americans should some day soon be able to communicate with the rest of the world as glibly as any Micronesians.

Whatever defects or lack of creature comforts the new schools may appear to outsiders to have, to many Micronesians they are unimaginably splendid. Not long ago, a thirty-year-old Ponapean stopped to gaze at one building that had just been put into use. He reflected about his own elementary education, given by an aged Spanish brother at a mission school, who taught him catechism in the morning and in the afternoon, while the boy sat on a cold cement floor in a somber Japanese building, taught him his ABC's, purportedly in English. "It was only after I grew up that I realized the brother couldn't speak English," the Ponapean said. "I can't pass one of these new schools without thinking, If only I could have gone to a school like this!"

As it happened, the school he was admiring also had a cement floor, and, because its furniture had not yet materialized, the children were sitting on the floor, some of them on mats they'd brought from home and some on pieces of cardboard torn from cartons. The furniture hadn't been delivered because when the building program was inaugurated, the Trust Territory administration, hoping to stimulate the regional economy, had invited Micronesians to bid on furniture-making contracts. There were two successful bids, one from Saipan and one from Palau. The Saipanese company subsequently had a change of heart and subcontracted its order to a firm on Taiwan. When the Chinese-made furniture finally arrived, it came in unassembled parts, and somebody had neglected to send along the hardware to bind it together.

The Palauans did a little better, but not without first giving the entire Trust Territory a fright. Half the coconut trees in Palau have been destroyed, in recent years, by rhinoceros beetles. They are formidable insects. A single beetle can swiftly kill a single tree, and they breed equally fast. This scourge had been confined to the Palau district, where an insect called the assassin bug had been imported to give it battle. In November, 1964, when a carton of Palauan furniture was unpacked at Majuro, in the Marshall Islands, twenty-seven hundred miles away, a live rhinoceros beetle was spotted clinging to a chair. The Marshalls produce more coconuts than any other part of Micronesia; if their islands ever became infested with the beetles, their straits would be dire indeed. The invader was summarily dispatched, and for weeks the Marshallese waited apprehensively for further evidence of the dread species. To their unbounded relief, subsequent deliveries of desks and chairs proved beetle-free.

Most school systems consider themselves well set up once they have enough teachers and classrooms to handle their enrollments. But in Micronesia, there are further essential considerations. "The big thing here is to get the teacher's house ready before the teacher arrives," one Trust Territory administrator said. Micronesia has relatively few homes in which westerners can live decently, and a concomitant of all the flurry of school-building, accordingly, had to be a flurry of house-building. By now, more than one hundred homes, either two- or three-bedroom affairs (with plumbing)—also fashioned out of the cement block that is rapidly becoming an American hallmark of this part of Oceania—have been constructed.

When the first batch of accelerated-program teachers turned up in the fall of 1963, however, accommodations were scanty. Some of them had to live in thatched huts until their more permanent quarters were done. Some moved into unoccupied classrooms, which, measuring nine hundred square feet, could with improvised partitioning be transformed into adequate, if makeshift, residences. Some moved into whatever buildings were empty and had reasonably leak-proof roofs. On Angaur, one young American couple from Connecticut, with two small children, was billeted in a vacant house the Japanese had put up before the war. Not long after they moved in, forty-six of the fifty-seven houses on the island were leveled by a typhoon. At the start of the storm, fifty or so Palauans came running to the Americans' home and asked to share their bomb shelter. They hadn't even known they'd had one; they had stored some canned goods on top of a small hatch that led to a two-and-a-half-foot-high basement the Japanese had constructed. The food was hastily removed, and the teachers and their children and their fifty neighbors crawled down into the cellar and squatted there for eight hours until the danger had passed.

Quite apart from the living, the teaching is not easy. Even experienced teachers find it difficult to instruct in what is for their students a second language. In the Trust Territory, the teachers mostly follow guidelines established by Dr. Charles C. Fries, who has written a number of books and manuals on the techniques of teaching English to Spanish-speaking Puerto Ricans being assimilated into continental United States life. Two Trust Territory American teachers—they have already expressed an intention to return to Micronesia—are at present taking graduate courses at Columbia and the University of Michigan in the philosophy and methodology of teaching English as a foreign language. At Trust Territory headquarters, more manuals on this tricky business are being turned out by an educational staff man named Gregory J. Trifonovitch, who has an apt background for the job; born in Palestine of Russian parents, he didn't speak any English himself until he came to the United States as an adult.

A good deal of the instruction is done by rote, which, however dreary it may sound to a passing observer, is what the Fries method advocates. "As nearly as we can tell today," Trifonovitch's major manual asserts, "memorization seems to be *the* way in which the raw materials of the new language can be fed into the nervous system of the learner in a form that we can begin analysis of them subconsciously—or, if you will, the way in which they are best 'programmed for his computer.' " The manual concludes, "Feed to your class orally and later in written form those English materials that lie closest to their interests, without regard to slang or colloquialisms that might be contained in them on the one hand, or complex grammar and rare vocabulary on the other, and it is our prediction that before the year is out you will be rewarded by hearing individual students use bits and pieces of what you have taught them in new combinations and in new situations. This is the experience of every parent, and should be the experience of every teacher of English as a second language."

Inasmuch as many of the teachers who are feeding in the raw materials on outlying islands are Micronesians who are not only totally unacquainted with computers but on far from intimate terms with the English language, the district centers have tried to help them by transmitting radio programs to their classrooms.

(Blackboards cannot always be used at such moments, because some Micronesian teachers are under the impression that a radio will stop talking unless you look it squarely in the eye.) On one kind of school broadcast, when the announcer wants the children in class to repeat a phrase, he blows a whistle, and when he wants them to answer a question, he rings a bell. This technique has resulted in some confusion among Micronesian children; practicing their English, they are likely to say "Good morning beep!" or "Brring! My name is Kasiko."

Those teachers whose students have achieved some reading capability find themselves hampered, like practically everybody in the Trust Territory, by their exceedingly limited funds. They can't get the books they want (some of them who don't understand the new math have been given no other kind of arithmetic books), and what they do get are books dealing with such unfamiliar concepts, to young Micronesians, as bunny rabbits, fire engines, and merry-go-rounds, or bearing such titles as "All About Dinosaurs," or containing such texts as "My name is Jane. I live in Philadelphia." (The American children for whom such books are written might well be baffled by some of the items displayed in a Ponape high-school science laboratory under the classification of "Common Pacific Roots": *karmihna*, *comphrena-globosa*, and *pwomwpwemw*.) Recently, on a small scale, the Trust Territory administration has been putting out some books on its own. One entitled "Here is a Family in the Marshall Islands" is all about a boy and a girl, Amram and Mary, their mother Ate (she cooks), their father Marcus (he fishes), their grandmother Ruth (she washes), and their grandfather James (he makes canoes).

Quite a few of the books with which the Trust Territory is obliged to make do are dog-eared hand-me-downs from the United States, of singular inappropriateness. There is a small island called Rumung, for instance, not far from the Yap district center. Rumung has one school building—a single-room affair with a tin roof, a bamboo floor, and crudely hewn desks and benches; one teacher—a young man of fierce countenance, but with two doves tattooed on his chest, who knows no English at all but is nonetheless gamely trying to teach it; and fifteen pupils —ranging in age from seven to thirteen and in grades from one to seven. This modest academy has a brand-new office-size typewriter, for some reason or other, but the machine has never been used, since there is no one on Rumung who can type. (Though none of the new elementary-school buildings has electricity, some of them have been equipped with new, expensive, and utterly useless electric tape recorders.) The Rumung school's small library of a dozen-odd volumes, on the other hand, is made up largely of discarded books from something called the California Developmental Reading Series, among them "Once Upon a Storytime," which contains tales about fawns and moose; "Our Good Neighbors" (this one about such neighbors as a football player, a circus performer, a fire chief, and a bus driver); and "Our California"—a title that may puzzle the children on Rumung when and if they get around to the study of both geography and personal pronouns.

Little though they know of fawns and moose, Yapese and other Micronesian children are being increasingly exposed, as part of the educational upheaval, to American fauna. One of their favorite tunes, which is played over and over on Micronesian radio stations, is a rendition of "Yankee Doodle" by a trio called the Three Little Chipmunks. The local announcers often precede its performance with an explanation of what chipmunks are. (They don't try to explain what a Yankee Doodle is; you can go only so far.) And at remote Rumung, as at just about every one of the dozens of widely dispersed islands where young Micronesians are coming to grips with the English language, never a day passes but that all pupils raise their voices in what has come to be the theme song of the Trust Territory educational revolution—"Old MacDonald Had a Farm." Micronesian children are unlikely ever to have much to do with sheep or ducks, but they can intone a baa baa here and a quack quack there with the best of them.

10.

Lo, the Rich Indian!

IN 1958, THE TRUST TERRITORY HAD NO HIGH SCHOOL. In 1962, it had a single one, with an enrollment of a hundred and eighty-six. By 1966, the enrollment jumped to twenty-five hundred—a fourteen-fold increase in four years. Each of the six district centers has a high school, with dormitories for students from outlying islands, who get no holidays during the academic year because there is no way of their traveling home and back within a reasonable period of time. The dormitories are unkempt and crowded. The Department of the Interior specifies for its Indian Bureau schools that each boarding student must have fifty square feet of living space. At Interior's Trust Territory dormitories, each student has twenty-five square feet. "I see no reason why we should provide less for individuals here than for individuals elsewhere," the Trust Territory's director of education recently said.

Quite a few Americans in Micronesia who are career men in

the Interior Department have worked in the Bureau of Indian Affairs, and while among most Americans, Indians are not generally thought of as leading an opulently subsidized existence, to these officials the contrast between our treatment of the one group of wards and of the other is striking and disheartening. (These officials are not unaware, of course, that Indians vote in United States elections and Micronesians don't, and that the source of both groups' funds is the United States Congress.) A number of Trust Territory administrators can and often do recite comparative statistics: that, for instance, Interior spends nearly ten times as much for the education of each Indian as it spends, accelerated program notwithstanding, for that of each Micronesian; or that, in a related field, the money appropriated by the United States for medical care and preventive health services averages out to $153.66 annually for each Indian, and twenty-four dollars for each Micronesian. The Trust Territory of the Pacific Islands is probably the only American outpost on earth where one hears the plaintive cry, "Lo, the rich Indian!"

In the spring of 1965, the district public high schools handed out one hundred and thirty-nine diplomas. An additional fifty-five were received at mission high schools. The principal one of these, Xavier High, where Bishop Kennally lives at Truk, is generally conceded to be the best school of any kind in Micronesia. It is the only school within the Trust Territory that has in its curriculum a course on the history of the area. Xavier offers this, according to its catalogue, "not merely to give the student a theoretical knowledge of the workings of democratic government, but to lead the student to a genuine appreciation of his obligations to justly constituted authority and to prepare him to participate intelligently in the self-governing political institutions that will be his responsibility in the future."

In some respects, the 1965 Micronesian high-school graduates were markedly different from their American counterparts. For all Palau's relative sophistication, its seniors in Koror had never listened to an assembly speaker until their last year of school. When they were exposed to their first one, their principal deemed it prudent to explain in advance that the rules of this particular American game prescribed that the students were not supposed to talk while the lecturer was talking. In many other respects, the graduates were indistinguishable from most Americans. A good many of the Micronesians, for instance, chose to wear caps and gowns at their commencement exercises, and some of them ordered class rings. In Truk, where there is a regional partiality toward glaring colors (the women go in for dresses of bright orange and fluorescent pink, and when their children fill in coloring books they learn strongly toward reds and yellows), the graduating class thought it would be nice to have pink robes, but they were persuaded by their stodgier educators to settle for dark blue.

In addition to the relatively new species of high-school students now studying within Micronesia, two hundred and twenty-four of them are in secondary schools outside the Trust Territory—most of these on Guam—and there are another one hundred and ninety-five at institutions of still higher learning. All in all, it is quite an accomplishment, considering that there was no Micronesian college graduate before 1958. (Nonetheless, there were more college graduates elected to the first Congress of Micronesia than there were in the territorial legislature of Hawaii when it first met in 1901.) Presumably a good many of today's college undergraduates will, on getting their degrees, come back home and teach. Nearly all of them are on Trust Territory scholarships, at about three thousand dollars a year apiece. Should they become qualified teachers and be able to replace an American, the savings to the administration, which spends just about the same amount a year to import one Stateside teacher and his household effects, could be substantial.

The question then arises: What if the American administration attains its professed goal of converting all Micronesians into English-speaking high-school graduates? What if a large percentage of them go on to college? A generation or so hence, educated Micronesians would be a glut on the teaching market, and at the moment there are no sure indications that, in a shaky economy, many other job opportunities will materialize. Nearly every forward-looking Micronesian wants to be educated himself, but not everyone is enchanted at the pospect of his putative scholarly eminence being universally shared.

One hears little outright left-wing talk in Micronesia, but there are more than a few natives who would concur with a professional man there who recently blurted out to a visitor, "What are you educating all of us for, anyway—to create a class of malcontent agitators? Why won't you give more money to our economy, so we can have something to work with? You give hundreds of millions of dollars to Vietnam because they have Communists. O.K., we'll get some Communists over here and then you'll give *us* more money. The biggest mistake you ever made was to teach us your ways."

One answer to the problems posed by intensive education is to try to balance the evolvement of a growing white-collar class by simultaneously encouraging the development of a blue-collar class. So far, though, there are just two vocational schools, one at Truk and the other at Koror. Since 1963, sixty boys have annually gone to the latter institution for a three-year course—one year of general shop training, and two years in carpentry, mechanics, or boat-building. After school hours, the carpenters have already built an entire home; being students, they receive twenty cents an hour for their labor, which is thirteen cents below the prescribed Trust Territory minimum hourly wage.

The boat-builders, both during and after school hours, have already completed a dozen craft, and one would think offhand that on graduating they'd have no trouble getting jobs. For one thing, Micronesia's greatest untapped assets are its marine resources, and the basic tool for harvesting these is a boat. For another, it so happens that the only boat-building business in the Trust Territory, a cooperative begun three years ago—in December, 1965, it finished a seventy-five-foot fishing boat, the largest vessel turned out by Micronesians in their recorded history—is in Koror, not far from the vocational school. Unfortunately for its students' chances of employment, however, they have been taught a Japanese method of construction—a method of which the cooperative boat yard, which has its own and different method, borrowed from Hawaii, strongly disapproves. For either institution to make a concession to the other's techniques would involve intolerable loss of face.

In the other districts, some of the regular high schools give a smattering of vocational training. The Ponape school, for instance, teaches a little carpentry. True, most of the machine tools on the premises are antiques that can't be repaired because parts for them are no longer made, but this hasn't overly bothered the educators in charge. "We want the students to learn to use basic hand tools, which is all most of them ever will be able to afford," one school administrator said. The girls enrolled in the Yap secondary-school system get a couple of hours a week of basket-weaving and mat-making, which is what some if not most of them will certainly be doing after they graduate; and the Yapese boys make fish traps and copra. At some other schools the students grow vegetables (on Saipan, one group reaped a 1,570-pound harvest of Chinese cabbage from a fifth-of-an-acre plot), and at still others they breed swine.

Perhaps the most notable integration of an academic and vocational program has been attained at a remote place outside a district center that has its very own high school. This is at Ulithi, which unlike the district centers, has no regular air service, although until recently the Coast Guard had a station there and its planes would periodically stop by. They still do, in emergencies. Recently, one Coast Guard plane en route from Yap to Guam made a detour to Ulithi on receiving a radio message from an American teacher there that a Ulithian had burnt his eye. The Coast Guard obligingly picked him up and took him to a hospital. (On July 4, 1965, the Coast Guard made a non-emergency mercy flight to Ulithi, delivering fifteen hundred hot dogs the students there wanted for a holiday feast.) The American on the radio was James C. Boykin, a bachelor from Georgetown, South Carolina, who has been largely responsible for Ulithi's independent accelerated education program. The atoll has twelve teachers; all are Micronesians except two—Boykin and an American widow from Guam named Mrs. Lavenia Stahl.

Boykin, a zoologist who has been too busy on Ulithi to finish his doctoral studies, went to that atoll in September, 1962, not long after a typhoon had left its inhabitants apathetic about life in general, let alone such particularities of it as education. To revitalize the natives, Boykin started off by persuading them to dump into the ocean a lot of rusty scrap metal that defaced their area—refuse from the Second World War that had been lying around, impervious to typhoons, for eighteen years. The natives were pleased at how much nicer their island looked, and their spirits perked up further when they realized that the land the scrap had occupied was now released for growing crops. Next, Boykin embarked on a sanitary crusade; he helped the natives fashion rat traps, and he invented an effective fly-catching device out of old glass fish-net floats.

By the time the accelerated education program came along, the Ulithians were all fired up and ready to tackle anything. They were so eager to have a new school that the Yap district center couldn't ship in building materials fast enough to suit them—and this in spite of the fact that they were digging foundation trenches with hand tools, were carting sand and gravel to the building site in baskets, and were performing all this labor without any pay at all. Soon they had two school buildings. The furniture for these was made, under Boykin's guidance, by the students who were to use it, and once they had a place to sit they proceeded energetically to construct themselves a dining hall and another big classroom building, so that more students could be accommodated and could share their good fortune. The students are highly self-sufficient; the boys catch the fish they all eat, the girls do much of the cooking, and boys and girls together tend an ever-expanding vegetable garden and orchard.

Ulithi has long been noted for its colorful dances. The square dance is now almost as popular there as are some of its traditional native counterparts, and the older children—while the younger ones faithfully run the gamut of "Old MacDonald Had a Farm"

—have become partial to "Won't You Come Home, Bill Bailey?" Ulithi itself has come to have so magnetic an attraction to teen-agers from nearby islands that practically all of them want to come to school there.

11.

Qualified Replacements

THE AMERICAN TEACHERS IN THE TRUST TERRITORY come from all over the United States, but of the other three hundred and forty-odd Americans working under the High Commissioner—there are also three thousand Micronesians on his payroll—a substantial number come from Hawaii. The fiftieth state, being only twenty-seven hundred miles from the center of Micronesia, is, as measurements go in the Pacific, practically a next-door neighbor. Hawaii is a mecca for Micronesians. One Marshallese chief toured the continental United States in 1964, and gazed upon such marvels of man's ingenuity as the new House of Representatives office building in Washington and the New York World's Fair, but what he wanted to see most of all was Waikiki Beach. He owned several beaches just as alluring and far less cluttered, but they didn't impress him because they were at home.

Hawaii is also the place where most Micronesians who aspire to higher education go to get it, although a few of them find the climate uncomfortably chilly. At the University of Hawaii, where Micronesian undergraduates, once a rarity, have become routine, there is an East-West Center, which offers six-week to six-month courses in a variety of academic and non-academic subjects. One hundred and fifty Micronesians now attend the Center annually, studying, among other subjects, nursing, business administration, commercial sewing, plant quarantine, extension agriculture, and environmental sanitation. There is also a course for waitresses. A 1965 enrollee in that one was the proprietor of a snack bar at Saipan; her patrons could hardly wait for her to get back and demonstrate her newly acquired skills.

Hawaiians, being themselves ethnically scrambled, have a built-in affinity with Micronesians, who even before they had Spanish, German, Japanese, and English strains fused with their bloodstreams were a mixture of Caucasoid, Mongoloid, Negroid, and Polynesian races. One of the many Hawaiians whose interest in Micronesians has impelled them to settle more or less permanently in Micronesia is J. Boyd Mackenzie, a district administrator who recently switched to Palau from Truk, which, with twenty-three thousand inhabitants, is the most populous as well as the most centrally located of the six Trust Territory subdivisions. Mackenzie is of royal blood; one of his grandmothers was an Hawaiian queen. An uncle of his, Tandy Kaohu Mackenzie, was Hawaii's most celebrated opera singer.

Trained as an agriculturist, Boyd Mackenzie first went to Micronesia in 1953. He was given the mission of finding new and improved methods of growing crops on low islands, and spent four and a half years on the Marshallese atoll of Jaluit, which had been the regional headquarters for both the German and Japanese overlords of that part of the Pacific (some Mikimoto pearls once came from Jaluit), but which in the American scheme of things had been relegated to the status of just another atoll.

Early in 1958 a typhoon hit Jaluit. Typhoons, with their aggressive tidal waves and slashing winds that reach two hundred miles an hour in velocity, are Micronesia's most feared and hated enemy. They not infrequently level every house and strip every leaf off every tree that they happen not to level. Mackenzie was visiting Majuro when Jaluit was assaulted. He rushed back on the first ship, and found that everything he'd done in those four and a half years had vanished—his experimental plantings, his house and all its furnishings, his office and all its records.

A less determined man might have returned to Honolulu, but Mackenzie stayed on in Micronesia and eventually wrote what came to be regarded as a definitive treatise on breadfruit. (For the seedless variety alone, Mackenzie revealed, the Marshallese had twenty names: *bukdol*, *bwilbwilkkaj*, *kitroro*, *maikwe*, *madik*, *majoklap*, *maron*, *majiloklok*, *kibwedoul*, *mabat*, *maddak*, *mejenwe*, *maijokaar*, *mamwe*, *medak*, *mejwa*, *petaaktak*, *mejid-duul*, *monnon*, and *ma*.) He married a girl from the state of Washington who was the High Commissioner's secretary, and his bad luck continued to plague him. On a honeymoon flight, the plane his bride and he were on had to make an emergency landing at sea, and before ditching the pilot ordered his cargo jettisoned, including the Mackenzies' wedding presents. In a subsequent plane crash, Mackenzie broke his back.

Like every other part of Micronesia, Truk, the district over which Mackenzie presided from 1960 to 1965, has its own peculiar and cherished legends. According to one of these, life began on Truk when a woman drifted in there on a large and uncommonly buoyant palm frond. Seventeen thousand of her descendants occupy the islands of the majestic Truk lagoon. (Its water is notoriously saline; a British manufacturer of outboard motors warns his customers at Truk to be sure to flush their engines every now and then with fresh water.) The Japanese converted Truk into an immense wartime base. They established their district headquarters on the Truk lagoon island of Dublon; the Americans have encamped on the nearby island of Moen. (In a cave on one Moen hill, commanding a sweeping arc of the lagoon, stands a British artillery piece; the Japanese moved it there from Singapore.) The native chief of Moen is a man of regal bearing named Petrus Mailo, now the acting Speaker of the

General Assembly of the Congress of Micronesia, who spent thirty days in the United States in the spring of 1965 at the invitation of the State Department. Away from home, he added to his normally formidable mien by wearing a broad-brimmed hat, which he kept on even while having lunch in the delegates' dining room at the United Nations.

Chief Petrus, who was born at the turn of the century, is an *itag* man—*itag* being a Trukese word that connotes both a lofty political philosophy and an arcane language known only to a handful of leaders. The language is supposed to be used prudently, because it can cast spells and make people sick. Not long ago, speaking in conventional Trukese, Chief Petrus talked to some high-school students at Moen. After describing himself, with characteristic Trukese diffidence, as a man ill-suited for his august position because he lacked wisdom, he discoursed at length and wisely about the history of Truk, and urged his listeners never to forget what their ancestors had learned: that there would be nothing more important in their lives than the soil they lived on and their relationship to it. "We take life from the soil of our land," he said, and added, "Don't reach beyond your grasp for what you don't have. If you reach beyond your grasp for the white man's knowledge but let go of your own knowledge, you will fall. . . . In the government a job assignment just hops from one person to another, but an assignment of soil cannot hop away. . . . Hold onto the Trukese pattern of things, the Trukese customs, the Trukese ways, the Trukese orientation."

At another public appearance, Chief Petrus shared the rostrum with a high-ranking American from Trust Territory headquarters, a man of such exuberance that he would scurry around Micronesia embracing august native elders in bear hugs and exclaiming, "You're the best friend I have!" (Trukese hate to have strangers' hands laid upon them; Trukese barbers customarily apologize to their patrons for having to touch their hair while cutting it.) The ebullient American, who in the pre-accelerated days would also roam around kicking at the walls of schools that he thought were of inferior construction (once he tried to kick down an interior wall of a private Micronesian home that he wanted to convert into a restaurant, and had inflicted a few nasty dents before anybody could make him understand he was in the wrong house), spoke before Chief Petrus did, and in his gushing fashion let loose a stream of heady prophecies about what the United States was doing, or was some day going to do, to make Micronesia a promised land. When the chief's turn came to talk, he said that the previous speaker had put him in mind of the *kuning*, or Pacific golden plover, a big, foolish, light-hued bird (some Trukese credit it with laying eggs in the sky) that "comes down to earth once a year and flaps its wings and makes a lot of noise and then flies away."

Chief Petrus, who has been a businessman since 1920, when he operated a trading boat for his father, was a founder, in 1948, of the Truk Trading Company, one of Micronesia's most thriving commercial enterprises. To promote purchases of shares in the company by his fellow Trukese, he once organized an all-day frolic during which sales spiels alternated with hortatory songs; one set of lyrics reflected the conventional Trukese self-derogation:

> Wake up, for the sun is rising;
> Get working tools and go to our place of
> work, and work hard.
> We're lazy but we'll try hard to work;
> We're stupid but we'll try hard in school;
> We're sinful, but we'll try hard in religion;
> For our land will progress through perseverance.
>
> Oh, we'll all be happy in our work;
> We will work for food and work for money, by
> cutting copra, gardening, and fishing.
> We will sell these things to build up our island,
> And so that our company will help us to progress.

On such occasions, the laying-on of hands is not deemed *de trop*. The more persuasive singers were rewarded by having their mouths and ears stuffed with coins, which muffled their delivery but helped the trading company. Other well-received performers were sprinkled with perfume and hair oil, which Chief Petrus thought was wasteful, or with water, which he thought undignified. Sales of shares were disappointing, however; the company would guarantee its investors no more than a ten-percent return on their money, and to many Trukese this was an uninviting prospect.

The Truk Trading Company began modestly enough, with only twelve thousand dollars in capital. It came to have more than ten times that amount of stock outstanding, total assets of close to a million dollars, and one hundred and thirty employees. All of these are Micronesians except for the manager, a Chicagoan named Henry Chatroop who has been in the area since 1946, when he did supply and accounting work for the Navy, and who lives over the company's main store in a commodious apartment with a panelled ceiling and, among other elegant furnishings, a grand piano. Chatroop's wife is a registered nurse from Scotland, who went to Fiji after the war with the Royal Nursing Corps. She is also a certified midwife, and she moved to Micronesia on being offered a chance to set up a midwifery school. But the Trust Territory administration then discovered it didn't have enough money to start one after all.

Chatroop is a real go-getter. He sells baseball uniforms, complete with thick woolen stockings, to out-islanders who normally wear hardly any clothing at all. He sells fancy foods that would be a credit to any gourmet shop, and keeps in stock a selection of wine and liquors of which any Stateside package store could be proud. The company has more books on sale than any other place in Micronesia, has a movie theater (unemployment in Truk is high, and it is open daily from 11 A.M. to 11 P.M.), and operates a bakery, a pool hall, a lumber yard, a restaurant, and a bar. Its bouncer is one of the largest men in the district; Trukese can get fairly rough on pay day. In the company's warehouses, because of the uncertainty of deliveries of anything in Micronesia, there is usually an inventory of half a million dollars' worth of goods.

Within the Trust Territory there a quite a few old-timers who, like Chatroop, have been on the scene for nearly two decades. The oldest-timer is a public-works mechanic at Koror, who as a Navy enlisted man took part in the American invasion of Palau in the autumn of 1944. He liked the place, stayed on, and married a native. He is the only American in Micronesia with betelnut-stained teeth. Most of the other veterans are former Navy officers who at the end of the war attended a School of Naval Administration at Stanford University. One of these, Roy T. Gallemore, who retired at seventy last year after serving as district administrator for the Mariana Islands, was a 1917 Annapolis graduate. He left the Navy seven years later to run a family newspaper in Florida, rejoined in 1940, and retired from that career in 1955.

Like most of the Trust Territory officials with lengthy service, Gallemore had been stationed at one time or another in nearly all of the districts, and he had come to react sensitively and sympathetically to many native beliefs and customs that people with less experience might be inclined to dismiss as myth or hokum. When he was district administrator at Yap, a few years ago, there was a long and depressing spell of rain. An elderly Yapese with a reputation for meteorological magic came to Gallemore's house one day, sat on his living room floor, lit a fire, delivered himself of some incantations, and departed after confidently announcing that the rain would stop at once. It did. Gallemore was, and remained, impressed.

Whether it is good or bad for foreigners to stay for protracted periods in outposts like Micronesia has been debated since colonialism began. It can be argued that people who want to help out natives cannot begin to do so until they are thoroughly acquainted with the natives' environment and, preferably, have learned their language. Some of the very best and most compassionate administrators in Micronesia are those who have tarried there the longest. On the other hand, the climate of Micronesia (the humidity is oppressive, and the temperature ranges between seventy-five and eighty-five), saps energy and reduces efficiency, and often people who spend long stretches of time in a hot, tiny, confining place get into ruts, or, once they have become big frogs in little ponds, are afraid to return to a different and more competitive society. One Hawaiian with fifteen years of Trust Territory service behind him said recently, "I'm beginning to think I'm a failure because I've been out here so long."

Micronesians are accustomed to living in small groups and to seeing the same few faces year in and out, but for foreigners on the islands the unvarying pattern of their social relationships can lead to disenchantment. Newcomers to Micronesia are pounced on by the residents; whatever sort of people they may be, they are new people, and for all anyone can tell may know some new jokes. They also usually receive an earful of old gripes. The Americans in Micronesia have a well-worked-over repertory of these. Some complain that they are being spied on, others that their mail is being opened before it reaches them, and almost all of them that they are the forgotten people of a forgotten land. When a disgruntled educator who'd been out there wrote a whole book full of gripes about the Trust Territory, his former colleagues griped about *that*.

The Micronesians, for their part, used to gripe that they were victims of discrimination. Until 1961, they were. They were not allowed to join the Trust Territory's social clubs, for instance, on the pretext that they wouldn't feel at home there because they were also not allowed to drink. The Navy had imposed prohibition upon them, and Interior had gone along with this restriction. High Commissioner Goding lifted it soon after he assumed office. Throughout Micronesia today, one sees signs saying, "This is a facility operated under the jurisdiction of the Trust Territory of the Pacific Islands. No discrimination by segregation or other means in the furnishing of accommodations, facilities, services, or privileges on the basis of race, creed, color, ancestry, or foreign origin is permitted in the use of this facility." Anybody who spots a violation of this decree is urged to let the High Commissioner know directly.

The clubs, one in each district center, are the social hubs of Micronesia. In the one at Yap, and also at Ponape's, movies are frequently shown. A recent favorite at Ponape was "The Pagan

Love Song," a thirty-year-old production that attracted a large and enthusiastic audience after being billed with the synopsis, "An American schoolteacher inherits a rundown plantation in Tahiti and tries to hire a native beauty for his housekeeper unaware that she is a member of the island's high society."

Back in 1952, an economist engaged by the United States to make a survey of Micronesia concluded that "care should be exercised, as it has so far been, not to advance wages beyond all reasonable hope that the productivity of the economy will be enough to sustain such wages. This is no idle caveat. Wage reasoning shaped by the cry of discrimination or by comparison with American wages could be ruinous to the Trust Territory economy in its present stage of productivity." Productivity hasn't yet reached a much more advanced stage than it had then, but, caveat or no caveat, the cry of wage discrimination is now often heard. The most that any Micronesian can currently earn as a Trust Territory administration employee, no matter how responsible a position he holds or how many years of seniority he has, is $10,300. Until August, 1965, the maximum for a Micronesian was $7,620, which is about where an inexperienced American schoolteacher starts. At the other end of the pay scale are the unskilled Micronesian laborers who get thirty-three cents an hour. This is by no means rock-bottom in their experience; under the Japanese, the minimum wage was the equivalent of forty cents a day.

Micronesians don't need as much money as Americans do. Most of the natives grow at least some of their food, hardly any of them pay income taxes, and they are not encumbered with insurance or social security, having instead a well-established clan system according to which all elderly people can count on being taken care of by their families. Some families, indeed, commandeer the wages of any of their members who happen to be employed; Micronesians in that fix who want to save some of their own earnings often ask their employers to deposit any overtime pay they may have coming to them in secret bank accounts.

Furthermore, few Micronesians have invested in their own education anything like the sums that Americans often must invest before they're eligible for a job. Nevertheless, the natives are increasingly articulating their dissatisfaction with a double standard of compensation. One highly rated and hard-working Micronesian currently holds a job that would pay an American thirteen thousand dollars, before taxes. The Micronesian gets forty-eight hundred, tax-free. What galls him perhaps more than anything else is that he is married to an American whom he met at the University of Hawaii and who works for the territorial administration, too. "My wife is only a clerk-typist and she gets more than I do," the Micronesian told an acquaintance. "Deep down, it hurts."

At present, it is the United States policy that every American employed in the Trust Territory is to be replaced, as soon as possible though not necessarily at the same pay scale, by a qualified Micronesian. In theory, a Micronesian is currently being trained to take over every position now held by Americans. Some of the Americans are displaying more eagerness than others are to lose their jobs. One of them, the Trust Territory entomologist, is so convinced of the rightness of this self-immolating program that he has *two* Micronesians studying entomology abroad—one in Hawaii and one in the Philippines—on the premise that this doubles his chances of obtaining a competent successor to himself.

It is not always easy, though, to find Micronesians who both want to assume responsibility and have the capability to do so. In 1962, an American who ran the Yap Trading Company (now called the Yap Cooperative Association) turned over its management to its native owners. They struggled along for three years, but as their business grew it became too much for them to handle, and they finally asked the American to come back. He did, but instead of reassuming the title of manager, he calls himself an adviser.

Micronesians are gradually playing an ever-larger role in managing their own affairs, however. Dwight Heine's appointment in August, 1965, as the first native district administrator was a major breakthrough. But Micronesians have mixed feelings about taking over their own reins. They are accustomed to working under people rather than over or even with them. One of the six assistant administrators was appointed in Palau to supplant an American of whom the natives had become extremely fond. The Palau district legislature, while it had nothing against the Palauan who had been singled out for the high post, passed a resolution deploring the switch and saying that "the stage of our development at this time is still such that it requires the knowledge and ability of a person experienced in handling major responsibilities, capable of handling various activities, and well experienced in human relations so as to be able to win the confidence of the people."

Some self-confident young Micronesians believe that they are ready right now to run the Trust Territory themselves—or at least to run it as well as the United States runs it—but their optimism is far from universally shared. The American in charge of seven Micronesians employed at a Weather Bureau station in the Marshall Islands asked them not long ago when they thought any of them would be ready to replace *him*. The most bullish among them guessed it would take ten years, the most bearish guessed fifty. In United Nations circles, the United States is often berated for not permitting Micronesians to assume responsibility for all their judicial affairs. When the principal native justice in the Yap district, an imposing man of seventy-nine named Joseph Fanechoor, was asked how soon *he* thought this change in jurisprudence could reasonably come about, he replied, "I don't know how many hundreds of years it will be."

12.

Customs, Courts, and Castes

THE ADMINISTRATION OF JUSTICE IN MICRONESIA IS A complicated business. The Trust Territory has its own Code, which was drawn up in 1952 and has since been slightly modified. While this is largely patterned after the United States Code, there are several notable differences. For one thing, there is no statute of frauds. Such a statute would have been pointless, because most Micronesians put no trust in written documents. To them, oral statements carry far more weight, and indeed if one of them insists on spelling out an agreement on paper, he is more often than not suspected of wicked ulterior motives.

Birth certificates issued by Micronesians are all but worthless. Even when a woman knows the name of her child's father, which is not always the case, it makes little difference to her what paternal name is entered on a birth certificate, since that is just a scrap of paper. Frequently, to save time and bother, Micronesian clerks filling out birth certificates will insert *their* name in the blank space set aside for "father"; by now some of the clerks, on paper at least, have become prodigies of paternity.

Another difference between the Trust Territory Code and its United States prototype is that in the former's version of the Bill of Rights the following notable exception appears: "Due recognition shall be given to local customs in providing a system of law, and nothing in this Chapter shall be construed to limit or invalidate any part of the existing customary law, except as otherwise determined by the High Commissioner." The two American judges in Micronesia try conscientiously to give the recognition due to local customs, but it is hard for them sometimes to ascertain just what local customs are. Since the natives distrust documents, few of the customs have ever been set forth in writing except by anthropologists. And anthropologists can be misleading; it is *their* custom on invading any area to get hold of some old and seemingly wise man, win his confidence, pick his brains, and record whatever he purports to remember and chances to say. Such documentation, from a judge's point of view, is far better than none; the only trouble is that should the same wise old man turn up on the witness stand during a trial, he is quite likely to testify that he knows of several dozen cases in which the custom in question was not followed and of no single case in which it was.

Along with local customs, the various districts of Micronesia have local laws. In Ponape, it is illegal to walk along a road holding an open can of beer, and one may not hunt pigeons in either June or December. In Truk, a husband or wife may get a divorce simply by, in the local phrase, "throwing away" his spouse—that is, walking out on his mate and sleeping with somebody else. This particular custom sometimes comes in handy for Trukese couples short of cash. The wife will entice another man into the bushes, and her husband will catch them there, throw the woman out, and sue the third party for alienation of affections in a community court. The limit on damages that can be assessed there is one hundred dollars, and not long after the alleged homewrecker has had this judgment levied against him—a stiff price to pay for one fling in a tropical land tolerant of promiscuity—the husband and wife will take up together again, one hundred dollars the richer for their mischievous deception.

One small island in the Truk lagoon has an ordinance against unfettered or unfenced pigs; violaters are theoretically liable to fines. But nobody pays any attention to the ordinance. There are some seventy pigs on the island, and they are raised to be sold. Their owners, from the chief of the island on down, figure that they can make a larger profit off their swine if they don't have to provide their own pig feed. So the animals roam around unchecked, eating up the community's stores of taro, rooting up preserved breadfruit that residents have buried against lean times, and even gobbling copra—the island's other principal source of cash income—off the racks on which it has been spread to dry.

There is some justice outside the law in Micronesia, too. A Yapese father whose son had been caught stealing warned the boy that if it ever happened again he would be severely punished; when it did happen again, the father chopped off the tip of one of his son's fingers. The Americans in Yap felt that the father had to be hauled into court and tried for assault, but he got off with a light sentence because, in the words of the American judge, it was "primarily a family matter to be dealt with as tradition decrees, within the family."

The Yapese put great store by their traditions. Three years ago, in a drunken brawl, a young man of low caste shoved a man of chiefly stature. The chief pulled out a knife and stabbed him twice. *He* was arrested for assault, tried, and found guilty. Before sentence was pronounced, his lawyer, hoping for mitigation (the knife-wielder finally got six months), put a couple of respected chiefs on the stand. The lawyer asked one of them what would have happened in the old days to anyone who shoved a chief. "We'd have killed him," was the reply.

The principal author of the Trust Territory Code was Edward P. Furber, a Harvard man, born in 1898, who after practicing law in Boston joined the Navy in 1942. Toward the end of the war, and for a year after its end, he was stationed at Okinawa and others of the Ryukyu Islands. In 1946, he moved to Guam. Two years after that, the Navy designated him Chief Justice of the Trust Territory, a position that he continued to fill when the Department of the Interior superseded the Navy in 1951, and that he has filled ever since.

Judge Furber and the one associate justice he has to share his work are the most independent Americans in the Trust Territory, being the only two who are responsible directly to the Secretary of the Interior and are not subservient to the High Commissioner. The two judges demonstrated their independence when a predecessor of Goding's, who was upset because thieves had broken into a couple of Americans' homes, decreed that anyone convicted of burglary in the Trust Territory would get a mandatory sentence of not less than a year's imprisonment. To the judges this seemed unreasonably harsh. A year in jail would be a stiff penalty for, say, a housemaid who found a bottle of her mistress's toilet water irresistible, and, what was more, among Micronesians it is sometimes difficult to ascertain what constitutes theft and what does not. Throughout most of the region, one is supposed to share whatever property one has with one's relatives. Accusations of theft have been countered with the defense that the individual caught red-handed was not committing a crime at all but was merely implementing a unilateral decision he had made to establish a relationship with the owner of the appropriated goods. The two judges, accordingly, lodged a strong protest against the decree about burglary, and they succeeded in having the one-year sentence made discriminatory instead of mandatory.

Judge Furber has considered it of the highest importance that the natives in his jurisprudential area, who have had a long history of subjugation under high-handed German and Japanese overlords and who are also inured to their own autocratic traditions, become accustomed to democratic concepts of justice. To instill respect for his High Court, and for all Micronesian courts, he himself issued a decree that his associate and he would wear black robes while sitting on the bench—a gesture of substantial sacrifice in an environment where men of high and low station alike usually wear merely an open-necked, short-sleeved shirt and slacks or shorts. The Chief Justice thought it would be nice, too, if his eighteen Micronesian associates in district courts also wore black robes. He besought their views on this, and all were agreeable save Judge Fanechoor of Yap, the dean of the indigenous judiciary.

A handsome patriarch with pierced earlobes and tattooed skin, Fanechoor had had little formal education and absolutely no legal training, but he was experienced in administrative affairs, having been an interpreter under the Germans and a policeman under the Japanese, and being the chief of one of Yap's principal municipalities. A daughter of his married an American anthropologist who served for a while as a district administrator. Fanechoor, who became a district judge in 1950, felt that he needed no ceremonial trappings to enhance *his* dignity, and he flatly refused to go along with Judge Furber's black-robe proposal. The Chief Justice agreed to accept a compromise submitted by Judge Fanechoor: that he and the other Micronesians would wear the vestments, but only while presiding over murder cases.

As part of his campaign to win respect for the law, Judge Furber also instituted the Territory-wide celebration of Law Day. It falls on May 1st, and is not widely observed in the United States, but it has become an important holiday in Micronesia. On its eve the High Commissioner annually and solemnly proclaims its imminence. The 1965 Law Day saw a spirited debate in the high school at Koror on the subject, "Be it resolved that the old Palauan custom of law enforcement is superior to the new Western common-law system with regard to the prevention of juvenile delinquency." A few years earlier, one Micronesian school teacher had been so moved by the High Commissioner's Law Day proclamation that he announced he was going to take his entire class to court to watch the Chief Justice in action. Judge Furber felt reluctantly compelled to ask the teacher to call off the excursion; there had been a logistical mix-up, and a suitcase containing his black robe hadn't yet reached the island where he was holding court.

The Chief Justice and his associate, like bygone circuit riders, spend most of their time on the road—or, to be more precise, in the air or on the water—carrying their robes, files, and other paraphernalia with them, and picking up interpreters at each stop. When Judge Furber wanted to distribute the text of some resolutions adopted at a Micronesian judicial conference a few years back, he sent out an instructional memorandum that went, "Each Clerk of Courts is requested to translate these [resolutions] into the local language, or languages, of his district and send a copy of the translation to each District and Community Court Judge and listed Trial Assistant in his district in a language which he believes the Judge or Trial Assistant concerned can read, or if he can only read English, then send him a copy of the English."

Judge Furber's High Court has jurisdiction over all criminal cases involving potential prison terms of five years or fines of two thousand dollars, and over all civil cases where more than a thousand dollars is in contention. One time the High Court, on reviewing the proceedings of one of the lower courts, was puzzled to find that a community-court judge had handled a false-arrest case on his own; false arrest is a serious charge and, the superior judges thought at first, should have been referred to them. On investigation, they learned that the case involved two men, one of whom had "arrested" a chicken belonging to the other, and had also cooked and eaten it.

The Micronesian judges who handle lesser litigation have all been trained by Furber, and like Judge Fanechoor they have had no formal instruction in law and have to compensate in common sense for what they lack in legal knowledge. Sometimes their judgments are exceedingly stern. When several young men were brought before Judge Kabua Kabua, the paramount native jurist in the Marshalls, after some New Year's Eve hell-raising, he let all of them off with a reprimand except for his own son, whom he sentenced to ten days in jail.

Most of the cases that come to any court in Micronesia are disputes over ownership or tenancy of land. In Yap, where a leader's authority derives from his acreage and there is an old saying, "The man is not chief, but the land is chief," the High Court heard a civil action in 1963 that stemmed from one man's having taken a single coconut from another's property.

Some of the strictest local laws relate to the use of taro patches, which generally consist of low, swampy tracts. In the Ponape district, where according to custom a male landowner must share his property with all his landless male relatives and with all his husbandless female ones, there was litigation as to whether one Pingelap man had actually given another man a four-row section of a taro patch or had merely allowed him to work those rows. After hearing the evidence, Judge Furber concluded, relying heavily for guidance on his familiarity with local lore, "It appears that under Pingelap custom it is usual for one who is making an outright gift of ownership of some part of a taro patch to give, at the same time, some dry land with it. An outright gift of the ownership of certain rows in a taro patch on Pingelap all by themselves is therefore not to be readily presumed."

The Micronesian courts have an easier time of it than some others because, for one thing, the environment itself is a deterrent against misbehavior. People on small islands cannot hope to get far away from the scene of a crime. Even so, there has lately been a troubling increase in burglaries that can by no stretch of the imagination be fobbed off as exchanges of familial possessions. The Truk Trading Company not long ago felt obliged to hire a night watchman, and its counterpart at Yap was thinking of following suit after prowlers twice broke into its thitherto unmolested premises. "We've had embezzlements before," the American adviser there said sadly, "but we'd never been robbed by people we didn't know."

Crimes of passion are rare, though every now and then two men enamored of the same woman will hack away at one another with machetes, and the Yap jail not long ago harbored a woman whose lover and she had murdered her husband and thrown his body into a swamp. She was paroled after fourteen years' internment, but by then she had become so fond of institutional life that she asked for and got a custodial job there. The public-safety department obtained a sewing machine so she could mend the prisoners' clothes.

Rape is all but unknown, and isn't even mentioned in the Trust Territory Code, since it is ordinarily considered natural enough for mature young women to engage in sexual intercourse. Why would anyone have to use force, some of the natives assert, to get a woman to do what she'd gladly do practically any time with practically anybody? When, however, some Yapese girls in their early teens were espied leaving a Coast Guard barracks, their families frowned upon this dalliance with foreigners, and although the girls had been willing enough, two of them were stabbed by their own brothers. In one rape case that did come into the courts, the American prosecutor, who from pre-trial conversations with the victim was confident of a verdict against her assailant, was dumfounded when the girl took the witness stand and said she wasn't sure what had happened to her because she'd been unconscious at the critical moment.

Because many of the natives are close-mouthed in public about what they consider their private business, it sometimes takes quite a while for the Trust Territory administration to learn that a crime has been committed, let alone do anything about its perpetrator. Two Americans visiting a Ulithian island for a few days asked for a housekeeper, and were surprised when an emaciated man, rather than a woman, was assigned to them. He was an outcast, they subsequently learned, who had once been a navigator, and as such was entitled to carry a rifle with him on canoe trips, to protect voyagers against sharks. He had set out some time before, the story went, in a convoy of two canoes, with thirteen passengers, among them a woman he coveted and her husband. There had been only three survivors: the woman, a close friend of hers, and the navigator. He had two tales: one was that the ten missing people had been engulfed by a wave; the other was that they'd died from eating poisoned shark meat.

The chief of the island he was staying on, though, believed that the navigator had murdered his companions. The chief wouldn't permit any of his constituency to discuss the episode, but he himself told the Americans that the man was available for domestic labor because nobody else would have anything to do with him. He had no woman to cook for him (the one who started all the trouble had moved to another island and married someone else), and would ultimately perish for his sins, of starvation and loneliness. The chief said he didn't mind if the Americans fed the pariah during their visit, because a few weeks one way or the other wouldn't really matter.

When Micronesians accused of crimes are dealt with in a fashion more to their Chief Justice's liking, they are usually represented in court by public defenders. (The only indigenous lawyer, a Palauan who got his degree from George Washington University in 1963, is Kaleb Udui, formerly an assistant attorney general on the High Commissioner's staff, who was recently named legislative counsel to the Congress of Micronesia.) One of the most effective of these advocates is Andon L. Amaraich, a Trukese who is a Congress Delegate—the Micronesian counterpart of a United States Senator—and the president of an organization that, although none of its members is a lawyer, is called the Truk District Bar Association. Amaraich once won an acquittal for a teenage client who seemed to be in a terrible jam: he had hit a cop over the head with a whiskey bottle. The public defender, by skillful examination and cross-examination, managed to establish that the policeman was drunk at the time and was trying to steal the bottle from the boy, whom he outweighed by fifty pounds and was throttling to boot; and that the boy, moreover, was of high moral character and was merely delivering the bottle to its rightful owner.

Until this year, all verdicts in the Trust Territory were rendered by judges. The new Congress has enacted a law authorizing trials by jury in certain limited circumstances, but most Micronesians are aware of the difficulties that might arise, in a region of marked consanguinity, from trying to empanel a jury with nobody on it related by real or adoptive kinship to a principal in the proceedings. Family bonds are so tight in Micronesia that one criminal investigator assigned to a homicide case had a suspect arrested whom he knew to be innocent; he knew that because he also knew that the actual killer was one of his cousins.

A good many of the crimes and altercations in Micronesia stem, as they do elsewhere on earth, from drinking. Under the Japanese, the natives could buy liquor, but only if they had a permit, and their permits could and often would be revoked for misbehavior. For the first fifteen years of American domination, beer was the only alcoholic beverage to which Micronesians had legal access. Prohibition didn't work much better there than it has worked anywhere. In the Truk district, for instance, natives on Moen were supplied by bootleggers operating on Dublon, where they brewed a concoction of coffee and yeast that enjoyed wide popularity. The stuff was so much in demand that a good deal of it was sold before the yeast had fully fermented; it was assumed by both producers and consumers that the process of fermentation was completed in the latters' stomachs. Moreover, Micronesians had for generations been addicted to a home brew called *tuba,* made from the sap of the flower buds of coconut trees. This versatile juice is used in its unfermented state as a tonic for babies; fermented, it is a toxicant for their elders.

When High Commissioner Goding abolished prohibition for the natives in 1961, local option came into being. Most of the district centers are wet, and most of the outlying municipalities are dry. (In the Truk district, only three of twenty-four municipalities have gone wet.) Where liquor is available, it is cheap; some Americans jestingly refer to the Trust Territory as a hardship post because the tonic in a gin-and-tonic coasts more than the gin. Some of the natives who after years of deprivation have had ready access to liquor for the last four years have reacted to it much as they reacted when in 1945 they were able to get some sugar for the first time since Pearl Harbor. They would put four heaping spoonfuls in every cup of coffee, and quite a few of the older men became diabetic. Cirrhosis of the liver is now gloomily predicted for their sons, some of whom gulp vodka for breakfast. Trukese are normally mild-mannered, but after downing a pint of 120-proof vodka imported from Japan, they can get pretty rough. In one barroom brawl, several of them held down one participant while another bit his eye out. In another fracas, at a bar in Moen, an out-islander who was getting the worst of it complained during a lull that his adversaries would never be able to whip him if they were fighting back on *his* island. He was promptly thrown into a canoe, paddled over there, and on arrival beaten up again. When Trukese are celebrating hard, motorists there have to be wary of young men staggering along roads brandishing rocks the size of coconuts.

Juvenile delinquency is getting to be a problem in Micronesia, and some of the older men, among them Chief Petrus of Truk, attribute this to drinking. (Judge Fanechoor of Yap is so concerned about the trend that he is in favor of jail sentences for miscreant fifteen-year-olds.) But alcohol is certainly only one of several contributing factors. As the younger Micronesians get better educated, they are also getting restless. The fact that many of them are unemployed would not have bothered them a generation ago. Living off their land, there was no particular reason why they had to have jobs, and unlike Americans, they had never believed in work for work's sake. They preferred leisure, an attitude that used to make people mistakenly think they were lazy. Indeed, among Palauans young men were never expected to do any work, even if jobs were available, until they were in their mid-twenties.

Now Micronesians are increasingly coming around to thinking that it is prestigious to have a job, and the young people who want one and can't get one are the trouble-makers. To give some of them something to do, Palau organized a Youth Corps two years ago, for idle boys between sixteen and twenty-four. Some districts have felt obliged to impose curfews to keep the peace. By decree of the Yap Island Congress, for instance, nobody under eighteen, unless accompanied by an adult, may be on the streets of the district center between the hours of 9:30 P.M. and 5:30 A.M.

In his recently published "The Challenge of Modernization," I.

R. Sinai says, "A new civilization can never arise without the disintegration of the old one." Many older Micronesians, who used to maintain firm control over their children, are bewildered by their inability to discipline them any more. Not long ago, a young man who wanted to get away from his seniors' authority had to travel by foot or canoe. Now, there is new-found mobility. In 1958, for instance, there was not a single motor scooter on the main island of Yap. Today, model houses being constructed on the main island of Yap come complete with scooter ports. The island has two hundred scooters, and nearly as many automobiles, and so many accidents have resulted that the adult-education staff of the Yap district education department felt it prudent to drop everything else a few months back and put out a booklet on traffic safety. One morning, shortly after this treatise was distributed, a seventeen-year-old Yapese boy came to the Yap hospital after a scooter accident. He was patched up, and then he patched up his scooter, and that same afternoon he was skylarking around the island's twisting roads with one girl riding behind him and another girl in his lap. For a Yapese boy to ride on a scooter with merely *one* girl would have been unheard of until recently. Dating was supposed to be conducted in secret. A girl on a Honda in broad daylight, with her arms around her young man's waist, and her bare breasts pressed brazenly against his back! In Yap, it was not only unthinkable, it was impossible.

Furthermore, the older Yapese shake their heads sorrowfully these days when they reflect how the younger ones have begun to talk back to them. It used to be the custom for young people to keep their mouths shut in the presence of their elders, and women up to thirty and men up to forty or fifty were considered young. Now, these uppity youngsters are not only speaking their piece but are articulating their distaste for a rigorously stratified society—nine castes, with two classes in each—that had been accepted by all Yapese for as far back as anyone can remember. There are even murmurs of unrest among the lowest of all Yapese, the Pimilngays, whose status is somewhere between that of a slave and an untouchable. Among the English-language books to be found in Trust Territory schools today is one with the unequivocal title, "You Will Go to the Moon." Some Yapese, in view of all the astonishing changes that their lives are undergoing, believe that if things have got to the absurd point where a Pimilngay may aspire to a motor scooter, there is no reason to doubt that the book's prophecy will soon come true.

13.

Reef Fever

APPROACHING ANY PART OF THIS VAST TRACT OF WATER lightly sprinkled with land, one never ceases to reflect how physically insignificant the Trust Territory islands are, and to wonder how any navigator manages to find them. Micronesian navigators have been doing just that for centuries. Intradistrict travel may entail a voyage of several hundred miles over open and by no means always pacific ocean, but the natives think little of embarking on a visit to distant neighbors in frail sailing canoes. To them, the ocean is not a barrier but a highway.

In water travel, as in practically every other aspect of life, there are variations from district to district. Palauans are partial to rafts. Yapese fancy a kind of canoe, called a *cugpin*, that has two gracefully arched necks, sometimes painted lively colors and bedecked with shell necklaces. Outboard engines are becoming more and more prevalent in Micronesia today, but the basic vehicle is still the canoe, plain or decorated, with, as a rule, a deep, narrow hull, a broad, steadying outrigger, and slim gunwales on which the native mariners perform prodigious feats of balance as they hop about on their broad, brown, splay-toed, confident, bare feet. On motor vessels and airplanes, though, they are prone to nausea.

The Marshallese are generally considered the best navigators. They use compasses now, but for years they relied on intricately designed stick charts. These consisted of slender, interwoven, curving pieces of wood, each one representing a wave pattern, with small cowrie shells tied to them representing islands or atolls. The prevailing waves in the Marshall Islands all have names, and to be allowed to learn these and to read and interpret stick charts used to be deemed a great honor. It was a privilege granted to only a few young men of noble birth. During their apprenticeship, they would be taken out to sea and would float on their backs to get the feel of the waves. With enough experience, they could tell where they were from the roll of a boat and the appearance of the waves that rocked it; they could also tell how far they were from an island they were seeking and whether—as happened now and then—they were lost.

Their navigational prowess has been much admired by American ship captains plying Micronesian waters who have been more conventionally trained in seamanship. One of these masters recently asserted that when the native navigators did go astray there were extenuating circumstances, and that the four main reasons were "1. Long periods of dead calm causing waves to flatten out and lose their pattern identity; 2. Leeway changes caused by the shifting of winds cutting across wave patterns, making them distorted and confusing to read; 3. Squalls, which, during their periods of intensity, result in their changing their direction of motion, sometimes as much as 180 degrees, making it imperative to lower sail and await the return of the original general winds and the reformation of the original wave patterns; and, 4. The above three situations occurring when canoes are too far distant from islands to see any wave patterns at all."

The Yapese are the farthest-ranging sailors. They have been

known to travel by canoe from their home islands to the Marshalls, fifteen hundred miles away. Even today, if the residents of one Yap district island run out of cigarettes, they will matter-of-factly take a canoe across the ocean to another island whose tobacco stocks, they hope, are not depleted. Micronesians are very fond of cigarettes. When a supply ship visits some of the outlying islands, the older natives will buy a couple of cartons and hide them. It may be months before another ship turns up, and toward the end of such intervals the shrewd elders will get tobacco-starved young men to work for them by dipping into their hoard and offering perhaps a half of a precious cigarette for a whole day's labor.

The three hundred inhabitants of the island of Fais, in the Yap district, are luckier. They grow their own tobacco, and spend so much time at it that they grow little else. They can count on being able to swap tobacco for, say, coconut syrup or candy, with smokers from Ulithi, fifty miles away. Ulithians periodically make a tobacco run to Fais, normally a five- or six-hour journey by sailing canoe. In June, 1965, five men and a woman trying to get from Ulithi to Fais didn't make it. After thirty-three days adrift, they were spotted by an American Air Force plane from Guam and picked up by a Coast Guard cutter. Their main concern was to get their canoe back to Ulithi.

In 1963, six Ulithian men had an even more grueling experience, when they set forth for Fais from their home island of Fassarai. They spent fifty-three days at sea. On the way to Fais, they ran into a typhoon, and when they turned around they missed Ulithi and kept going west until they hit the Philippines, fifteen hundred miles from home. They would have been in worse straits than they were had they not taken with them, as barter for the tobacco they hoped to get, six hundred smoked fish and three hundred doughnuts they'd made in a machine the United States Navy had abandoned at Fassarai. The most discomfiting part of their experience came at their landfall, when the Philippine Constabulary gave them a hard time, being unable to communicate with them and somehow concluding that they were

Communist spies.

Even at unsqually times, it is difficult, and it can be costly, to travel around Micronesia. The Trust Territory, like Alaska and other huge tracts, relies heavily on airplanes. In 1951, when the Interior Department took over from the Navy, Interior arranged for the air service to be provided by Transocean Airlines, but in 1960 Transocean went out of business. Since then, the Trust Territory has had its own airline, operated by Pan American. Passengers are charged twelve cents a mile—the highest air-fare rate anywhere on earth—but the distances are so vast and the equipment on hand so uneconomical that the line nevertheless shows an annual deficit of half a million dollars.

The ideal plane for Micronesia would be a jet that could carry thirty passengers and ten thousand pounds of cargo and land on a five-thousand-foot-long grass runway. Unfortunately, no such plane exists. The Trust Territory has been making do instead with four hand-me-down planes: two small twin-engine Grumman amphibians and two relatively commodious DC-4s. Until the first DC-4, which has a capacity of fifty-seven passengers, was added to the fleet in 1962, the amphibians had to provide all the air service there was in Micronesia. It was—in terms of area, if not of population—as if the entire United States were dependent for rapid transit on a pair of small two-engine craft. The second DC-4 joined the modest fleet in the winter of 1966. It was dubbed the "Congress of Micronesia" (its forerunner never had a name), and when it made its first appearance at a couple of district airstrips the overjoyed natives engulfed its passengers and crew with fragrant leis and draped one oversized lei, sixty feet long, over the nose of the plane itself.

The amphibians have been essential, because up to 1963 only three of the six districts had landing fields. Now there are five, and a sixth is under construction at Ponape. The field at Majuro had to be closed for a while to the first DC-4, though, because of a glorious instance of bungling among federal agencies, including two that function independently of the Trust Territory administration. The Weather Bureau, which built a station alongside the

Majuro air strip in 1954, resolved ten years later to put up a newer and bigger structure. Somebody sometime must have approved the plans, but it has been hard to get anyone to admit he even saw them. In any event, the building was half completed when the Federal Aviation Agency decided it was closer to the strip than that agency's regulations sanctioned. The F.A.A. said the DC-4 couldn't land there until the offending edifice was removed. The new weather station had been too solidly constructed to shift it a few feet. So after spending some twenty thousand dollars to put it up in the wrong place, the United States had to spend as much again to tear it down.

The Trust Territory airline has a printed schedule, and in theory makes a trip to each of the six district centers at least once a week. The service is apt to be irregular, though. Even when a pilot is all set to take off he cannot be certain that he won't be asked to spend an hour or so searching the ocean for a canoe that has gone astray. The amphibians can carry only a dozen passengers, and space aboard them is usually in such demand that priority lists have had to be established, as in wartime. Passengers with low or no priorities may spend weeks waiting to go to the next island. Not long ago, a California man of modest means became bewitched by Ponape, having read about its lush, exotic foliage, its craggy hills, and its serene, mangrove-edged streams. Determined to visit the place, he saved up for several years, and finally headed west. He got as far as Guam. After being bumped off the weekly flight to Ponape three times in a row, he ran out of funds and out of patience and went back to California.

The capacity of the Trust Territory planes is further limited because there are hardly any maintenance facilities at Micronesian airfields, and each flight has to carry its own mechanic. Veteran patrons of the airline hardly raise an eyebrow when, a few moments before departure time, they see a pilot slicing off a frayed bit of tire with a penknife. The cargoes, which in the two smaller planes ride in the same compartment with the passengers, are varied and can sometimes be unsettling. (Trust Territory headquarters at Saipan felt obliged not long ago to remind passengers on its flights that no fish may be taken aboard except in leakproof containers.) There may be a stretcher patient, or a corpse. There may be a crate of live chickens or a container of sterile male fruit flies; these last, sent to Micronesia by the Department of Agriculture, are released in crop-producing areas to mate with gullible fertile females, in an anti-population-explosion drive that one United Nations report on the Trust Territory has described as brilliant, though the reporter could not refrain from also describing this deception of the female sex as an "effective though sad technique."

Except in emergencies, the Trust Territory airplanes serve merely the district centers. To shuttle people and supplies around the dozens of other widely dispersed communities of Micronesia, the administration has a fleet of nine ships, the largest of which is a four-thousand-tonner that the Interior Department's Bureau of Indian Affairs once used on the Seattle-Alaska run. The passengers—mostly Americans—who occupy the few cabins these vessels have pay four cents a mile for their berths and five dollars a day extra for their meals; the deck passengers—all Micronesians —pay three cents a mile and bring their own food. Until 1965, all the ships' captains were non-Micronesians except Robert de Brum, a member of a distinguished Marshallese family of seafarers. The de Brums are descended from, among others, a Portuguese trader and a German trader who, late in the nineteenth century, jointly founded a dynasty that is still powerful in Marshallese affairs. The captains have duties beyond those of other master mariners; some of them leave their bridges long enough to collect fares from their deck passengers and then rush back to their posts— much like small-town movie-theater proprietors who singlehandedly man both the ticket counter and the projection booth.

All the captains, moreover, lead a harrowing life, because some of the channels through which they must thread their vessels to reach atoll lagoons are exceedingly narrow and, even at high tide, dismayingly shallow. There is only one captain around who at one time or another has not had the sickening experience of feeling the bottom of his ship crunch on a coral reef; he is Dewey Huffer, a rotund, cheerful seafarer who is known throughout

Micronesia as The Virgin Captain.

Captain Huffer is all the more revered because of a feat of nautical derring-do he performed in the fall of 1964. When he learned by radio that a twelve-year-old girl on an isolated Trukese island had been seriously burned and had to get to a hospital at once if she were to survive, he undertook to steer a five-hundred-and-sixty-ton vessel into a formidably reef-ringed lagoon in the middle of a moonless night. He got through without losing his celebrated briny maidenhood, and he saved the maiden's life.

In 1964, five Trust Territory sea captains checked in concurrently at a hospital in Guam. This occupational coincidence aroused the curiosity of the hospital psychiatrist, who stopped by to chat with each of them. He surmised afterward that, although they complained of a variety of aches and pains, all five were probably suffering from what for want of a better name could be called reef fever.

The reefs of Micronesia have plagued natives and foreigners alike for centuries. The reefs are treacherous and, some mariners think, sneaky. One sea captain in the Trust Territory is convinced that these coral snags have a magnetic attraction that throws compasses out of whack and lures innocent ships into their jagged snares. The history of the area abounds with nautical stories. The hero of one is Horace Holden, a twenty-five-year-old hand on a New Bedford whaler, which went aground in 1832 on Ngaruangl Reef, off the big Palauan island of Babelthuap. Holden, who became known as "the tattooed man," subsequently spent years in slavery on the remote island of Tobi, Micronesia's westernmost bit of land.

More recently, on the southernmost bit of land within the Trust Territory, the atoll of Kapingamarangi, the tale has been told of a contemporary woman who, desolate because of a separation from her husband, decided to do away with herself. Without any provisions, she took a canoe and headed out across the lagoon toward the ocean, to starve or drown. But her canoe got hung up on a reef at low tide, and while it was stuck there her brothers sailed out and dragged her back to shore. Quite a few Micronesian islands have foundered ships cluttering their approaches; the water route to Ponape leads past a boat that for the last ten years has sat straight upright, though its bottom is completely gone, on a reef that trapped it in a gnawing, mortal grip.

Reefs or no reefs, Trust Territory ships continue to make their interminable rounds, for they are the only lifeline between the district centers and the outlying populated islands. None of these last have docks, and many of them don't even have safe anchorages. At nine of the twenty-four regular stops of the Truk district's field-trip ship, its captain is obliged to drift offshore; all loading and unloading has to be done by transferring passengers and cargo between the ship and a bobbing fleet of canoes.

In theory, a ship touches at every Micronesian settlement at least once every two or three months. In practice, the interval may be six months or more. In Palau, there is an atoll called Helen Reef. It is a miserable spot, almost bare of vegetation except for a few dozen coconut trees, and it is normally unpopulated. Its shallows, however, are a lucrative hunting-ground for trochus, a shell that until recently—when it couldn't compete with plastics—was much in demand for shirt buttons. A couple of years ago six natives, four men and two women, asked to be set ashore there, with a few implements and a scanty store of food, to harvest trochus. They were to be picked up on the ship's turnaround, the following week. But the weather turned nasty, and nine months went by before another ship got to Helen Reef.

By then, it was assumed that none of the six trochus-collectors would be alive. The ship captain who expected to collect their bones was greeted instead, though, by eight robust and animated Palauans—two of them infants—who were living in eye-popping splendor. A Japanese ship had gone aground there years before, and they had dived into its murky hold and fetched up canned goods and chinaware and toys and bolts of cloth and, in all, a couple of tons of assorted household effects. The resourceful castaways had also found an American flag, which they were waving cheerfully from a stick to welcome their rescuers.

14.
From Saudeleurs to *Nanmwarkis*

FOR MOST OUT-ISLANDERS, THE APPEARANCE OFFSHORE of a ship is a momentous occasion. It provides them with their only opportunity to buy goods beyond what their own tiny stores may have in stock, and with their only opportunity to acquire cash in return for their principal export crop—copra, the dried white meat of the coconut.

The coconut tree is indispensable to Micronesia. It can be traced back, according to one Marshallese legend, to a woman named Limokare, who lived on the island of Likileo on Ailinglapalap atoll. She had two children, the second of whom, named Debolar, was a coconut. The mother was taken aback by his appearance, but Debolar told her not to worry; she should, the boy said, bury him alive, and he carefully explained to her the many uses to which she could put his parts when he materialized again as a tree. The coconut tree has more than redeemed that pledge of utility. From its nuts come, among other Micronesian staples, meat, milk, jam, butter, lard, and vinegar; from its husks come rope fiber and charcoal; from its leaves thatch and sheathing; from its trunk all-purpose lumber.

Copra, the dried meat of the coconut, which is used for making margarine, cooking oil, soap, cosmetics, and a protein-rich animal feed, has been a Micronesian cash crop since 1864. Seventy-two thousand acres within the Trust Territory—one-third of its productive land—are devoted to coconut culture. Lately, Micronesia has been exporting fourteen thousand tons of copra, all of it—because of high Amercian tariffs—to Japan. Micronesia accounts for less than one percent of the world's output of copra—the giant land masses of Indonesia and the Philippines are far and away in the lead—but the two and a quarter million dollars that this annual production brings in represents earned income without which the Trust Territory would be an economic nonentity. (It isn't much of an entity even with the copra money.)

In 1964, on a visit to the Philippines, High Commissioner Goding dropped in at the Manila office of the Copra Producers Association to find out how things were going generally in the coconut world. He was met with gloomy faces. Things were terrible, he was told; a typhoon had raised havoc with Filipino copra production, and political instability was having dire consequences in Indonesia. Goding, on hearing what for the rest of the copra industry was bleak news, could hardly refrain from cheering.

Even during times of comparative meteorological and political tranquillity, the copra market is volatile. Postwar prices per ton to growers in Micronesia have bounced back and forth between forty and one hundred and thirty dollars. To help blunt the effect of sharp changes in the open-market price of the commodity, the Trust Territory administration has set up a Copra Stabilization Board, which guarantees Micronesian coconut growers a fair price for their output, and, in good times, stores away a surplus to prop up prices that would otherwise sag in lean times.

In 1962, forty-two high-school students in Ponape were asked what future activity would, in their opinion, contribute the most to the economic development of Micronesia. Twenty-two of them—all of them, that was, excluding girls, who don't ordinarily work on copra, and Palauans, who don't have many coconuts to work with because of the rhinoceros beetle—said that increased productivity of copra was the answer.

Coconut trees do not grow wild. They must be cultivated and nurtured; in Palau, it used to be the custom for every male to drop whatever he was doing when the moon shone full and to spend three days planting seedlings and tending his mature trees. Whether or not Micronesians will ever learn to raise coconuts according to the most efficient known methods is debatable. When one American agriculturist chopped down some trees that, according to all the tenets of coconut science, were crowding out other trees and impairing their productivity, the agriculturist came close to being massacred. But suspicion of outside experts and their newfangled ways is gradually abating. Today, Trukese Boy Scouts, when they are not tying granny knots and identifying bird calls, are being instructed in modern techniques of coconut-planting.

Coconuts thrive on littoral soil, and the low-lying Marshall Islands, which are almost entirely littoral, account for more copra than any other Trust Territory district. On the high-rising island of Ponape, almost any kind of crop will flourish. Ponapeans sometimes call their district seat the Garden Isle. In testimony to its lush productivity, many of them adorn themselves daily with a home-made headband of fresh flowers, called a *mwaramwar*. The Trust Territory has a twenty-seven-hundred-acre Farm Institute on Ponape, where improved methods of growing coconuts, cacao, mahogany, and rice are being studied, and from which, since 1964, two dozen trained Micronesian farmers have been graduated each fall. On Ponape, too, is the Territory's principal agricultural station, which recently announced that anybody who was interested could have for the asking some of its surplus plants—among them guava, star apple, breadfruit, cherimoya,

Surinam cherry, mangosteen, Malabar chestnut, pink shower, ti lead, bougainvilla, St. Thomas, tiarre gardenia, ixora, alamanda, star fruit, and sour sop. The fruits of some of these are so delicious that the station has had difficulty propagating them; scarcely will a batch of, say, mangosteens ripen when the neighborhood kids sneak in and joyfully gobble them up.

In 1954, hoping to find a crop that could readily be grown in Ponape and could profitably be exported, the agricultural station hit upon pepper as a likely prospect. The project got off to a limping start; it wasn't until several years after the first plantings that the men in charge realized they were using a variety of pepper unsuitable to the local environment. By the fall of 1962 they had themselves straightened out and were in a position to send five pounds of dried Ponape pepper to the American Spice Trade Association, in New York, to see if the product would pass commercial muster.

On receiving the Association's blessing, the Trust Territory administration began to export pepper, imprinting on its packages the name "Micronesian Spice Association," which sounded impressive even though no such organization existed. In 1964, Ponape shipped out slightly over one ton of pepper. This was only one eighteen-thousandth of the amount of the condiment that India and Indonesia together exported, but many Micronesians viewed the achievement as a promising start toward a new income-producing venture. In Ponape, the *Guam Times Weekly* asserted, "pepper has a bright future."

Ponape's fertility is attributable to its dampness. Ponapeans like to say jokingly that they have only two kinds of weather: Either it's raining or it's just about to rain. It is a rare day when a bank of clouds is not draped menacingly on the peaks of Ponape's hills. In the soggier sections of the island the average annual rainfall is three hundred inches. In July, 1965, the skies dumped 37.2 inches of rain on Ponape.

The climate is more than some foreigners can bear. One American schoolteacher's wife after a few weeks became so distraught about her musty mattresses and limp saltines that she took to attending six-o'clock mass every morning and praying for a single day's uninterrupted sunshine. Next she began dropping in at the home of the district administrator after church for a cup of coffee and a dollop of sherry. Pretty soon she was on pre-breakfast whiskey. After three months of supplication and stimulation had had no discernible effect on the moist environment except to reduce her to copious tears, her husband decided he had better take her home.

The main island of Ponape consists of one capital town, called Kolonia (not to be confused with the capital of Yap, which is Colonia), and five municipalities—Sokehs, Kiti, Net, Metalanim, and U. Their names can be spelt in various ways. Sokehs is also Jakejs, Kiti is Kitti, Net is Nett or Not, Metalanim is Madolenihmw, and U is Uh. Metalanim was once the scene of a battle in the American Civil War; in 1865, the Confederate warship Shenandoah turned up there and found two New England whalers at anchor. The Shenandoah's captain told the natives he'd give them some arms if they'd destroy the Union vessels, and the natives obligingly set these afire. It was just about the only time, during all of the alien wars that over the years have affected Micronesia, that any Micronesians have taken aggressive action against foreigners. U, for its part, is celebrated for a one-time chief who was so determined to resist getting involved in outsiders' affairs that he made a point of publicly lighting his pipe with pages torn from a missionary's Bible.

Ponapeans have an elaborate system of chiefly hierarchies. Not unlike the British, they have two lines of nobility, with titles in the one being attained through birth, and in the other through achievement. (In at least one other respect, Micronesia corresponds to the United Kingdom: The occupant of the English throne is entitled to all the sturgeon his subjects catch, and the occupant of one Yapese seat of majesty gets all *his* subjects' whale meat.) The chiefliest of Ponapean chiefs is called a *nanmwarki*, and he is a powerful figure. Until the end of the nineteenth century, he owned all the land in his province. It was lese majesty for women not to double over when they passed his house; and if a *nanmwarki* chanced to walk past some women, they were expected to squat. The inhabitants of Net always reverently lowered their sails when their canoes went by their chief's house.

All *nanmwarkis* are still tendered a fixed number of ceremonial feasts a year, and their subjects annually pay tribute to them in the form of the first and finest fruits of their harvests. Yams are an especially prestigious crop in Ponape. There are at least eighty varieties of yam in the district, and they are graded by size and by age. Some are left in the ground to mature for twenty years, and some attain such bulk that it takes six men to carry a single tuber. The most proficient yam-growers tend their crops in secret and conceal their techniques from their neighbors. The heaviest and hoariest yams unearthed in Ponape end up, more often than not, in the larder of a *nanmwarki*. Indicative of the respect that Ponapeans continue to confer on yams was a colloquy not long ago between an old woman and a young man holding a Trust Territory administrative job in Kolonia. He told her that he was about to get married. "How many yam plants do you have?" the woman asked him. The young man said he didn't have any, but hoped to get a promotion soon. "You'd better start planting some yams," the woman said, unimpressed, "because you'll need lots of them when you're married."

The highest-ranking chief on the island of Ponape is traditionally the *nanmwarki* of Madolenihmw. (In Ponapean, *madolenihmw* means "space between houses"; Ponapeans, unlike the inhabitants of low-lying Micronesian atolls, do not live all clustered together, but build homes on scattered farm-sites.) The holder of the title for thirty-four years, until his death early in 1966, was a non-English-speaking man with the non-Ponapean name of Moses Hadley. One of his paternal great-grandfathers was an American who reached Ponape in 1836 aboard a whaling ship, decided to stay there, and set up shop as a provisioner for other whalers. He even advertised in Honolulu newspapers, urging ships to put in at Ponape for "refreshments."

Moses Hadley inherited his title through his maternal ancestors in 1932, when he was thirty-eight. He had twenty-seven hundred subjects, and twelve children of his own. Two of his sons, one employed at the Farm Institute and the other at the agricultural station, have become quite westernized, but their father continued to lead an old-fashioned Ponapean chief's life. The Hadley home is a dirt-floored, thatched hut at the edge of an inlet of the sea. Next door is a canoe house; paddles and sleeping mats are stored on the rafters of his dwelling. The residence is modestly proportioned, but it is usually filled with a couple of dozen retainers and relatives, not to mention a flowing undercurrent of dogs and pigs. One of the *nanmwarki's* principal aides was known as "Two-horsepower." He once acquired a three-horsepower outboard engine, and went for a ride on a blustery day when, his neighbors warned him, he would probably capsize. He did, and on being fished out acquired his nickname.

In his last year of life the chief was asthmatic and infirm, and rarely went out. Mostly he held court—clad, like as not, in a flower-patterned blue shirt and bright pink shorts—on a raised bamboo platform at one end of his house. He had acquired a few Western ways himself: he was a chain-smoker, and he was henpecked. His wife used to sit alongside him on his dais, and whenever anybody asked him a question, she answered it. There is a legend in Ponape that if someone tells a story erroneously, it will rain. Some Ponapeans affected to discern a casual connection between their weather and the gabbiness of the *nanmwarki*'s wife.

As busy a place as the chief's house was on ordinary days, on feast days it was bedlam. The resident pigs were joined by fat swine brought in slung from poles, and other faithful subjects arrived with fat yams bending their carrying poles. The yams at least were quiet. The pigs squealed in fright, the dogs yapped at the humiliated pigs, and if a *sakau*-drinking party was in progress, as it almost surely was, the din was nearly enough to drown out the chief's wife.

Sakau, sometimes known as *kava,* is a beverage esteemed in many parts of the Pacific; among Micronesians, Ponapeans are its principal addicts. It is a mildly narcotic brew made from the root of a cultivated pepper plant: one's lips turn numb from drinking it, and it often makes westerners' stomachs turn, for it is a slimy, gray concoction with a taste as dismal as its looks. It is indisputably fresh. The natives make it in full and sometimes horrifying view of its consumers. Kneeling or sitting near a big flat stone, they pound the roots with smaller, specially selected stones, in rhythmic, tuneful fashion. So pleasant and familiar is the ring of *sakau*-making that the Ponape district administration has recorded it to use as its radio station's musical theme.

The crushed roots are wrapped in the inner bark of hibiscus fiber and squeezed into halved coconut shells, along with, as often as not, some dirt, animal droppings, sweat, and spittle. The hibiscus tree, if not quite as versatile as the coconut, has many uses in Micronesia. From *its* various components come carrying poles, fertilizer, medicine, and canoe lashings. Its inner fiber can be converted not only into *sakau* but also into wallboard. Disagreeable as the potion may seem to some unacculturated Western palates, it would have been impolite for anyone calling on the *nanmwarki* of Madolenihmw not to sip from each of the five cups proferred to him according to a strict protocol in which the first serving was handed reverently to the chief by a venerable henchman who solemnly intoned, "The tide is high." The visitor could always steel himself by reflecting that *sakau* is accounted an excellent sleep-inducer, dental anaesthetic, and antidote for rheumatism.

A short boat ride from where Moses Hadley reigned from his princely perch is the strangest and most celebrated landmark in the entire Trust Territory—the fabled ruins of Nan Madol. They represent one of the biggest and most puzzling relics of aboriginal architecture. The ruins cover an area of about a square mile, and embrace close to one hundred islands, most of them semi-artificial. Nan Madol was built of basalt crystals—volcanic rock that cooled slowly—carved by means unknown today into huge and heavy logs, which were stacked up in cribs, much like log cabins. There are walls still standing that measure twelve feet in height and that contain rock timbers twenty-four feet long.

Nan Madol was the headquarters for many years of Ponapean rulers known as Saudeleurs, whose power was so supreme that no one within their orbit would presume to harvest lice from his own head without bringing the biggest louse to court. Among the most celebrated Saudeleurs was one of such cruelty that he forbade his subjects to eat head lice. Another, known as The Cannibal, was reputed to have turtlelike teeth, and he would only eat fat people. Still another, according to Ponapean lore, contritely set fire to his home and himself on discovering that his mother-in-law was a crocodile.

The last Saudeleurs were conquered by a tribe from the island of Kusaie, two hundred and sixty miles away. The tribe turned up as guests (three hundred and thirty-three of them in a single monstrous canoe, one story has it), led by one Isokelekel, and after winning the confidence of their hosts suddenly staged an insurrection. Isokelekel lost an eye while winning Nan Madol, and the title of the man who put the eye out is held today by one of most revered aides of the ruler of Madolenihmw, who customarily gets to proffer the *nanmwarki* his *sakau* cups.

In its prime, Nan Madol had quarters and reception halls for the Saudeleurs and their ranking generals. It had harems, and cemeteries, and special halls for pounding *sakau.* It had one pool reserved for a sacred eel, which had its own kitchen and was placated with frequent servings of baked turtle and baked dog. How all this came into being is uncertain. One legend has it that two brothers, Olosihpa and Olosohpa, built the massive enclave without any trouble, having the power to make stones fly through the air. It is as good an explanation as any other that has been devised. Whatever the facts, Nan Madol is man-made, and mysterious. A German governor of the area who had the temerity to disturb some of the ruins died shortly afterward, and no Ponapeans were surprised.

Nan Madol would probably be a great tourist attraction were it not fairly inaccessible; except at high tide, the ruins, lying along the shores of mangrove-bordered streams, can be approached only in a canoe. Notwithstanding, attempts have been made to exploit the place. In the nineteenth century, evangelists from the Boston Mission Society, displaying a commonsense New

England attitude toward pilgrimages, prevailed on the then reigning *nanmwarki* to charge visitors to the site five dollars a head. When the Japanese held sway in Micronesia, they took schoolboys there on outings, free of charge. As recently as 1935 skeletons were discovered. Even today, visitors to Nan Madol can find loose beads from some of the jewelry that adorned Saudeleurs and their courtiers.

Nobody even knows for sure how old Nan Madol is. Until recently, archaeologists and anthropologists had been poking around the ruins for years, inconclusively. The most extensive early research was done by the Polish-German Johann Stanislaus Kubary, who went to the Caroline Islands in 1872, when he was twenty-six, and stayed in Ponape until he died there at fifty, of excessive drink. More recently, and more soberly, Nan Madol has been scrutinized by three cultural anthropologists from the Smithsonian Institution. In 1963 they dug some trenches at Idehd, where the sacred eel was berthed, and by carbon tests subsequently determined that someone had been cooking something there between A.D. 1120 and 1240.

Spurred on by their interest in Nan Madol, the Trust Territory administration embarked on a program to disentangle the ancient ruins from some of the vegetation that had all but smothered them in eight hundred years or so of uninhibited proliferation. A task force of thirty men was recruited to tidy up the area. But after they had done a good deal of clearing, the Trust Territory, which had and still has hopes of some day converting Nan Madol into the Micronesian equivalent of a national park, ran out of funds for the project. The jungle at once began to reclaim the ruins, to the regret of the caretaker in charge, who now, when an occasional tourist stops by, can provide little more edification than to pose for souvenir photographs wearing a relic extricated from the ancient shrine—a man's grass skirt the date of which, like so much about Nan Madol, is unestablished.

15.

The Southern Field Trip

The outlying islands of the Ponape district receive what outside supplies they get by ships that make periodic field trips. One trip goes almost due east, to Mokil, whose inhabitants are uncommonly enamored of outboard engines and tend to look down on Micronesians who make do with paddles or sails; on to Pingelap, with its land-usage rules nearly as old and entangled as the ruins of Nan Madol and its baffling local breadfruit-blight called Pingelap disease; and finally on to Kusaie, where one's rights to land are contingent on not having been absent from it for longer than ten years at a stretch.

Kusaie, one of the most fertile of all Micronesian islands, is notable for its secular laxity and religious firmness. Prisoners there are released at night, on the premise that it is unthinkable to expect a man to sleep in a jail. The island is also a staunch stronghold of Protestantism. It used to be a favorite stopping-place for whalers, who behaved so naughtily—the worst being a man who hung around for a long time and became known as Bully Hayes—that emissaries from the strait-laced Boston Mission Society found the native population highly receptive to conversion. Two spinster missionaries from New Jersey, the Misses Jane and Elizabeth Baldwin, lived on Kusaie for nearly thirty years.

Kusaieans are now led in worship, and led on a tight rein, by indigenous clerics. To the dismay of schoolteachers there, it is considered a sin to study any book on Sunday except the Bible. The first Monday of each month is public-confession day, and everything else comes to a halt. Going off into the bushes with a girl, though normally condoned in Micronesia, is considered so heinous a sin for Kusaiean men that it can't even be confessed openly. When young lovers are caught *de flagrante*, they are sometimes taken aside by compassionate elders and advised that inasmuch as they had better own up to *something* sinful when Confession Monday comes around, they can mitigate the wrath of their religious leaders by confessing to the lesser, but still grave, sin of smoking. At the start of every month there is a good deal of abashed avowal, by hotblooded young Kusaieans, of an uncontrollable addiction to the weed.

The other district field trip goes south, from the lush island of Ponape, to the three atolls of Ngatik (the "g" is silent), Nukuoro, and Kapingamarangi. Many Ngatikese have British surnames and Anglo-Saxon features. Eighty years or so ago an English whaler slipped into the Ngatik lagoon. The crew got into a skirmish with the natives, killed off most of the men, and appropriated their wives. Present-day Ngatikese, conceivably because of the Allied blood that flows in their veins, were extremely hospitable during the Second World War to American pilots, who when their aircraft were disabled would try hard to ditch them at that atoll. In gratitude for the warm reception their fellow flyers received, the pilots of non-disabled planes would from time to time skim over Ngatik and drop cigarettes and other gifts. The only known Ngatikese war casualty was a native who, avid for a smoke after a long spell of involuntary abstinence, rushed out to retrieve a bundle of cigarettes about to hit the ground and suffered a dislocated shoulder when the bundle hit him first.

While I was visiting the Trust Territory, I was anxious to get away from the district centers, which are comparatively sophisticated communities of three or four thousand inhabitants and which provide most of the amenities of contemporary living. So I was glad to learn that it would be possible for me to spend a few days at Kapingamarangi, which, like Nukuoro, is a Micronesian atoll that was settled untold years ago by Polynesians. Everybody wants to stay at a Polynesian island at least once in his life. And to most travelers in Micronesia, Kapingamarangi is considered far and away the most alluring spot in the entire area. It is far away, for one thing. This southernmost of all Trust Territory land is only sixty-five miles above the Equator and a hundred and seventy-two miles from Nukuoro, its nearest neighbor. Isolated and relatively primitive, Kapingamarangi not only has no outboard engines; it doesn't even have a wheel. And the very name of the place is romantic. It was less romantic under the Japanese, who called the atoll, as some prosaic-minded Kapingamarangans still do, Greenwich—a name first conferred on it by British whalers.

Kapingamarangans, like most Micronesians, are fond of travel. Some three hundred of them—nearly half of all the Kapingamarangans there are—have migrated to the island of Ponape, five hundred miles from home. They do not mingle much there. They have established a village of their own on the shore of the Kolonia municipality, whence nearly every morning a fleet of a dozen or more Polynesian canoes, with billowing white sails, takes off for the open ocean, to catch fish. Living in that village while I was in Ponape was a Kapingamarangan named Apinel Mateak, who was enrolled in the adult-education program for native schoolteachers, and from him I gleaned some advance information about Kapinga, as we who have come to know the atoll call it for short.

Apinel, like most Polynesian men, is tall and stout. He was

born in 1933, and is one of the best educated Kapingamarangans, having finished high school. He has been a student on and off since he was enrolled at home at the age five in a class run by a Japanese copra buyer. Today, Apinel is more fluent in English than any other Kapingamarangan teacher. His salary is eighty dollars a month. He normally turns over half of this to various distant relatives, and with the other half supports his wife and their four children. (He has another child, a daughter, born of a youthful dalliance, but she doesn't really count as she lives with her mother.) By Kapingamarangan standards, he is well off. A family of six on his home atoll can get by nicely with a hundred dollars in cash a year, and this, at the going price for copra, represents less than two bags a month, which any able-bodied man can make without overexerting himself. Kapingamarangans can obtain for free all the building materials, fish, fruits, and vegetables they want. With whatever cash they have, they mainly buy cloth, rice, sugar, corned beef, curry, pepper, and cigarettes. They normally spend all the money they have on hand whenever a field-trip ship brings some trade goods to their islands. Saving money is unheard of among them; to that extent, at least, they are indistinguishable from most Americans.

Apinel's needs are simpler than some of his fellow Kapingamarangans' because he neither smokes nor drinks, having joined the Christian Endeavor movement, which forbids such scapegrace behavior, and which also bans the use of dirty words. He has inherited this strong religious bent; his father, Duiai, was a Sunday-school teacher. Moreover, Apinel is of royal blood. His father's half-brother David was for nearly twenty-five years, until his death in 1949, the sovereign ruler of Kapingamarangi. Some called him King David. Duiai was one of the very first Kapingamarangans to get any kind of formal education. Just after the First World War, the Japanese took him and two other Kapinga boys to Ponape and let them attend school through the fifth grade. It was a big move for a Kapingamarangan, for the atoll people then believed that leaving home was tantamount to dying. Duiai succeeded David, and in 1958 Apinel succeeded his father, who was by then titularly known merely as Chief Magistrate. Apinel relinquished that post when he moved to Ponape in 1963, but when he returned home expected to reassume his chiefly and magisterial status. Even when away from his home atoll, he would refer to all Kapingamarangans as "my people."

Apinel's domain is not statistically impressive. The merely four hundred inhabitants of Kapingamarangi have thirty-three islands they can call their own, but one is so small it has just a single coconut tree on it, and all of them together have an area of a fraction more than one half of a square mile. The existence of this fragment of the earth first became known to the Western world early in the sixteenth century, when a Spanish ship sailed by, and the name "Kapingamarangi" is supposedly a corruption of the name of a Spanish seafarer named Captain Mariano. The natives couldn't understand the Spaniards at all. The voyagers had some iron on their vessel, but when the Kapingamarangans, who admired the toughness of this material, stole some of it and planted it, nothing grew.

Even in the sixteenth century, as far as Apinel knows, Polynesians had long been in residence on Kapingamarangi—since the year 1200 is as good a guess as any. The foremost, if not first, of them, according to the most popular belief, was a man named Utamatua. *His* father was a fisherman on a distant Polynesian island, the name of which has come down as Taman. He found a woman in one of his traps one day, and since she was not a fish, he cut her in two and threw the halves away. The next morning she was there again, intact, and he repeated the operation. When she materialized a third day, she was escorted by three white terns, who told the fisherman to take her home whole and mate with her.

Utamatua was born of this winged counsel. He grew up, survived a number of gory massacres, and married one Onotok, who got mad when he proved unfaithful. She took off to sea in a canoe. Utamatua and five friends set out after her, and found her by means of magical powers of divination, which also guided him to the nearest land—Kapingamarangi. Onotok by then was weak, and died; the remorseful Utamatua slept ever afterward with her skull beneath his pillow. The atoll turned out to have other inhabitants, led by a woman named Korae, but Utamatua soon showed her who was boss when they had an island-moving contest. She stirred up a lot of wind and rain, but the island in question wouldn't budge. Utamatua dislodged it with merely a moderate-sized wave.

Then he built an island, called Soho or Touhou, and divided it between Korae's people and his own; the legend goes that on her side, if men sleep in the daytime, they'll be killed by female ghosts, and that on his side, if women sleep in the daytime, male ghosts will kidnap them. Kapingamarangans of both sexes have since become so emancipated from their ancient superstitions that they sleep whenever they feel drowsy, and they no longer take too seriously another divisive system that was established for them by a son of Utamatua: He separated everybody into "Rights" and "Lefts," and he decreed that only Right people could make canoes and catch fish.

Utamatua also founded what was for seven hundred years or so the Kapingamarangan religion, and built a cult house, called a *heleu,* into which no one but priests could with impunity venture; the gods of the sea were supposed to have helped construct this shrine and to sleep in it after dark. It remained the principal Kapingamarangan place of worship until 1923. Then a Nukuoroan missionary named Henry Noah, who had been converted to Christianity by a sea captain, visited Kapingamarangi.

Henry Noah arrived the day before Christmas, which gave him a chance to introduce his hosts simultaneously to Jesus Christ and Santa Claus. Within a few days, the newcomer said that if the Kapingamarangans had any hope of salvation or Christmas presents, their heathen cult house would have to be demolished. When nobody else would lay a hand on it, he demolished it himself. When nothing happened to him for that blasphemy, it was easy for him to substitute his gospel for the Kapingamarangans' long-cherished notions.

Kapingamarangans swiftly began to adopt Biblical names like

Noah—David, for one, and, among today's residents of the atoll, Adam, Jonah, Matthias, Moses, Jeremiah, John, Isaiah, and Solomon. Apinel—whose name was Apiner until a schoolteacher changed its spelling to conform with the Japanese style of pronunciation that most Kapingamarangans follow—was probably named for Abner, and he has friends named Billimon, Mikel, and Anaisai, whose scriptural counterparts would appear to be Philemon, Michael, and Ananias. Apinel's surname is his paternal grandfather's name; he adopted it, as other Kapingamarangans have done, only so he would be able to accommodate foreigners with forms to be filled out.

Western theology notwithstanding, Kapingamarangi has harbored few westerners. Since a British copra trader who lived there died early in the twentieth century, the atoll until recently had no white-skinned persons in more or less permanent residence. In 1956, the United States Air Force set up a weather station, which functioned for two years. Apinel was fascinated by this development, decided to become a weather man himself, and spent eight months studying meteorology under the newcomers' tutelage (he became the first Kapingamarangan ever to measure the atoll's annual rate of rainfall), but after the Air Force pulled out he decided to become a teacher instead.

The Kapingamarangi lagoon covers twenty-two square miles of water, and it is a six-mile canoe trip from the atoll's central island, Soho, to the island—now called Air Force Island—on which the weather men set up shop. In bygone times this island was called Funatahat, Pumatahat, Matahat, and, by the Japanese, Funatahachi. Kapingamarangans, in the pre-Christian days, had to observe a lot of existential proprieties; their lagoon contained magic points, and as they approached any one of these in their canoes they were required to sing a chant to tuna fish, or whatever was appropriate. What is now Air Force Island was a taboo island, because their founder Utamatua allegedly stopped there first when he came in from the sea. It became a Kapinga tradition that anyone who picked a single coconut there would surely die, and his whole family, too. The Air Force survived.

As a rule, the southern field-trip ship out of Ponape stops at its destinations only long enough to let off passengers, pick up new ones, unload trade goods, and load whatever copra the natives have waiting for it. The whole operation rarely takes over a day. I would have a chance to stay at Kapingamarangi longer than that, I learned, because the field-trip ship had been privately chartered from the Trust Territory government to make a round trip from Kapingamarangi to Rabaul, the capital city of the New Guinea island of New Britain, five hundred miles southwest of Kapingamarangi.

The charterer was a thirty-seven-year-old woman, Yvette Etscheit Adams, the only Caucasian ever to have become a naturalized citizen of the Trust Territory of the Pacific Islands. (Of the one hundred and sixty-four individuals who took out citizenship in the first thirteen years after naturalization was sanctioned in 1951, half were Guamanians. The others came from Japan, Korea, the Gilbert and Ellice Islands, the Philippines, Taiwan, China, Hong Kong, Okinawa, and New Guinea. It is almost impossible for United States citizens to become Trust Territory citizens.) Married to an Australian engineer, Mrs. Adams had good reason for becoming naturalized. By Trust Territory law, in most instances only citizens of the area may own land, and she, born in Belgium, wanted to be certain of inheriting some of the property that for many years has belonged to the Etscheits—one of the best known families in Micronesia.

Her father, Carlos Etscheit, now sixty-four, and his brother Leo, now sixty-eight, are both prominent businessmen in Kolonia, Ponape. Kolonia is a small place, and the Etscheits are the only non-Micronesians engaged in commerce there, but the two brothers are fiercely competitive. They run rival general stores and import-export businesses only a few hundred feet apart. The non-Micronesian colony in Kolonia numbers so few persons that one is apt to see everybody one knows every day, but Carlos and Leo, though both have dwelt on Ponape for most of their adult lives, have for most of that time been barely on speaking terms.

Their father—Yvette's grandfather—was Dominique Etscheit.

Dwight Heine, the first Micronesian to be appointed a Trust Territory district administrator, is congratulated by fellow Marshallese on returning to his home atoll, Majuro.

Like most Yapese, this surveyor, clad in a *thu,* never strays too far from his betelnut bag.

Prelude to legislative history: Members of the Congress of Micronesia arrive at Saipan for their first session. Welcoming them (in black tie) is High Commissioner M. W. Goding.

An American home economist, Mrs. Hattie Baker, supervises a sewing class at the Yap High School.

Start of a new school: Lumber shipped from Ponape is carried ashore at Ngatik after being off-loaded by outrigger canoe from the field-trip ship *Kaselehlia,* riding at anchor in the atoll lagoon.

Dockside at Majuro: the island-hopping ship of the Marshall Islands Import-Export Company unloads cargo at its home port.

At school in Yap. The zoris at left are the habitual footwear of those Micronesians who don't go barefoot.

Rongelapese children – offspring of the hydrogen-bomb fallout victims – play with pandanus-leaf boats.

Many Micronesian children contribute to their own subsistence. These Yapese exhibit their day's catch in a mangrove-lined inlet.

At the Palau boatyard, wooden vessels up to 125 feet are built and repaired, and a skilled boat builder teaches modern boat building skills to local craftsmen.

Making copra—the first step.

A copra production line at Dublon, Truk: separating the coconut meat from its husk.

On the island of Dublon, a Trukese family makes copra—drying coconut meat in an oven stoked with coconut husks and shells.

A *sakau* party in Ponape: the mouth-numbing beverage is made by pounding roots with special stones.

A Trukese agricultural-extension worker removes beans from cacao pods.

At the government agricultural station on the garden isle of Ponape, fresh pepper is harvested. Lately, Micronesia has been exporting a ton of dried pepper a year.

Black pepper garden at the Ponape Agricultural Development Station. The conical shapes are mature black pepper vines growing on fern posts. In the center foreground is the black pepper cutting garden where new pepper plants are produced for distribution to local farmers.

The air strip at Yap is just about the only spot left on earth where sightseers can still inspect the remnants of Zero fighter planes used by the Japanese during the Second World War.

Housing, at Truk, for a Micronesian employee of the Trust Territory government. In the background a cave in the hill still harbors a Japanese artillery piece trained on the Truk lagoon.

Courthouse square — or the front entrance, at any rate — of the Marshall Islands Court at Majuro.

A typical Micronesian beach scene—this one at Rongelap, in the Marshalls.

Leaning against a characteristically steep-roofed Yapese house is a piece of the famous old stone money of that district. The bicycle is newer.

Main Street, Rongelap, the Marshall Islands.

Two visiting United States Congressmen pose precariously atop the fabled stone-log ruins of Nan Madol, in Ponape.

When and if tourism becomes a major Trust Territory activity, it is a sure bet that visitors will want to have their pictures taken, like this Micronesian, in the embrace of a piece of Yapese stone money.

The son of a German lawyer, Dominique studied business in London, went to Australia with a gold-rush party, and toward the end of the nineteenth century turned up in Manila as the resident agent for a German firm. Later, he became secretary to the Spanish governor of the Philippines. Dominique was in Manila in 1899 when Germany bought Micronesia from Spain. A lot of Germans were opposed to this far-flung real-estate venture, but the Kaiser fancied it; Germany was already established in Rabaul and the southern Solomon Islands, and the Micronesian islands looked like good intermediate ports for German trading ships. Dominique Etscheit, tipped off by the German consul at Manila that Micronesia was about to change hands, astutely bought land from the Spaniards before they moved out, and from the Germans after they moved in. He ended up with a whole island in the Truk district, and three thousand choice acres on the island of Ponape, along with various other minor holdings. (Much of his Ponape land had earlier belonged to the scientist Kubary, who explored Nan Madol.)

Dominique owned an ocean-going schooner, the *Germania*, which ranged all over the western Pacific—it made the Ponape-Hong Kong run in twenty days—and at least once, his son Leo believes, got as far east as San Francisco. Dominique married a Belgian woman, and during the First World War, when Germany disowned him because he declined to serve in its armed forces, he acquired Belgian citizenship. He died in 1925 at seventy-one. His widow stayed in Ponape until shortly before the Second World War, and then moved to Brussels. While she was in Micronesia, she, too, had a business in Kolonia, so there were three competing Etscheit establishments in the same village.

Of the Dominique Etscheits' children, two were born in Ponape; one of these is now a plastic surgeon in Dusseldorf. The other was Carlos. He was taken to Brussels, as, a small boy and raised there. In 1925, he returned to Ponape to take over his father's business affairs. Leo, who was both born and raised in Belgium, arrived two years later. It was the brothers' original plan to work in partnership, but they couldn't get along, and each went his own way. Carlos has a wooden leg; his leg got caught in a hawser back in 1937 and was sliced in two.

Both brothers were constantly bedeviled by the Japanese, who at one time or another "bought" a good deal of their land at prices arbitrarily set by the purchaser. The brothers have since recovered most of their property, after long and not altogether tranquil negotiations with the Trust Territory administration. During the Second World War, the Japanese regarded Carlos and Leo as Allied spies and interned them. It was bad enough for the non-fraternal brothers to be cooped up; it was worse that the Japanese cooped them up together. They received no mail between 1939 and 1945. Later, both of them worked for American military-government officials, Leo as an adviser on Ponapean customs, Carlos as an interpreter. For a while nearly all Ponapeans who spoke English spoke it with a Belgian accent.

The Etscheit brothers began rebuilding their businesses after the war, and they prospered again, although Carlos bewails the wages that now prevail for coconut-plantation hands. Leo lives the more stylishly of the two. At the end of the war, he took over the residence of the Japanese governor of Ponape, or what was left of it, got hold of the original plans, and hired a Japanese carpenter to rebuild it. The house now boasts hi-fi, a piano, and a wine cellar. Outside it are the only pecan trees in Ponape, the only private swimming pool anywhere in Micronesia, and a cage containing an equally unique pet deer. (A German governor brought deer to Ponape, and a Japanese governor brought carabao. Both species now run wild in the Ponapean hills.) Leo is also a bibliophile; he is an ardent devotee of the collected works, translated into German, of Dr. Frank G. Slaughter.

When the Etscheit brothers reached their sixties, their neighbors and friends in Ponape began hoping they would mellow toward one another. The outlook brightened during a recent New Year's Eve party at the community social club in Kolonia. Both Etscheits were present. At midnight, "Auld Lang Syne" was played, and everybody began kissing everybody else. At the height of this spirited random osculation, Carlos and Leo were suddenly seen in a smacking embrace. It made the whole future of Micronesia seem more promising.

Yvette Etscheit Adams' purpose in chartering the field-trip ship for the Kapingamarangi-Rabaul-Kapingamarangi run was to pick up some merchandise for her father's store, which she helps to run, and also to pick up a new propeller shaft for a ship, the *Tungaru*, that Carlos bought in 1962—a one-hundred-and-twenty-foot-long Australian-built vessel that is one of the very few privately owned ships that big in Micronesia. The *Tungaru* had backed onto a reef at Pingelap and broken its original shaft, and a replacement for that had been lost when, insecurely lashed to the deck of the ship delivering it, it slid overboard.

The ship that Mrs. Adams chartered was the M/V *Kaselehlia*. Its name is the Ponapean equivalent of "Aloha." (In Yap, one says "Kafel," in Truk "Ran Annim," in Palau "Dimeikun," in the Marianas "Hafa Dai," and in the Marshalls "Yokwe Yuk.") The *Kaselehlia* is a relatively new vessel. It was built for the Trust Territory at Shimizu, Japan, in 1958, and its reef-conscious owners specified that it must have a double bottom. This proved to be sound planning, for the *Kaselehlia* has already gone aground five times. But it is a sturdy ship; it once unconventionally bounced right over a reef and landed safely in a lagoon. By Western standards, it is not large for open-ocean traveling. One Britisher who sailed Micronesian waters in 1903 described the vessel he was on, a five-hundred-tonner, as "tiny." The *Kaselehlia's* displacement is three hundred and sixty-two tons. It is a hundred and thirty-one-feet long (or one foot longer than Robert Fulton's *Clermont*), and twenty-eight feet wide, and has a ten-foot, one-inch draft. Its top speed is ten knots, but it rarely exceeds nine. It can carry one hundred and fifty tons of general merchandise or one hundred tons of copra, which is bulky. It can accommodate ten cabin passengers, and a theoretical maximum of twenty-five deck passengers, though it often squeezes aboard more. It carries a complement of fifteen: a captain, two mates, three seamen, a chief engineer, two other engineers, three oilers, a cook, a galley hand, and a steward.

The hazards of navigation being what they are in Micronesia, the *Kaselehlia* had gone through half a dozen captains in two years. The incumbent was Ian Donald Morrison, an Australian. He was to be succeeded, after a relatively long command of fourteen months, by his second mate, a portly, efficient Kusaiean named Tetrick Melander, who came from a seafaring family. Melander's paternal grandfather was a Swedish-born naturalized American, who settled at Kusaie and married a native after assuming command of a ship out of Hawaii whose captain died at sea. The grandfather had once built an ocean-going schooner at Kusaie called the *Palango*—a name derived from a Kusaiean word that means, roughly, "So that's how it's done!" and which was uttered over and over as the schooner took shape.

Trust Territory ships acquire their masters' personalities. Some field-trip vessels have captains who care about the cuisine and even have menus prepared for their cabin passengers. Under a former captain, the *Kaselehlia* had written menus, deck chairs, and round-the-clock coffee service in the wardroom. Captain Morrison, an expert seaman, did not bother with such fripperies. I was told in Kolonia, by a man who had been aboard the *Kaselehlia* not long before, that when Morrison, who rarely visited his galley or wardroom, chanced to observe a meal his passengers were eating, he had cheerfully remarked, "If I ever served this stuff to Australians, I'd have a mutiny on my hands." (I was soon to find out for myself what he meant. After I was at sea a couple of days, the sole Australian among the passengers had given up on the tea that was served and switched to coffee. At the same time, several of the American passengers, including myself, gave up on the coffee and switched to tea.) Captain Morrison would sometimes refer to his ship as "Old rock and roll," and sometimes as "a vile little bugger." Still, from the outside it is not unhandsome, having, like the rest of the Micronesian fleet, a natty white superstructure, and a single blue funnel that sports a circle of six white stars, emblematic of the official Trust Territory flag. And what is more to the point, the *Kaselehlia* usually gets where it is supposed to go.

16.

From U to Kapingamarangi

THE *Kaselehlia* WAS SCHEDULED TO SAIL FROM PONAPE at six o'clock one evening. That morning, in the dining room of the Kaselehlia Inn, where I was staying, I saw six large cardboard cartons with my name crayoned on them. They were my provisions for the trip, the hotelkeeper told me. I also got a mimeographed sheet entitled "Operations Instructions, Southern Field Trip No. 641127-A/C," which was couched in military prose ("Routine Duties: All field-trip personnel carry out assigned duties for their respective departments and submit report in accordance with CPM 59-2-AD revised."), and which listed most of the passengers and gave their cabin assignments.

The leader of our party, invested with the rank of Field Trip Officer, would be a thirty-year-old Micronesian I had already met in Kolonia. He was Kasiano Joseph, the community development officer on the district administration staff, a member of the district legislature, and president of both the Kolonia Credit Union and the Kolonia Consumers Cooperative Association. His features have a markedly Asian cast; his father was Japanese and his mother Ponapean. He speaks excellent English, although, he told me, he had to struggle to learn it. At fifteen, he won a scholarship to the College of Guam, where all the courses are given in English, and at the time he matriculated he had had only one year's schooling in the language. His two principal non-routine duties during the trip, he told me as we were being ferried from Kolonia to the *Kaselehlia's* dock, would be to explain to the people of Ngatik, Nukuoro, and Kapingamarangi the Territory-wide elections scheduled to be held soon for the Congress of Micronesia and then to register voters; and to arrange for the distribution of some food at the last two stops. A tidal wave that originated off Ecuador had swept across the Pacific in 1963, and had inundated some taro patches at Nukuoro and Kapingamarangi. Until the patches were declared salt-free and fully productive, the people dependent on them were periodically being given free quantities of food allocated to the Trust Territory by the United States Department of Agriculture.

On this occasion, Nukuoro and Kapingamarangi would each receive one hundred bags of rice, five sacks of flour, and twenty cases of dried milk. One of the passengers on the *Kaselehlia* was an agriculturist from Ponape, Oliver Arten, who was supposed to check on the salinity of the taro-patch swamp water, and to decide whether it was time for the Trust Territory administration to take the islanders off its dole. Arten seemed a fitting choice for this assessment; he had once worked for a soil-service agency in the Department of Agriculture. A fifty-year-old Minnesotan, he had also spent six years as a Lutheran missionary at Madang, New Guinea, and he was going on to Rabaul from Kapingamarangi, to revisit a region he had once called home. Of solemn mien, he was something of a tropical dandy; I had admiringly noticed him at a party in the Kolonia community club, wearing crisp white shorts, natty white knee socks, and gleamingly polished black loafers.

Arten and Kasiano Joseph, I gleaned from the Operations Instructions, were sharing the largest of the *Kaselehlia's* four passenger cabins with Carl Kohler, the district judge for Ponape, and Gaius Edwin, the district economic and political adviser. I was in a cabin with the then associate justice of the High Court of the Trust Territory, Paul Kinnare, who was to be let off at Ngatik to hold a session, and would be assisted by Judge Kohler and Edwin. Judge Kinnare also had with him a native clerk of court, a bailiff, and a court reporter, Nancy Hattori, a grandmother from Hawaii who had never before been on a field trip. She was nervous.

Judge Kinnare, on the other hand, was a veteran island-hopper. A sixty-two-year-old, pipe-smoking bachelor from Chicago, he had been on the Micronesian jurisprudential circuit for more than three years. This was to be one of his last out-island excursions; he was scheduled for retirement in the fall of 1965. Like many Trust Territory officials, he had spent a good deal of time in the Pacific. During the war, he went to New Guinea with an amphibious engineer outfit, and after the war he practiced law in Okinawa. For a while, too, he was general counsel and sales manager for a Guam distributor of beer and spirits. One time, the chief of the Trukese atoll of Lukunor visited Guam, and Kinnare took him to dinner at Agaña's fanciest restaurant, the Surf Club. After the chief had lip-smackingly consumed his second rich dessert, he asked Kinnare what the name was again of that brand of beer he distributed. Budweiser, Kinnare told him. The chief forthwith proclaimed that as long as he had anything to say about what went on at Lukunor no other brand of beer would be allowed within its outer reef. Having no idea how long he'd be at Ngatik, Judge Kinnare was taking aboard the *Kaselehlia* a half ton or so of impedimenta—several crates full of law books and court records; cots and bedding for his party; a kerosene stove and a large drum of kerosene; a box containing his judicial robes; a dozen or so cases of food; and five cases of Budweiser. Judge Kinnare and the other passengers would have found the southern field trip less agreeable after the *Kaselehlia* changed skippers; one of Captain Melander's first general orders was to forbid the consumption of alcoholic beverages aboard his ship by either passengers or crew.

Mrs. Hattori was sharing a cabin with Yvette Adams, who, like the judge, had an entourage aboard. Small though the *Kaselehlia* was, it carried merchandise and attendant supercargos from three Kolonia stores—Carlos Etscheit's, Leo Etscheit's, and a cooperative. The cooperative also had a copra buyer on the ship. He would inspect the copra that the natives had made and classify it according to one of three grades. The best-grade copra would fetch five and a half cents a pound, the next best five cents, and the poorest four and a half cents. The copra buyer had four thousand dollars with him, for on-the-spot cash purchases; as soon as most of this money was disbursed, it would go to the three supercargos in payment of trade goods.

The trade goods—rice, flour, sugar, cloth, rubber zoris, and, above all, cigarettes—were stored in the hold, just forward of the bridge, much of the merchandise encased in stout wooden sea chests. Two of the supercargos were men. The third was Mrs. Neomy Johnny, a cheerful young woman whom Carlos Etscheit likes to send on the southern field trip because she is a Kapingamarangan and seems to know instinctively what goods her prospective customers will want. She makes sure to have in stock little necessities like scissors, and little frivolities, like brassieres.

In Yvette Adams' retinue, moreover, was the Australian who couldn't stomach the *Kaselehlia's* tea, a young man named Roy Robertson. He was on his way home, with two assistants, after spending six months teaching Ponapeans how to weld galvanized-iron sheets together to make water-catchment tanks. Rabaul has three dry months a year, and its residents are dependent on such tanks, often hitching several of them together. Ponape, for all its rainfall, had never had adequate facilities for catching and storing water, and Yvette Adams' husband had had the idea of importing catchment tanks from Rabaul. But these were bulky, and hard to transport on smallish freighters, so Carlos Etscheit had begun importing sheets of the metal and assembling them, under Robertson's direction, at Kolonia. Robertson's two helpers were bushy-haired Papuans from New Guinea, a mild-mannered pair of young men whose presence in Kolonia had, unjustifiably, frightened a good many of the permanent residents; some of the more gullible Ponapeans had been persuaded by other mischievous Ponapeans that all Papuans are cannibals.

The fourth cabin was occupied by still another family with New Guinea connections—the Robbert Kummers and their two sons, Peter, aged four years, and Job, aged three months. Kummer was a doctor from Holland. His wife Tekkie, a lawyer, was from Borneo. Dr. Kummer, who was in his mid-thirties, had spent five years in Dutch New Guinea, leaving when Indonesia took over the area. He was a specialist, understandably, in tropical medicine, and he had become inured to the compromises that medical men often have to make in areas whose people are inclined to believe in medicine men. In New Guinea, he had learned to accept resignedly the refusal of some highland natives to let relatives who were desperately ill with, say, pneumonia, be moved to a clinic over which he presided. If a sick person died in the clinic, their relatives would miss a gala funeral feast that would be held should he die at home. The highlanders would rather lose a life than a feast.

Dr. Kummer had gone back to Holland for a couple of years after the Dutch ceded New Guinea, but he couldn't practice much tropical medicine there, and he had applied for a post in Micronesia. Until 1963, the only non-Micronesians who could hold jobs in the Trust Territory were United States citizens, but in the case of physicians the administration found it expedient to be less exclusive: there are few American doctors who are willing to take a position that pays only fourteen thousand dollars a year. So the Kummers had ended up at Ponape, where their second son was born.

The doctor had a good many reservations about the state of medical affairs in the Trust Territory. He had delivered his baby at his home, because his wife, after taking a look at the shabby delivery room at the hospital where he worked, had burst into tears. This was Dr. Kummer's first field trip. His wife and the baby would be going on to Rabaul, where Tekkie had friends; the doctor and Peter, a red-haired, freckle-faced boy, would be staying at Kapingamarangi. Accompanying Dr. Kummer were a laboratory technician and a supply man. They were going to check on health conditions generally at Ngatik and Nukuoro, and to inspect the dispensaries there, staffed by resident health aides. At Kapingamarangi, they hoped to make a comprehensive survey of the health of every inhabitant. Dr. Kummer had a large trunk full of medical equipment and supplies, and he had also brought along, to facilitate his survey, a height-measuring device and his own bathroom scale—the type one stands on and peers down at to ascertain one's weight.

Our departure was a lively occasion. A good deal of the excitement was provided by a couple of dozen natives who, laden with sleeping mats, taro roots, and coconuts, had hoped to go with us as deck passengers, but learned at the last minute that there wouldn't be room for them. Yvette Adams' husband, Jack, and their two small children were there to see her off; Jack Adams told me not to be surprised if I got stuck at Kapingamarangi for two weeks or more before the ship returned from Rabaul. Various Americans in the Kolonia community thrust letters and packages upon me to deliver to the Lee Milners, a teaching couple at Kapinga. Oliver Arten was taking them a three-foot Norfolk pine from the Ponape agricultural station. I found myself the custodian of a dozen or so bottles of liquor (Kapingamarangi is dry, at least when it comes to buying bottled goods), several parcels of fresh vegetables, a case of popcorn, and a dozen eggs raised by Robert Halvorsen, the district administrator. Dr. Kummer had brought along four small green tomatoes, not to mention a large supply of baby food; the tomatoes weren't much, he told me on deck as we were waiting to cast off, but they were the first fruits of a garden his wife and he had planted, and he didn't want to go off and leave them on the vine.

In the water below us, a number of sharks were swimming around lazily. The medical supply man, a rotund Micronesian named Katao Eliam, told me the sharks were harmless, but I wasn't sure whether or not he was kidding. Micronesians are fond of little jokes. When Nancy Hattori, the apprehensive court reporter, asked one of them whether she'd need a mosquito netting at Ngatik, he said to her, "Oh, you won't need it for mosquitoes, but it may come in handy for keeping the rats off." Nancy laughed, nervously. I went down to my cabin in search of a spot to store the eggs and found Judge Kinnare there, with a bottle of 120-proof vodka. I was pleased; I like vodka and had brought along a couple of bottles myself. The judge poured us each a stiff slug from his bottle and we wished one another bon voyage.

We were soon under way, sailing out at dusk past the shores of U, past the outer reef, and into the ocean. We were due to reach Ngatik, slightly over one hundred miles away, at daybreak. Regular meal hours on the *Kaselehlia* were seven-thirty for breakfast, eleven-thirty for lunch, and five for dinner. We cabin passengers were already over an hour late for dinner, so at Captain Morrison's direction we proceeded at once to the wardroom, which could barely accommodate fourteen people. I forget what we had to eat, but it was probably some kind of stew, because that was what we usually had for dinner, and for lunch, too. The best food at any time of day was the bread, which was baked on board.

After dinner, I wandered around the ship, which didn't take long. The crew's quarters were up forward, beyond the cargo hatch, across the top of which was lashed a tubby whaleboat. The deck passengers were astern, in a jumble of food and bedding. The wardroom and galley were amidships, just below the passenger cabins. The captain's cabin, appropriately, was the largest one aboard, and the only one with a private bath. Just outside his door was a stairway that led directly up to the bridge. My cabin was across a corridor from the captain's. On the walls of the corridors a number of maritime certificates and notices had been posted. One notice asserted that any member of the crew who, while ashore, was injured in a two-wheel-vehicle accident would be relieved of duty, lose his pay, and have to defray his own medical expenses. We passengers were advised in a memorandum signed by the chief steward to "remove shoes, zoris, outer pants and shirts before laying on bed," to refrain from vomiting out of portholes, and not to leave soap scraps on the shower-room floor. "The next person in the shower may slip on these scraps and break their back, that next person may be you," I read. I was subsequently to leave a whole cake of soap in the shower-room soap dish. By the time I remembered this and went to retrieve the soap, somebody had swiped it. It was a transgression not covered by the rules.

While I was thus briefing myself on shipboard protocol, Captain Morrison stuck his head out of his cabin and invited me in for a beer. He had thick black eyebrows and a thin black mustache, which combined to give him the air of an amiable pirate. He was in his underwear, his favorite off-bridge garb, and was stylishly tattooed from stem to stern. He was fifty-five, he told me, and was born in Scotland, in the Hebrides islands. Now he lived just outside Sydney, Australia, and considered himself an Australian. "I never want to see the Atlantic again," he said. "And I certainly never want to see Halifax, Nova Scotia, again. When the temperature gets below sixty, I begin to shiver. Thirty-five years ago, I was on a whaler in the Atlantic, and even in my young days it was a bit too cold there for my blood. I reckon now that where you can see the copra palm trees growing is a good place to be."

Captain Morrison had been married twice. His first wife had taken off fifteen years before with their two children, and he had no idea where any of them were. He hadn't seen his second wife, an Edinburgh woman named Lena, for eight months, and for all he knew might not see her for another eighteen. This didn't bother him especially, and he told me it didn't trouble Lena, either. "She knows I'm a seafaring man," he said. She must have been an understanding wife; from time to time she would send him pinup pictures to brighten his cabin walls. Alongside his berth was one of the latest: a photograph of a naked, astonishingly big-breasted Japanese girl.

Captain Morrison got around. He'd been caught in a terrible

typhoon in East Pakistan and in an almost equally nasty one at Hong Kong. He spent May Day, in 1963, looking at the Great Wall of China, having got there by virtue of being master of an Indonesian troop transport. "I had a seven-thousand-ton ship, and its crew, which was all Chinese, was the worst crew I ever had," he said. "Some were from north China and some from south, and when you get a mixed Chinese crew there's bound to be trouble. It's got to be all the one or the other." He had been a Trust Territory skipper for nearly a year, and liked the crew he had on the *Kaselehlia* much better. His chief mate and chief engineer were both Filipinos; the others were Micronesians—mostly Kusaieans, Mokilese, and Nukuoroans.

When I asked Captain Morrison how long he thought we Kapingamarangi passengers would stay there, he guessed about six or seven days. He hoped to get in and out of Rabaul in thirty-six hours. But he cautioned me not to count on that. What was more, he added, he was going to worry about one stop at a time. Ngatik, which we were due to reach at daybreak, was an especially tricky atoll to deal with. The entrance to the channel into its lagoon is only two hundred feet wide, and the tides there are strong, running at five or six knots, which is close to the *Kaselehlia's* top speed. It was then nearly eleven o'clock, and I was tired, so I excused myself. The captain said he needed only four hours' sleep, and would see what he could get on his shortwave radio. As I was dozing off across the corridor, Captain Morrison was, he told me elatedly the next morning, getting excellent reception from Addis Ababa.

It was five-thirty in the morning when the captain told me that. He had just awakened me by coming into my cabin and shaking my shoulder. He ran a taut ship, and had a tight grip. We were approaching Ngatik, he said, and he thought I'd like to see it. I went up on deck. The islands of the Ngatik atoll, from several miles away, looked like tiny blobs of green dripped into the ocean. As we drew nearer, we could see a ship stuck on the outer reef. It was a Japanese tuna boat that had cracked up several weeks before. Its bad luck was to bring Nancy Hattori a measure of good luck; when the Ngatikese learned that Judge Kinnare had a female court reporter with him, they paddled out to the tuna boat and brought ashore one of its doors, which they installed in one room of a native house that had been designated to shelter the judicial party, so that Nancy would have some comparative privacy.

As we entered the channel, I could see what Captain Morrison meant about its hazardousness; on both sides of the *Kaselehlia,* jagged coral was clearly visible and uncomfortably close. A minute or two later, we both felt and heard what everyone dreaded; we had scraped the reef. But it was only a fleeting brush, and the captain didn't seem rattled. Soon we were safely inside the lagoon, and a fleet of Ngatikese canoes came out to greet us. The natives had had no idea that we were coming until they saw us. They tied up alongside the *Kaselehlia* and clambered aboard. Quite a few of them had towels bound around their heads; like other Micronesians, the Ngatikese consider towels attractive as headgear, and they can also be temporarily removed and used to sop up sweat.

At breakfast Kasiano Joseph, our field trip officer, announced that anyone who wanted to go ashore was welcome to. He also said that we'd be leaving at six o'clock the following morning and that anyone who wasn't back aboard would be left behind. Judge Kinnare, who was expecting to be left behind, was busily supervising the transferral of all his paraphernalia from the *Kaselehlia* to a half dozen of the canoes, and after a while we all boarded one or another of the little boats and were paddled to Ngatik island, the principal island of the atoll. We waded the last fifteen feet. The island is not terribly large. One can circumambulate it in less than an hour. Judge Kinnare liked that; most of the cases that would come before him, he knew from previous experience, would be disputes over land, and the smallness of the island would make it easy for him to make a first-hand inspection of the property in contention.

Ngatik has no land vehicles, but a smooth dirt path encircles the island, with bushes neatly planted along both sides. On the water side of the path is a stone wall low enough so human beings can scale it, but high enough so pigs can't. The four hundred inhabitants of Ngatik have among them about one hundred pigs whose meat they eat mainly at feasts; but since the animals can't get to the central part of the island, Ngatik is one of Micronesia's tidiest spots. Dr. Kummer was pleased by this civic sanitation. He was less happy when he saw the dispensary, a one-room shack with rusted, torn screening, and no source of water except a rusty tank outside for catching rain. Attached to one exterior wall of the structure was a canvas stretcher; it was rotted through.

Dr. Kummer examined some thirty patients whom the resident health aide rounded up for him that day; after ministering to an infected ear, the doctor handed a used cotton swab to his Ngatikese assistant, who disposed of it by poking it through a hole in a window screen and letting it drop to the ground. The doctor winced. "Horrible!" he said. This, I was to realize, was one of two words that Dr. Kummer alternately employed to express his view of Micronesian medical practices. The other was "Awful!"

I wandered down the pleasant dirt path to the house that had been assigned to Judge Kinnare, a simple wooden building with a corrugated tin roof. Three Ngatikese were building a cubicle outside it; this was to be a bathhouse for Nancy Hattori. The judge was unpacking some of his crates, and was bemoaning his failure to bring along a fire extinguisher. Nancy was preparing lunch for him and her and anyone else, including me, who happened to be around. Lunch consisted of hardtack, slices of *sashimi* that she deftly carved from a fresh-caught yellow-fin tuna some hospitable Ngatikese had brought the judge, and warm beer. The judge was no less hospitable than his native hosts; at that very first meal, we cut pretty deeply into one of his five precious cases of Budweiser. Judge Kinnare asked Judge Kohler, his Micronesian associate, where their bailiff was. Judge Kohler pointed to a Ngatikese girl who was standing nearby and replied, "Bailiff single man—not so good." Eventually the bailiff turned up, smiling broadly.

Kinnare asked Kohler to find a girl for him—to act, he added hastily, as housekeeper for the judicial party. He said he'd be willing to pay her five dollars a week. Judge Kohler frowned and said that was far too much. They were still arguing the point when I took leave of them in mid-afternoon and boarded a canoe that was going back out to the *Kaselehlia*. Captain Morrison invited me into his cabin for a chat, and after a couple of beers he impulsively raised up his undershirt and revealed the chef d'oeuvre among his tattoos, a palm tree that spread luxuriantly across his chest. Above the tree was inscribed "I love you Lena-san," and below it "But I'm just a lonely drifter."

The next morning I awoke on my own at six, when we were supposed to leave. I saw a pair of big brown feet dangling out of what had been Judge Kinnare's berth. They belonged to Kasiano Joseph, who had apparently moved in during the night. I dozed off for half an hour, and was surprised to notice at six-thirty that the ship wasn't under way, although I had been aware of a good deal of commotion outside our cabin. A little later the chief mate stuck his head inside our door, saw Kasiano, and exclaimed, "*There* he is!" It turned out that our departure had been delayed while a search had been on for my new roommate, who everyone assumed had spent the night ashore and overslept.

We cleared the reef channel, without bumping into anything, at eight o'clock, and set our course for Nukuoro, one hundred and eighty-five miles southwest. It was a quiet day. The Kummers carried their baby's bassinet up on deck and rigged an umbrella over it. Oliver Arten, the agriculturist, had a cribbage board with him, and he invited me to play. I hadn't played cribbage for thirty years, but he retaught me. He didn't suggest that we play for money, and since he'd been a missionary I didn't suggest it, either. It was just as well; he proved to be my better. The two Papuans tied fishing lines to the stern of the ship, and late in the afternoon one of them hauled in a fine fat tuna. I never did find out who ate it. Probably the deck passengers; we who were on wardroom fare had stew.

After dinner I fell in with Dr. Kummer's jolly supply man,

Katao Eliam. He was looking forward to Nukuoro; his in-laws lived there. I complimented him on his command of English, and asked him how many other languages he knew. His answer was impressive. "Ponapean, Kusaiean, Trukese, Pingelapese, Mokilese, Nukuoroan, and Kapingamarangan," he said. I asked him how he had found the medical-supply situation on Ngatik, and he said that the health aide had requested a roll of screening, but everything else seemed to be satisfactory. (Robbert Kummer told me later that it was his observation that Ngatik had no decent supplies of any kind, unless you could count an ordinary needle and some dressmaker's thread that the aide had been using for sutures; the doctor summarized the supply situation there as "just plain awful.")

Kasiano Joseph materialized on deck, and I asked him what a field trip officer's main routine responsibility was. "To arrange departures," he said, straight-faced. The weather was beginning to turn squally, and nearly all the deck passengers, Kasiano said, were already seasick. I hadn't seen Yvette Adams for some hours, and gathered that she had taken to her berth in similar misery. Before I turned in, feeling fine but rocked and rolled every which way, Captain Morrison told me that our arrival would probably not take Nukuoro by surprise, since he had transmitted word by shortwave radio to an American anthropologist, Vern Carroll, who was living on that atoll, and who the captain hoped had had his set turned on.

The captain's hand clamped firmly on my shoulder at five-fifty the next morning. He thought I might like to see Nukuoro on his radar screen. Radar isn't terribly effective in most of Micronesia; atolls like Nukuoro are so low-lying that a ship has to be quite close to them before its scanning device can pick them up. I scrambled up to the bridge and peered at the radar screen. Nukuoro looked like a doughnut with a small bite out of it; the bite was the channel, a ninety-foot one, through which we would soon be snaking our way.

There are forty-six islands in this atoll, strung in a nearly symmetrical circle—strung, as one Catholic missionary has put it, like the beads on a rosary. The lagoon they engird is small, only two miles in diameter. From outside the reef on one side, surf can be seen breaking on the reef on the other side. The *Kaselehlia* once went aground there, and as we approached the channel, we could see that the Nukuoro reef, like Ngatik's, had some time before captured its own Japanese fishing vessel. Much of the flooring in contemporary Nukuoroan homes comes from the decks of that wrecked ship.

We drifted off the channel entrance for a while, waiting for high tide. At seven-forty, Captain Morrison ordered the whaleboat lowered. His chief mate and a seaman hopped into it and chugged off toward the channel mouth several hundred yards away. They carried two flags. If they waved a white one, it would be prudent, in the mate's opinion, for the *Kaselehlia* to enter the channel. If they waved a red one, we should steer clear of it.

For about an hour, the signal was red. Then there was a flutter of white, and we nosed our way toward the lagoon. On an island at the channel mouth, not many yards from our hull, was a refrigerator under a palm tree, and alongside were four men in United States Air Force uniforms. We learned later that they were assigned to a mapping project and had arrived the day before by helicopter. The Nukuoroans had had no idea they were coming, and when the helicopter whirred down over their heads, one excited native fell out of a coconut tree.

Nukuoroans like to paint their canoes gay colors, and by the time we'd anchored in the lagoon we were surrounded by a flotilla of blue, white, yellow, and green boats. We had also acquired a big bird, which at the moment of our entering the channel had swooped down upon us and perched itself on an upper-deck rail, like a harbor pilot. Aboard one of the first canoes to tie up alongside the *Kaselehlia* was a white man. It was the anthropologist Vern Carroll, and he wondered if we had any mail for him. We did—four large sacks. It was the first mail he'd had in three months.

Carroll had received one of the *Kaselehlia's* radio messages, and the islanders were expecting the ship. The Nukuoroans welcomed us ashore with fragrant leis, and the anthropologist, once his mail had been dumped on the wraparound porch of his house (the place therewith had the appearance of a rural post office at Christmas time), with the laconic observation that he happened to have some Asahi beer on ice. Carroll, it developed, not only had a kerosene refrigerator but a small generator. Electric lights are a rarity on a Micronesian field trip.

Carroll had been living on Nukuoro for fourteen months. A lean, calm, competent man in his early thirties, he was born in Brooklyn, served as a Marine fighter pilot in Korea, attended Yale, Cambridge University, and the University of Chicago, and was working leisurely toward his Ph.D. in anthropology. The National Institutes of Mental Health had underwritten his trip to Nukuoro, where he was studying kinship and family structure. He told me during the course of the day that there were only fifty families on Nukuoro, but that some of them professed not to know some of the others, having the same attitudes of fear and incomprehension that are exhibited by ethnic groups in large American cities toward different ethnic groups. He had also observed that, to avoid the trouble they'd get into with their religious leaders if they commit incest, most Nukuoroans never mentioned their ancestors' names.

Carroll's own family consisted of his wife Raymonde, an attractive Frenchwoman who was born in Tunisia and had an M.A. from the Sorbonne; and a baby girl who was only five months old when they arrived at Nukuoro, where no white people had ever lived before. Vern and Raymonde had both become fluent in Nukuoroan, and Raymonde was teaching school there. He had already compiled a Nukuoroan grammar and was working on a dictionary; with his wife, he had not long before conducted a four-day seminar on the local language, and all but six Nukuoroan adults had attended—the same six noncomformists, he said, who regularly skip church.

Carroll had also contributed a scholarly monograph, "Place Names on Nukuoro Atoll," to the Atoll Research Bulletin Series of the Pacific Science Board of the National Research Council. It was the anthropologist's conclusion that most of the maps in current usage, including those in the chart room of the *Kaselehlia*, had most of the place names wrong. The two islands of the Nukuoro atoll between which our ship had passed to enter the lagoon, for instance, were, according to the United States Navy map on which Captain Morrison relied, Kaujema and Shenukdei. Carroll's research, however, had disclosed that they actually were Gausema and Senugudai.

The Carrolls had considerable prestige, I was to learn, on Nukuoro. For one thing, they were light-skinned, and to Nukuoroans all light-skinned people are beautiful. It has nothing to do with race; it is merely a matter of aesthetics. For another thing, among Nukuoroans, a man's stature is measured by the number of people he collects. It is a feather in your cap to have people living with you—even living off you. Nukuoroans watch closely to see who among them acquires the passengers debarking from incoming ships. Carroll's house stands only a few yards from a pile of stones that serves as Nukuoro's dock, and nearly everybody calls on him first. The natives had been especially impressed, a few months before, when an American destroyer came by and its captain stepped ashore in starched whites, to be received by the anthropologist clad only in a lava lava. The Nukuoroans concluded that Carroll must be the more important of the two, since he hadn't felt obliged to dress up for the commander of so mighty a vessel.

As the proprietor, moreover, of Nukuoro's only two-way radio set, Carroll was the atoll's communications link with the rest of the world. Except late at night, there would almost always be a half dozen or more natives sitting on a log bench outside his house, hoping a crumb of news would drop their way, or merely basking in the beautiful white family's aura. Before Carroll came to Nukuoro with his radio, the natives' only source of information about ship arrivals had been the speculations of their own divinators. Carroll's information proved, not surprisingly, to be far more accurate than the magicians', and they sulkily spread the word that he was some kind of spy and not to be trusted.

In due course, he won general acceptance, but then he ran into another problem: he would pass along some item he'd heard, and as the news was relayed from mouth to mouth it would be embellished and twisted so that by the time it reached the far end of the small island it would be hopelessly garbled. At one point, as a reprimand for this infidelity to the truth, he stopped giving out news for a whole week. He resumed his service only after his neighbors promised that they would refrain from annotating his commentaries.

After glancing through some of his mail, Carroll took me on a walk around Nukuoro. He said he had no idea how the Polynesians had got there. One Nukuoroan legend mentions a place called "Hiti," and this has led some scholars to surmise that the first settlers of the atoll came from Tahiti. Carroll was more inclined to think that "Hiti" was a corruption of "Fiji," but he had no proof that the Nukuoroans had come from there. Nukuoro had no walls, like Ngatik, to restrain its pigs, but it was nonetheless admirably clean, and it was crisscrossed by broad, moss-covered roads that a former chief had laid out with geometrical precision. Several of the roads had no buildings alongside them and led to nowhere; it was as if a Florida developer had been there and gone bankrupt.

The island had no dogs; it had had them, but when one dog bit a child, the same chief who laid out the roads decreed that all dogs on Nukuoro must be destroyed. We walked past a cemetery, with upended beer and wine bottles used to decorate the grave sites; and past some undecorated earthen mounds. Carroll had no idea what they were and said his neighbors didn't know, either; he had written to an archaeologist in New Zealand who he hoped might turn up some day, or year, and study them.

Carroll had quite an establishment on Nukuoro. He had a latrine that jutted out over the water, and a study alongside it. He had a cookhouse with a washroom attached. There was no plumbing—one simply took a bucket of water in there and sloshed it over one's head—but the place had a shower curtain.

His wife and he were living a good deal more comfortably now, he said, than they had for their first year on Nukuoro. They slept on the floor then, on mats, and subsisted mainly on rice, corned beef, and fish. He lost twenty pounds. Toward the end of that austere period, the Carrolls intensively pored over the Sears, Roebuck and Montgomery Ward catalogues and ordered two beds and fifteen hundred dollars worth of assorted foodstuffs. After the *Kaselehlia* delivered his purchases, during the field trip before ours, life became a good deal more comfortable.

We sat around for hours, eating fish cooked with coconut cream and drinking cold Asahi. "It's kind of weird, living on a small island like this," Carroll told me, "but I couldn't miss civilization less." He thought he might stay for another year or so. When he first arrived, he said, and wanted to supplement his family's monotonous diet of canned foods, he had asked some of the natives who went fishing if they'd sell him some of their catch. They were reluctant, and he soon discovered that they didn't care about cash. Then he asked them if, as friends of his, they'd give him some fish. They gave him more than he could use. Then they asked him, as their friend, to give them some cigarettes, and he did. "I never offer anybody wages any more," Carroll said. "When my neighbors work for me, doing carpentry or whatever, I pay them off in things they need, like cigarettes." Dr. Kummer had by then finished his inspection of the Nukuoro dispensary and had joined us. "Things they *need!*" he snorted. "Things they *think* they need."

Carroll went on to say that he'd been impressed with the Nukuoroans' social organization. Except when a field-trip ship is in port, they stick to a strict schedule. They are extremely religious. Sunday is God's day, and they spend most of it in prayer. On Monday, they gather food. On Tuesday, they work in cooperative groups on homes or canoes or roads. On Wednesday, they work on church affairs. Thursday they devote to community affairs. Friday is another cooperative work day, like Tuesday. Saturday is another food-gathering day. The pattern hardly ever varies. Carroll said that most Polynesians like to have their lives thus planned, and that when he had asked one native friend about his sex life, the man had replied, "It all works out all right if I put it in my program."

Oliver Arten came by then and said the taro patches looked in fair shape to him. Carroll said they'd never been badly hurt by the tidal wave in the first place, but that if the United States wanted to keep sending in emergency rations, Nukuoroans were certainly not going to refuse them. As a matter of fact, he continued, the taro patches were worse than they could have been, not because of salt-water damage but because of the surplus rice, flour, and other edibles that America had handed out. The Nukuoroan women who would ordinarily have weeded the taro had found it less arduous to open cans of peanut butter. Then the men who would ordinarily have gone fishing while the women were weeding got mad at the women and refused to fish. Then the women got mad at the men for not fishing. Carroll rather hoped that to restore Nukuoroan equilibrium the United States, in its distant wisdom, would mitigate its generosity.

Before breakfast the next morning, Kasiano Joseph told me that he had had an extremely successful political meeting in the Nukuoro school house the previous afternoon. All but half a dozen or so adult Nukuoroan men—and, to his surprise, some women and children—had turned out to hear about the forthcoming congressional elections, and he had been impressed by their interest. He said he was planning a similar session for Kapingamarangi, and would let me know about it in advance. He didn't think, though, that Kapingamarangans would be quite as concerned about high-level politics as Nukuoroans were. I recalled that Apinel Mateak had expressed much the same opinion back at Kolonia. "Kapinga is so isolated," he had said, "that the people there don't really understand what the Congress of Micronesia is. All they know is that somewhere a group of people are going to be making laws and that they're going to be expected to follow them."

Breakfast was chaotic; the wardroom steward was a Nukuoroan, and he had made the most of a night at home. We got out of Nukuoro without incident, and traveled that whole day and night. At one point, I asked Kasiano Joseph what he thought about the future of Micronesia. "I'm tired of having the question asked," he said. "We'd like to be independent some day, but to run a government, you need money, and we don't have any money. Most of what we have is water, and we don't yet know how to get money out of water."

17.

Dashing Through the Snow

We were due to reach Kapingamarangi the following morning, and we hit it squarely, though Captain Morrison said he'd had to cope during the night with a southwest wind, the first southwest wind he'd ever encountered in those waters. When I asked him if he'd heard any world news on his radio, he said that according to a New Zealand broadcast a canoe with five persons aboard was missing off Johnston Island, more than two thousand miles to our northeast; and that some Tahitians were complaining to General deGaulle because French troops were building barracks and barbed-wire fences on one of their beaches, to the ruination of the tourist trade. The whaleboat was lowered, the white flag was soon waved, and we slipped into Kapinga's lagoon, the helmsman spinning his wheel furiously as he tried to hold the *Kaselehlia* in the middle of another narrow, tugging channel.

We headed toward the three adjacent islands of the atoll that are inhabited, Soho, Ueru, and Taring. All but a few Kapingamarangans live on Soho and Ueru, which are about one hundred feet apart. The two had once been connected by a stone causeway, but a tidal wave reduced it to rubble. In Polynesian fashion, most of the straw and thatched homes of Kapingamarangi were built in clusters at the lagoon beach, and as we approached what most people who never see it visualize as a South Seas paradise, Dr. Kummer looked at the huddled homes and remarked, "It's very difficult to fight tuberculosis when they're packed together like that, but then to change people's habits is very difficult, too." He didn't yet know that Kapingamarangi has only half a dozen overwater latrines; most of the natives simply wade out into the lagoon to relieve themselves.

Polynesians are large. One of the biggest of the natives who, for all their size, scrambled nimbly aboard from canoes when we dropped anchor was the incumbent chief magistrate of Kapingamarangi, a bulky man named Hyup with a broad pandanus-straw hat on his head and gray stubble on his face. He was wearing a white T shirt and long gray pants, and he was shoeless. (Kapingamarangans think nothing of stubbing out cigarettes with their bare, callused feet.) He was the highest-paid official of the atoll, receiving fifty-four dollars a year from the local treasury, whose funds derived from an annual two-dollar head tax levied on every male over eighteen. The atoll's recording clerk, or scribe, got thirty-six dollars a year, its solitary policeman got thirty, and each of the eleven members of its local governing body, a municipal council, got a dollar a month.

Other Kapingamarangans swarmed aboard the *Kaselehlia,* and most of them went directly toward the now opened cargo hatch. A rickety iron ladder led from the deck down into the hold. Half a dozen natives followed the supercargos down. One Kapingamarangan clung to the ladder. The men below would hand items to him and he would pass them up to other men on deck. First came empty copra bags, and then cans of coffee, bolts of cloth, bottles of soy sauce, and, above all, cartons of cigarettes. Kapingamarangi had been out of cigarettes for five weeks. It was rough even in the lagoon that morning, but the natives seemed unperturbed as they transferred merchandise from the rolling ship to the bobbing canoes alongside it. Up from the hold came rice, and up came sugar, and up came soup, and in the middle of it all down from the sky came a torrent of rain.

A thin, fidgety, deeply tanned white man, wearing only a pair of khaki shorts, had also come aboard. He was Lee Milner, the schoolteacher, and on learning that Dr. Kummer and his son and I would all be staying at Kapingamarangi, he graciously asked us to live at his house. We'd had no idea where we'd be sleeping, and quickly accepted his invitation. Kasiano Joseph, who would otherwise have had to find us accommodations, looked relieved at this turn of events. Milner, who was forty-four, and his wife Nancy, twenty-five, had been at Kapingamarangi for six months. They were living on Ueru, which is the site of the atoll's taro patches and of its baseball field, too. The field has a large breadfruit tree where a shortstop would normally stand; a batted ball hitting the tree, according to local ground rules, is an automatic single.

The Milners lived in a frame house, with a cement floor, on the ocean shore of the island, only a few feet, at high tide, from the breaking surf. They had built the house themselves, using materials they'd brought with them. They also imported a trained carpenter from Pingelap, who supervised a construction crew of six Kapingamarangans. Both the size and the design of the house were determined by its available components: sixty-seven two-by-fours and forty-eight two-by-sixes. The house, put together without a plumb, a level, or a tape measure, was a two-story structure. Downstairs were a living room, a dining alcove, a kitchen, and a bathroom. The kitchen had a kerosene stove and kerosene refrigerator. The water for it, and for the bathroom, which had a basin, a tub, and a vertical iron pipe that served as a toilet, came from a garden hose hooked up to a cistern outside the house.

The cistern was fed by rain running off the tin, V-shaped roof. The roof leaked. When it rained, as it did steadily during our visit, water would spill into the house through a half dozen crannies; in a heavy downpour, a stream would gush onto the living-room floor. Downstairs, also, was a small room that the Milners used as an office, with bunk beds in it. Dr. Kummer and his son got that room. A steep, ladder-like flight of stairs led up to the Milners' bedroom and an adjacent landing. They set a cot up on the landing for me.

There were no other houses within a hundred yards of the site, but as the Nukuoroans liked to hang around the Vern Carrolls' establishment, so had the Kapingamarangans gravitated toward the Milners'—or had until they were told not to. The Milners had not learned the native language, though they talked vaguely of doing so when they found the time, and they had some difficulty communicating with all but the handful of natives who knew English. Soon after the American schoolteachers settled in, they were disturbed by the Kapingamarangans' habit of peering in at their living room through its screens, or of climbing palm trees to peer into their bedroom, or of simply strolling in through the front door whenever they were in a mood to. Milner tried to get Chief Hyup to hold this traffic down to reasonable proportions.

The chief, misunderstanding and thinking that the Milners wanted to be left alone outside of school hours, had convened the municipal council, and the council had forbidden all Kapingamarangans to go near the teachers' house, which was not what the Milners had wanted at all. However, a good many natives ignored the restrictive edict, among these most of the younger children and one old man named Ciro, who for hours at a stretch, by day and night, would station himself outside their house. He talked to himself a good deal, but that was no particular nuisance, because he couldn't be heard over the interminable pounding of the surf.

During the day, as canoes went back and forth between the two main islands and the *Kaselehlia*, our gear was ferried ashore and hand-carried along a palm-shaded dirt trail to the house. Milner told me that when he and his wife first arrived to stay, with, of course, considerably more impedimenta than any of us had, their belongings were strewn for several days over the three inhabited islands. They had had no place to live—they occupied a vacant native hut for the two months it took to get their house up—and it had looked as though they might never assemble all their possessions, and when the *Kaselehlia* pulled up anchor and sailed off and they knew they were utterly on their own, they sat down on the ground with the only liquor they'd brought with them, a half-full bottle of vodka, and drained it then and there. Then they felt better. I had a bottle of vodka in my suitcase, and broke it out then and there, and we all had a drink and we all felt better.

Opening up the cardboard boxes with my name on them as they were carried in, I found I had some bedding, a case of paper towels, a case of toilet paper, two frying pans, fifty pounds of rice, five pounds of sugar, a hurricane lantern, and enough assorted canned goods to succor a castaway indefinitely. I didn't quite know what the protocol was, so I just gave everything to Nancy Milner, who said they had plenty of food as it was but she sure could use the frying pans.

This being ship-arrival day, the whole pattern of Kapingamarangan life was dislocated, and council edict notwithstanding, the house was surrounded by onlookers, many of them staring in amazement at Peter Kummer, the first white child they'd ever seen. Quite a few of the older girls and women among the spectators were wearing gaudy brassieres—white with colored cups being notably in vogue. These are usually donned, I was to learn, when a ship is in the harbor; most of them are doffed as soon as the ship leaves. Strangers make the women shy.

In deference to this trait, Milner had not long before told a little white lie, he confessed to me, to an officer off a Navy patrol boat. The officer had come ashore to find out if some of the crew on his vessel could visit the atoll for a few hours' liberty, and had put the question to Milner, as the senior white man on the scene. Not wishing to disrupt the small community any more than necessary, Milner had replied, untruthfully, that as far as he was concerned the sailors were welcome, but that the officer probably ought to know that burial services had just been held for two

Kapingamarangan women who had died from a particularly virulent strain of gonorrhea. The officer fled back to his ship and the ship fled out to sea.

We spent most of that day getting unpacked, and conveying to the Milners the gifts for them that had been entrusted to us. I needn't have worried about the eggs, all but one of which I delivered intact; the Milners had a chicken house of their own, and were getting two or three fresh eggs a day. Oliver Arten ceremonially handed over the Norfolk pine, and Milner said he'd get it into the ground just as soon as he had the time. As he was murmuring appreciatively about some of the bottles of liquor that friends at Ponape had sent, Milner remarked that he and his wife had only once had to cope with pilferage—when somebody cut through their kitchen screen and filched a bottle of poisonous methyl alcohol off a shelf. Fearful that the culprit might drink it, they had rushed off to get word to Chief Hyup, who is an unflinching prohibitionist and announced, after hearing of the incident, that if the thief did swallow the stuff and die, he would get just what he deserved. Everything worked out all right; at any rate, there were no unnatural deaths in the ensuing few days.

While we were all inspecting some of the Milners' other gifts—among them a tape recording of a broadcast of a World Series game that had been played three months earlier (they had a battery-operated machine), and a travel folder about Paris—I suddenly noticed that the winding stem on my wristwatch was broken. I decided not to have it repaired until I got home, and asked Arten if he'd buy me a cheap watch in Rabaul. I had no idea how I'd make out at Kapingamarangi without a watch, but soon came to realize that it is one of the few places on earth where a timepiece is absolutely dispensable. On the atoll, Milner told me, it is 6 A.M. whenever the sun rises, and 6 P.M. whenever it sets. It was a good thing that the old British name for Kapingamarangi was no longer in wide use; otherwise there might be two horological systems known as Greenwich Mean Time.

With only twelve hours of daylight, and no electricity, the Milner household was geared to the sun. After a daybreak breakfast of fresh eggs and canned Spam, the Kummers and I—a train of Kapingamarangan toddlers following the Dutch boy—walked over to the lagoon shore of Ueru and watched the *Kaselehlia* sail away. We would have to stay where we were until the ship came back, and there would be no point in our changing our minds, for there would be no way of letting anybody in the world outside of Kapingamarangi know about it.

When the departing ship was only a speck on the horizon, Dr. Kummer rounded up his resident health aide, a lethargic young man named Maita, and went off toward the dispensary. En route, they passed a teenage boy whose skin was scaly. The doctor stopped to peer at him, and asked the health aide how long the boy had been afflicted. For as long as anybody could remember, Maita answered. "*Tinea embricata*," Dr. Kummer said confidently, and told Maita to have the boy come around and he'd cure him. The doctor's eye next lit on a fat baby who looked in the pink of condition to me. "Anemic," said the doctor, frowning. He walked past five girls who were eating pandanus out of a basket. The sugary fruit was covered with a thick, swarming blanket of flies. The doctor shuddered. "Horrible!" he said. "Awful!"

Dr. Kummer was pleased to discover that the dispensary, a shack of wooden siding and a pebble floor, was considerably more sanitary than Ngatik's or Nukuoro's. The dispensary was located on the Ueru side of the strait separating Kapingamarangi's two main islands. At this busy terminus of traffic to and from Soho, there was usually a crowd of people hanging around, most of them in no need of medical attention. The building was furnished with a cupboard containing a few drugs and bandages, and a rusty metal operating table, a hand-me-down from a military field hospital. A clean straw mat was spread on the table. After looking the place over, Dr. Kummer decided he wanted some space where he could examine people in relative privacy, so he rigged up a curtain he borrowed from Nancy Milner as a partition. Then, while seeing patients, he himself could only be seen by the half dozen or so natives who could simultaneously stick their heads through a window.

Outside the dispensary, a tall young Kapingamarangan came up to me and said that Chief Hyup had told him to show me around Ueru. His name was David; he had the surname Madakilar, but rarely used it. (His first name was also sometimes spelled "Tavid" or "Tavit"; Kapingamarangans, lackadaisical about many things, are inconstant about consonants.) David, who was twenty-seven, had gone to a Catholic mission school on Ponape for three years and spoke fairly good English. One of the first Ueru sights he showed me was the Catholic church, which was set apart from the buildings around it only by a wooden cross at its summit. In predominantly Protestant Kapingamarangi, there are only forty avowed Catholics, and they have no priest, so David, as the most erudite member of the flock, usually reads the stations of the cross and says rosaries.

As we strolled around at a leisurely pace, David introduced me casually to several of his fellow islanders. A few women—now that the ship was gone, they had discarded their bras and were comfortably bare-breasted—were making straw mats from strips of dried pandanus leaf. In nearly every hut where there was a woman there was a baby, like as not cooped in a straw hammock slung between roof posts; every so often, a woman would reach out and give the hammock a firm push. One hut harbored two swinging babies and two baby swine—the pigs snoozing motionless with both their snouts cupped in a single big clam shell.

David told me that if I'd like to take a mat home he could arrange to have one woven for me, at the going charge of twelve cents a square foot. Whenever we passed a house where somebody was eating something, David would matter-of-factly help himself to a portion—a slice of taro, a piece of breadfruit, or a coconut. He told me that this sort of free-loading is perfectly acceptable, provided one is related to the people whose food one takes; I deduced after making the rounds with him for several days that the size of his appetite was matched only by the size of his family, for there seemed to be hardly a house at which he could not, and did not, pause for a snack.

At one fueling stop, David introduced me to an English-speaking Kapingamarangan of whom I was to see a good deal. His name is Elison and he pronounced it, as if he were Japanese, "Erison." Elison, a chunky, powerful man, was in an ebullient mood; he was devoting this particular morning to sampling a new batch of *tuba*, a mildly alcoholic drink derived from the cornucopian coconut tree. On one muscular arm he had a tattoo consisting of the letters "E," "N," and "K." The "E" and the "N" were for his name, and the "K" was for his atoll. Some Kapingamarangans tattoo themselves with ball-point pens; the arms of others bear what appear to be a cluster of vaccination marks, but these as often as not are actually scars evolving from a romantic local custom: Lovers pledge their passion by pressing the lighted end of a cigarette against one another's biceps.

Elison was an uncommonly materialistic Kapingamarangan. On a chain around his neck he wore four keys. They were, he said, for two houses he owns, for his tool box, and for his clothing chest. He was the dude of Kapingamarangi. Elison was the only resident of the atoll who boasted a turtleneck sweater, and he wore the gayest lava lavas of any one around. Sometimes he would make known his presence in one of his homes by flying one of the more colorful of his wraparound skirts from a pole at its door. Elison told me that if I were interested he'd take me out some night on a lobster hunt. He said that the Kapinga way to get lobsters is to walk along the shore in shallow water until one of them nips one's bare toes, but that, since my feet were palpably more tender than his, I might be happier if I wore shoes. I thanked him and said that as far as I knew my calendar was clear.

David led me on to one of Ueru's two school buildings. The older children have classes on that island, and the younger ones on Soho. At the Ueru school, an open-sided structure with a thatch roof, Lee Milner was presiding over an eighth-grade class. There were fourteen students, sitting on the ground around a table that had once been the deck of a boat the Milners had brought down. The boat cracked up just about the time that the schoolroom needed some furniture. Decorum was first-rate; the students, their teacher told me afterward, had elected their own counterpart of the local government—a chief magistrate, a secretary, and a policeman. The class policeman, however, unlike the atoll one, was not allowed to club anybody over the head.

The students, who ranged in age from twelve to twenty-two, were about to sing "Old MacDonald Had a Farm." This was a warm-up for a practice session of Christmas carols. On a blackboard was chalked "Dashing through the snow, in a one-horse open sleigh." None of the students had ever seen any kind of a sleigh, or a horse, or snow, and when it came to that, the concept of dashing was unfamiliar in their easy-going environment. Milner told me, further, that the idea of "cold" was so difficult for some of his pupils to grasp that he had to explain it over and over again. Some things, he said at dinner that night, were far easier to teach than others. He had made little headway with doorknobs, for instance, inasmuch as nobody in his classes had ever seen a doorknob, but he was doing quite well with satellites. For not only did the natives see them, but they had found it necessary to think about them; when they went out at night to catch flying fish they navigated by the stars, and anybody who mistook a man-made star for a real one might get confused.

That night, the Milners told me a little about themselves. Both were midwesterners—he from Missouri, originally, and she from Michigan. Nancy had graduated from the University of Michigan in 1961, and after teaching elementary school at Flint and Grand Rapids, had decided it would be edifying to travel. She had applied for a job in the armed forces overseas school system, and the next thing she knew had received a letter from the Trust Territory administration. Lee, who had an M.A. from the University of Iowa, had come to Micronesia after the breakup of a first marriage. They met in Ponape and, deciding to get married, asked the district administrator, Robert Halvorsen, to perform the ceremony. District administrators, like mayors, have that right. (They also function ex-officio as United States consuls and can grant visas.) Halvorsen is a veteran Trust Territory official. A bachelor from Chicago, he was studying fine arts at the University of Wisconsin when the Second World War began. He became a naval officer, served in the Pacific, attended the Navy course on Micronesian affairs at Stanford in 1946, and has been immersed in Micronesia ever since. He lives with a pet baboon. Halvorsen has performed quite a few marriages, and couples whom he has wed have often named children after him, or what they hope is after him. There is a native boy on Kapingamarangi now with the testimonial name of Alperijon.

When the Milners told Halvorsen their plans, he suggested that they get married at the ruins of Nan Madol, and they did, the bride in her white gown and veil being escorted to the exotic site by a flotilla of outrigger canoes, whose native occupants blew trumpeting salvos with conch shells. (Halvorsen couldn't officiate after all, having broken a leg while trying to retrieve his baboon from a roof, and rock-strewn Nan Madol, a menace to the sure-footed, is no place for a man on crutches.) For their honeymoon, the Milners took a cruise on a field-trip ship that touched at Kapingamarangi. They were enchanted by it, and on hearing in 1964 that the Trust Territory administration planned to assign an American teacher or two to that lovely but lonely post, they volunteered.

Partly deaf since childhood, Lee had worked for many years with handicapped children in special schools of the Iowa public-school system, and he felt that this experience had helped him deal with Micronesian children who were handicapped at least to the extent of having to be educated in an alien language. He had taught some Kapingamarangan children the manual alphabet used by the hard of hearing, and they had caught on very quickly. When, however, he tried to teach his older students an American game that involved hand-clapping, he got nowhere; it was his conclusion that the girls sat on their hands because of their belief that all Americans are like gypsies and that if the teacher had too close a look at their palms he'd learn what mischief they were up to after school.

After meeting and marrying at Ponape, the Milners had been

assigned to the Sokehs municipality there. The roads were nearly impassable. (After the Milners left Sokehs, one of its villages, Lukunoht, decided to build itself a decent stretch of road 2,909 feet long. It assigned portions of this road to each resident male, whose wife and children were expected to help him do his communal bit.) The Milners had to commute to work by canoe, and since Nancy, like so many midwesterners, can't swim, they had decided that Kapingamarangi, for all its inaccessibility, would be safer than Sokehs because the water she'd have to ford on her way to school was only waist-deep. (This very day, Nancy said at the dinner table, she'd been accompanied by two native children who were carrying a pig across. The pig was slippery, and they kept dropping it into the water, so she finally fished it out and toted it over herself, as a result of which she was obliged to teach in some disarray.) Their Kapingamarangan students, raised in a one-name society, called Mrs. Milner "Nancy," and they called her husband "Milner."

Both the Milners looked tired, and Nancy was pale. What with teaching school and keeping house, she rarely got out into the sun. All in all, though, she had found that her travels, while in the circumstances they could hardly be called broadening, had been stimulating. And a few of her experiences had been as interesting as they'd been upsetting. It had taken her some time, she told me, to persuade her second- and third-graders to refrain during classes from pelting their peers with stones plucked from their schoolroom floor. Not long after she'd finally persuaded them that human beings who aspire to the finer things of life simply do not go around throwing stones at one another, their mothers were invited to school one morning, as observers. Some of the women thought the place was too noisy, and in an attempt to help Nancy maintain discipline, the mothers picked stones up off the floor and hurled them at their children.

18. Coral in the Ears

THE NEXT MORNING, I WADED OVER TO SOHO. IT WAS food-distribution time. The rice, flour, and dried milk our ship had brought was stacked inside the community house, a big, open-sided hut that is the lay hub of Kapingamarangi. Several yards away is the Protestant church, the religious hub. Outside the community house, a group of village elders were sitting around. Two of them were playing a game somewhat like Chinese checkers. Their board was a flat piece of breadfruit wood with a design scratched on it; one player's pieces were small stones, and the other's larger stones. Each had twelve pieces, and nearly as many kibitzers. Near them sat some older, more industrious men, making rope out of coconut fiber that had been soaked in salt water and dried in the sun. They would coil the fibers together by rubbing them back and forth against their bare, glossy thighs. Other elders were fashioning fish nets from the new-made rope. I asked one of the thigh-rubbers on this efficient assembly line approximately how much rope he could turn out in a day; one hundred fathoms, he told me.

There were other, far younger and sprightlier men hanging around, doing nothing. Several of these were young bucks with long sideburns, wearing bowling shirts with inscriptions on them like "Clearlite Trophies, Borba Manufacturing Company, JU 9-1542, South San Francisco," or "Kehner Manufacturing Company, Industrial Sheet Metal." They didn't seem interested in what the older generation was doing, and as I learned subsequently, few have troubled themselves to acquire their fathers' and grandfathers' skills. Indeed, there are only about fifteen or twenty Kapingamarangan men who are considered steady, reliable workers at any time. Apartness can generate apathy. There isn't much that most Kapingamarangans have to do in the course of a day, and there isn't much that they can do, so a good many of them get in the habit of doing nothing. Sometimes, the Milners told me, they would dismiss school and an hour later find their students still in the classroom, having no reason to go anywhere else. On the previous United Nations Day, part of the celebration had been a track meet, but by the Americans' standards the affair had been somewhat less than a rousing success because none of the contestants had tried especially hard to win any of the races.

My friend Elison was generally accounted one of the more energetic Kapingamarangans, but this morning, suffering from a *tuba* hangover, he was dozing on a bench at the entrance to the community house. I offered him a cigarette, and he thanked me with a broad, bleary smile. Inside, Chief Hyup and David, my guide of the day before, were at a long table, figuring out how to allocate the free food. The chief could not speak English, but he was adept at long division. As the representatives of different families appeared, he would tell them how much to take, and make a suitable notation on a list before him. I never did comprehend what formula he was using for the dole, but David told me as we were wading back to Ueru that *he* had received for a family of seven—himself, his wife, two children, and three relatives who happened to be living with them—ninety pounds of rice, forty pounds of flour, and twenty pounds of dried milk.

We stopped at the dispensary to see how the doctor was doing. He was examining a few old women of massive obesity. Two young girls were watching him through a window, one of them solicitously picking lice out of the other's hair. The harvester's family had evidently got in early on the food distribution, for she was wearing a tiara made of empty rice bags. Still another girl in Dr. Kummer's audience that day had a doughnut on her head, like a halo. While she was jostling for position outside the dispensary, the doughnut fell to the ground where David, who had a chronic cough, had been spitting a good deal. The girl retrieved the doughnut, broke it in two, and gave half of it to a boy alongside her. They ate their pieces. Dr. Kummer, fortunately, did not witness the incident. He was too busy, inside, trying to hoist an elephantine breast off a woman's chest so he could touch a stethoscope to her heart.

Later in the day, the doctor said he was concerned about the natives' diet. Near as he could make out, they ate very little except pandanus, breadfruit, coconut, and taro. Unlike Nukuoro, Kapingamarangi had no bananas or limes, and its fish, the doctor was convinced, were more abundant in the water than on the table. He had noticed a disturbing number of dental cavities, and a high incidence of anemia. He asked Nancy what sort of breakfast the younger children had before they came to school, and whether she would encourage them, whatever they had, to eat more fish and boost their protein intake. Nancy said it was her impression that many of the children didn't bother to eat *any* breakfast (several Kapingamarangans I spoke to said this was not so), and that the best she'd been able to do about it was to get their parents to send some powdered milk to school. She mixed it there with water from a rain barrel, and served it in receptacles that each child kept on the premises—a cup or jar or, more often, halved coconut shell on which the teacher had inscribed its owner's name with nail polish.

The following day was a Sunday, and Nancy offered to escort me over to Protestant services at Soho, which was a real sacrifice for her, inasmuch as it was one day in the week when she could have stayed snug and dry on her own island. Services began at nine o'clock—or, at any rate, three hours after sunrise. The church, the biggest building at Kapingamarangi, lay almost exactly in the center of Soho, a few feet from a single limestone slab that marked the location of Utamatua's pre-Christian *heleu*, and beneath which, some Kapingamarangans believe, are buried their progenitor's remains. Built of cement, the church was also Kapingamarangi's most solid structure. It was austerely fitted out inside with a plain wooden altar and some backless wooden benches. The sexes were segregated. The women sat on benches at the right hand of the minister, a handsome, huge, white-haired man wearing a long-sleeved white shirt and white trousers; the men occupied the benches at his left. Behind the women were the girls, sitting on the bare cement floor; behind the men were the boys. There were twice as many females, shrouded from neck to ankle in bulging Mother Hubbards, as there were males; I was not surprised not to see Elison present.

There were two choirs—one from Soho and one from Ueru. Both sang in the harsh, strident, nasal manner that is popular throughout Micronesia. They sang some hymns in Ponapean, some in Kapingamarangan, and one, for reasons beyond me, in Trukese. (Outside of church, Kapingamarangans also sing English spirituals; children at the edge of the strait between Soho and Ueru like to spur on waders of the watery gap with "When the Saints Go Marching In.") The Bible had never been rendered into Kapingamarangan; the minister had a Ponapean version and translated into the local language as he went along. His text was Romans: XII, 1–21, which concludes, in English, "Be not overcome of evil, but overcome evil with good." At the end, the congregation sang the doxology, in Kapingamarangan.

After the service, I wandered over to the community house. A sign in the local language had been newly posted on a bulletin board there. Elison, now clear-eyed and upright, was nearby, and

I asked him to translate it. The message was that all children should report to the dispensary at seven-thirty the next morning. When, back at the Milners', I mentioned this to the doctor, he winced. He had already had one unsettling experience. He'd spotted a boy hanging around the Milner house with what he thought was a pet bird. Then he'd discovered that the boy had snared the bird and had broken its wings so he could torture it further without its escaping.

Now, Dr. Kummer said, he was going to have to try to get the bulletin countermanded, because he didn't want every Kapinga child at that morning hour; he merely wanted pre-school children. Lee Milner, whose wife had just reminded him that he really ought to do something about planting their Norfolk pine, said he'd be glad to go off and try to find somebody who could straighten out the situation. It began to rain, and the roof began to leak. While we were scurrying around stationing buckets and cans in strategic spots, Robbert Kummer espied a chess set. "How's your game?" he asked me.

"Awful," I said. "I haven't played since boyhood."

"Mine's horrible," he said, looking cheerful for the first time all day.

After dinner Nancy went to bed with a headache, and Lee said he had to get some letters written before the *Kaselehlia* returned. Robbert and I, by the light of a kerosene lantern, played chess for several hours, with the surf beating against the rocky shore outside, with the ever-vigilant Ciro now and then pressing his face against the living-room screen to see how we were doing, and with, just before we decided to turn in, two cats getting into a screaming, snarling fight on the tin roof overhead.

It didn't matter much who turned up at the dispensary at seven-thirty the next morning, because the doctor couldn't find Maita, his health aide. Maita had overslept. Things were so hectic there that when Elison materialized and offered to take me by sailing canoe to Nonuket, one of the atoll's small uninhabited islands, I leapt at the chance. His canoe, he said, was forty years old. I raised my eyebrows; I told him I had read in an anthropological tome that Kapingamarangan canoes have a maximum life expectancy of ten years. Elison laughed, in a that's-anthropologists-for-you way. He said the canoe had been built before he was born, and he was thirty-eight. He was also, he revealed, one of a mere three contemporary Kapingamarangans who were skilled canoe-makers. He and the other two experts hoped to train some of the younger Kapinga men to carry on after them, but he didn't think the prospects were especially good.

Nonuket differed from any other atoll island only in that it had once been the scene of a small Japanese military installation. The remains of a concrete barracks building were there in the underbrush, and of a Shinto shrine. And there was a crumbling concrete tower at the water's edge, fifteen feet high, that the Japanese had used as an observation post for spotting enemy ships. They pressed Kapingamarangans into service as sentries, Elison said, but the natives got bored with that duty, and when the Japanese weren't looking substituted dummies with coconut-frond bodies and coconut heads. The island was deserted except for some coconut crabs and wild chickens, which went squawking every which way when we accidentally flushed them. On the ride back to Soho, Elison said he might take me out after flying fish that night. He said it was quite a sight. A fleet of canoes would set forth after dark, with a torch man at each bow standing on a special footrest called a *sahia;* attracted by the torches, schools of fish would come skimming and skipping toward the boats, to be scooped up, hundreds at a time, by net men perched at the gunwales.

Back on Ueru, I dropped by a sixth-grade science class being conducted, in halting English, by Deruit, one of three indigenous teachers who helped the Milners tend to the education of the one hundred and five children in the Kapingamarangi schools. Deruit also taught art, and was an accomplished draftsman. He had learned perspective at Ponape, where he went by accident—specifically, by falling out of a coconut tree and landing on a rock. He broke both arms and smashed up his face. This happened while the Air Force weather team was around, and when an American supply plane came along a couple of days after he was hurt, he was flown to Ponape. He was to have been flown back once he was healed, but in the meantime the Air Force left Kapingamarangi, so he stayed in Ponape and went to school. His fractured arms had originally been set by a Kapinga medicine man, and had been reset at Ponape. It was Deruit's contention that the native bone man had done the better job.

Now, for want of any other furniture, Deruit was sitting on a coconut grater, talking about the difference between simple and complicated animals. But he was having trouble; his students didn't know what "simple" and "complicated" meant. I moved on to the other Ueru schoolroom, where Lee Milner had some eighth-graders singing again. "I have that joy, joy, joy, joy, down in my heart," they were chanting nasally. "I have that peace that passeth understanding down in my heart."

I swung around—there could be little variation, because of the size of the islands, in one's daily itinerary—to the dispensary. Robbert Kummer had begun giving his physical exams. His health aide was measuring heights and weights. His laboratory technician was doing haemoglobin tests and handing out paper sputum cups, in which he hoped subsequently to receive stool specimens. The doctor himself, behind his curtain, was giving once-over-lightly general physical exams. He invited me in. "I've never seen so many umbilical hernias in my life," he told me, poking one. He had been somewhat slowed down, he said, because the parents of babies who ordinarily run around naked all day had brought them swathed in clothing, which he had had to remove. A lot of the children, he said, had a lot of coral in their ears. "Good lord!" he exclaimed, squinting into one captive infant ear. "A whole reef in his head!"

But by the end of the day, notwithstanding everything, the doctor had managed to complete one hundred and seven physicals. He had seen seventy-seven pre-schoolers, and in this group alone had found twenty-eight umbilical hernias, an identical number of cases of rotted teeth, eighteen of pyodermia (impetigo, skin ulcers, and the like), four of fungus, two of bronchitis, one of heart disease, and one of diarrhea so aggravated that he had already told Maita to have the afflicted child ready to board the *Kaselehlia* and go to the Ponape hospital.

Robbert hadn't kept statistics on anemia, but he had on ears: six children had *otitis media*, and fifteen others had coral in their ears. His hopes of obtaining some comprehensive data on the physical make-up of all Kapingamarangans, moreover, had been dashed by one unforeseen circumstance: It had quickly become apparent that it would be impossible to ascertain the exact avoirdupois of two-thirds of all Kapinga women beyond the age of eighteen, because Dr. Kummer's bathroom scale could not register any weight over two hundred and fifty pounds.

Elison showed up at dawn, with a sack of lobsters over his shoulder. He'd stopped by in the middle of the night to pick me up, he said, but I'd been asleep, and he didn't have the heart to wake me. Lee was skipping school to do an errand for the Ponape district administration, and I decided to join him. Ponape wanted to know whether any of the buildings the weather men had left on Air Force Island six years earlier were salvageable; specifically, whether they could be disassembled, floated across the lagoon to Soho or Ueru, and used for some community purpose. Our escort for the six-mile canoe trip was Isaiah, the head of the Kapingamarangi municipal council. He was, for a Polynesian, uncommonly lean; his grandfather, or great-grandfather, was reputed to have been a Western trader.

As Elison, for a status symbol, carried his keys around his neck, so Isaiah—at least while they lasted—carried in the hip pocket of his khaki shorts a whole carton of cigarettes. They were Camels, which were by far the most popular brand on the atoll, except among a few sophisticates who had been to Ponape and acquired a taste for Salems. Elison's brother Werson had once had a small store at Kapingamarangi, and he ordered a case of Philip Morris Commanders one time, liking the authoritative sound of the name. But nobody would buy them, so Elison smoked up the stock, while his fellow islanders hooted at his eccentric behavior. He lost a good deal of face, but regained it, at annual lava-lava-making time, when his wife stitched him a dazzling skirt of yellow, black, and red stripes.

The six galvanized-iron buildings the weather people had left on Air Force Island proved useful right away, for the weather was dreadful, and, except where falling coconuts had drilled holes in metal roofs, the abandoned structures sheltered us from the rain. What a trove of ruined, rusty equipment there was! Presumably because it would have cost more to move the stuff out than it was worth, the Air Force had left behind, among other things, generators, refrigerators, and some desalination equipment. (While the weather station was in operation, its complement had motion picture shows; to share in the fun, Kapingamarangi children, who hadn't seen any movies before, and hadn't since, would run ten miles along the inner shore of the lagoon, barefoot, unconcernedly skipping from island to island en route over ridges of coral.) We had brought along a crowbar and a machete. With the crowbar, Isaiah and Lee pried a few plywood panels off interior walls; they concluded that it would be possible, though by no means easy, to break up some of the structures into portable and rejoinable pieces. The floors were cement, and would have to be left where they were. With the machete, we hacked open a coconut apiece for lunch.

By the time we returned to Ueru, we found Robbert Kummer in a tizzy. He had scheduled some examinations for early afternoon, and he needed the aid of his health aide, but his man Maita had disappeared. The doctor had got to know Maita well enough by then to surmise that he was probably asleep, but Maita was no fool. Instead of napping at his own house, where the doctor could be counted on to track him down and make him get to work, he had crawled into a dark recess of a friend's house, and it had taken a posse to find him. To add to Robbert's discomfiture, he had just found some coral in one of his own ears.

After living together for five days, the Milners and Kummers and I all got to know one another fairly well. Night after night, after the doctor tucked young Peter into bed, we would sit around and talk, raising our voices to compete with the surf and the rain, swapping war experiences (Lee and I, like Robbert, had our own reminiscences about New Guinea) and family histories. I learned more about the education of handicapped children in the state of Iowa than I'd ever have thought possible. Peter, who was bilingual (sometimes he would switch from Dutch to English within a sentence), had rapidly become adjusted to the Kapinga environment. He would chew away at fly-strewn pandanus sections like any native boy, and his father was becoming adjusted to that. Robbert told us one night, graphically, about his boyhood sufferings during the Nazi occupation of Holland, and both Milners, in the best Trust Territory tradition, groused a good deal about the inadequacies of the administration of Micronesia. Lee confessed that while they were living on Sokehs and Nancy had to commute by canoe, he learned that the public-works department at Ponape had some life jackets stashed away in a warehouse. He went around there to try to get one for his nonswimming wife, but was told that he couldn't have one because he didn't have the proper requisition, or some such, so when nobody was looking he simply swiped one.

The Milners were fairly indifferent to what was going on in the rest of the world. They had brought a short-wave radio with them, but it had soon stopped working, and they hadn't taken any steps to replace it or get new parts for it. They hoped that district headquarters at Ponape would send them a two-way radio some day; it would be nice in emergencies. Meanwhile, they were inured to ignorance. They hadn't learned until a month after election day in 1964 that Lyndon Johnson beat Barry Goldwater. While I was visiting them, they suddenly reminded one another that two months before *that* an odd-looking submarine had poked its conning tower up out of the ocean a few hundred yards from their house. It hadn't seemed to them to be an American ship, and now Lee told Nancy that if he had time before the *Kaselehlia* returned he probably ought to get off a letter to the United States Navy about the baffling bygone episode.

During a lull in the day's downpour, I splashed over to Soho.

Chief Hyup was walking around there with Kasiano Joseph and the copra buyer from Ponape. They had a pole with a scale hung from it, and as they went from house to house they weighed and checked whatever copra bags were on hand. I hadn't seen our field-trip officer for a couple of days, and Kasiano looked abashed when he saw me. There had been a meeting about the congressional elections the day before, he told me contritely, and he'd forgotten to let me know. He said it was a good enough meeting, but not up to Nukuoro's. "These southern low-islanders have had relatively little contact with white people and don't care much about political progress," he said. "There are too many old people here, and old people have no interest in change."

Meanwhile, back on Ueru, Dr. Kummer, who rightly prided himself on his gentle handling of the native children, had just suffered a blow to his morale. Nancy Milner, unable to shake her headache, had stayed away from school for a couple of days. In her absence, one of the indigenous teachers had taken over her classes, and she'd been puzzled, on her return, to observe how unusually docile her children were. The explanation soon came to light: her Kapingamarangan colleague had told the kids that the white doctor had come to the atoll to chop off the hands of any of them who misbehaved in school.

When the news was relayed to Robbert, he was understandably dismayed. He had realized at about the same time, moreover, that the health statistics he was conscientiously compiling might not be unassailably accurate. For on going over some of the records his assistants had compiled for him he had found that there were supposedly eighteen seven-year-old children on Kapingaramangi, and fifteen nine-year-olds, but not a single eight-year-old. Being a scientific man, he couldn't accept so implausible a deviation from the laws of probability.

Outside the dispensary, a feast was in progress. It was an important occasion—a first-birthday party. When a child reaches twelve months, the time has come, the natives believe, to assume that he will survive, to stop coddling him, and to begin subjecting him to family disciplines. It is weaning time, too; the child's mother rubs a bitter salve on her nipples, to discourage backsliding. (The mother also resumes sexual intercourse, which is frowned upon while she's nursing.) To celebrate so big an event, food preparation starts at dawn, and consumption lasts till dark. Sometimes a pig is slaughtered (the natives tether their animals by looping a leash around one forepaw), and today there were heaping bowls of pork, and slices of fresh raw red tuna steak, and slices of taro basted in coconut oil and baked in a fire pit, and huge, rocklike doughnuts, and pandanus and coconuts galore, and hot baked flying fish with a sauce made from flour and curry. Several dozen people were enjoying the festivities, including, inevitably, David, who after helping himself to a slice of tuna graciously helped himself also to a slice for me. He remarked, between bites, that his one ambition in life was to get a pair of low shoes, size 7¼ medium, to wear to church.

The guest of honor, a plump baby girl, looked glum. She had been imprisoned in a long-sleeved, ankle-length, red dress, while all the other small children were running around free and naked. Dr. Kummer emerged from the dispensary to pay his respects to the birthday child, and on glancing at her *he* looked glum. "Clear-cut case of malnutrition," he remarked. I asked him if he'd been to many feasts in Micronesia, and he said the last one that came to mind had been at the home of the *nanmwarki* of Madolenihmw. The doctor had brought the ailing old chief some ampules of drugs to ease his asthma, and when Robbert left he discovered that the *nanmwarki,* in grateful reciprocation, had had a live pig trussed and dumped into the visitor's boat.

The following morning, Robbert and I, who had been harboring the same silent thoughts, both began to wonder aloud when the *Kaselehlia* would return for us. I sought out Kasiano Joseph and put the question to him. He said he thought tomorrow, maybe, or if not tomorrow maybe the day after that, maybe. By now, as I walked around the two little islands, I could recognize and identify a good many of the people who smiled and nodded greetings, and even some of the tethered pigs were beginning to look familiar, like suburban neighbors' dogs. The sun was out, for a change, and it was a hot and humid day, and I stopped off in the shade of Lee's classroom roof. His seventh- and eighth-graders were painstakingly chanting, in unison, a dialogue from a textbook that went:

Mrs. Miller: I don't like cold weather.
Mrs. Perry: My son doesn't like cold weather, either. He's in Alaska with the army. He wrote yesterday. He said that it was snowing there.
Mrs. Miller: Does it snow very much in Alaska?
Mrs. Perry: Yes, but they have clear, sunny days, too.
Mrs. Miller: Does your son like Alaska?
Mrs. Perry: Yes, he likes snowy weather. He doesn't like hot weather.

I had to leave before Lee got around to what I imagined might be a challenging explanation of that colloquy, because I had agreed to accompany Robbert to an appointment with the Chief. Hyup's house, on Soho, was quite near Nancy's first- and second-grade classroom, and as we drew near our destination we could hear her pupils singing. "This is the way we go to school, go to school, go to school . . ." (Except when the children were spitting on the floor, her classroom was a tidy place, with "jobs for month" written out on a bulletin board: Kesin and Walden were in charge of crayons, Septina and Emerina of mats, Eluru of Cuisenaire rods—a method of teaching arithmetic to toddlers—Usuru of ringing the bell, and Nena of art supplies. Kalina and Kimson were line leaders, and Naker and Ugo were supposed to pick up paper.)

Chief Hyup received us—Robbert, myself, and David, who was acting as interpreter—in magisterial style. Attired for the occasion in a shocking pink lava lava, the chief was sitting, Buddhalike, on a raised wooden platform in his house. He had a bad cough, and was drinking something, conceivably medicinal, from the spout of a teapot. Periodically, he would clear his throat and spit on the floor. The doctor made no remonstrance; after all, he was a guest in Hyup's house. Robbert got down to business at once. He had concluded that Kapingamarangi had an intolerably high incidence of perinatal deaths, and he thought (his own wife's experience notwithstanding) that the reason for this sad state of affairs was that the local women had babies at home. The doctor wanted a delivery room built as an annex to the dispensary, and while he was at it he advocated the construction of an entirely new medical building. The chief, a man of few words, grunted occasionally during the doctor's exposition, and finally nodded his assent and suggested that perhaps such an installation would be created out of the Air Force Island structures.

That being settled, at least on a policy level, Robbert said he hoped to put an X-ray machine aboard the *Kaselehlia* its next trip south, so that the islanders could be checked for tuberculosis. He told the chief that the equipment would be too cumbersome to ferry ashore; the natives would have to paddle out to the ship to be examined. The chief grunted, coughed, spat, and nodded. Finally, the doctor said, he had found the condition of most Kapingamarangans' teeth to be awful—just horrible. He wanted to send a dental team out on the *Kaselehlia,* too, and to have it remain on the atoll for at least a month. Meanwhile, he hoped the chief would initiate a propaganda campaign in favor of toothbrushes. Hyup looked dubious. The doctor added hastily that not only would the chief, by plugging dental prophylaxis, do his subjects a service, but that he understood the chief ran a store, and what better way could there be to combine business with uplift than for the chief to sell toothbrushes?

The chief's expression brightened. He hauled himself up from his perch, and showed us his emporium—a six-by-twelve-foot annex to his house. It was so full of crates and boxes (not to mention a desk with a briefcase and a Trust Territory flag atop it), that there was barely room to walk inside. The merchandise on display included small quantities of flashlight batteries, sugar, cloth, lanterns, chewing gum, cigarettes, several sheets of tin, two onions, and a pair of rubber zoris. Seeing these last, I was reminded that the only footwear I'd brought along, some sneakers and leather sandals, had been wet throughout my stay, so I asked the chief if he had any zoris my size. He didn't; the only ones he had were three sizes too large. I bought them anyway. When he had a full line of zoris, he told me, his charge for them was based on their dimensions. The charge for a size-10 pair would be a dollar, for a size-10½ $1.15, for a size-11 $1.30, and so forth. It seemed like a sensible way to price shoes.

At the Milners', Nancy was holding a library class on her living room floor, with seventeen third-graders in attendance, around ten years old. She had made them all wash their hands in the ocean before picking up any books. Today, she was trying to teach her charges, none of whom could read English, that books were to be looked at, not thrown. She was also trying to get them to come to grips with the alphabet. To that end, she had put the words "cat," "fish," "all," "jump," "eat," "let," and "house" on a large sheet of paper. She gave each child a piece of paper and a pencil and asked the class to write down the seven words, in alphabetical order. She explained at great length what alphabetical order was, and then had an eighth-grade girl who was helping her repeat the explanation in Kapingamarangan. Not one of the children came close to solving the problem, but most of them seemed to be trying hard, except for one boy with a slingshot around his neck. He was the one who had turned up earlier with the maimed bird.

Deruit, the art and science teacher, dropped in after the library session. He was nearly twenty-two, had a wife, a child, and a steady job (he earned $10.40 a week), and thought he was in a rut. He told me that his ambition was to get back to Ponape and resume his education where he'd left off—on the threshold of tenth grade. "I want to help the people of my atoll," he said, solemnly. Specifically, he wanted to instill in them a sounder appreciation of health and sanitation. He thought too many Kapingamarangans were indifferent to germs and flies. As he was leaving, I asked him if there was anything I could send him from the outside world, when and if I returned to it. Yes, he said; he would like a subscription to *Time*.

19.

The Ship! The Ship!

There was exciting news the next morning. Elison had got Port Moresby on his radio, and although the reception had been poor, he thought he'd heard in a broadcast of ship movements that the *Kaselehlia* had left Rabaul the night before that. There was a stir of activity among a dozen or so natives who hoped to obtain deck passage to Ponape. Some of them had been on a waiting list for more than a year. Now, as they had done in vain half a dozen previous times, they were assembling food and clothing and sleeping mats, on the chance that they could get aboard. I learned for the first time that a ship may not enter a Trust Territory port from outside waters without medical clearance. Were not Robbert on Kapingamarangi, the *Kaselehlia* would have to go first to some island where one of the five doctors in Micronesia was present. I felt boundless gratitude to Robbert for being where he was, even though he had trounced me brutally at chess the night before. In any event, there was no rush, for this was a Saturday, and even if the ship appeared within the hour, it wouldn't leave before Monday. For all their dependence on copra as a cash crop, Kapingamarangans are not permitted by their spiritual leaders to load cargo, or do any other gainful work, on Sunday. It was raining hard, but just on the possibility that we might see something on the horizon, Robbert and I walked to the shore and looked long and longingly out toward sea. Nothing.

It rained all night. Two empty coffee cans, a ten-quart bucket, a mixing bowl, and an ashtray, strategically emplaced, collected most of the water that dripped into my sleeping quarters, but the living-room floor was awash. Shortly before dawn, the rain stopped, and when we got up the sky was clear and the sun was out. It was the second most beautiful sight Robbert and I could conceive of—the first, of course, being the lovely, lovely *Kaselehlia*. By now, I could not imagine how Captain Morrison could ever have described this precious link to life as a vile little bugger.

Robbert and I went out to look for the ship, to no avail, before breakfast. Lee went out to plant the Norfolk pine. *For* breakfast, Nancy opened up a case marked "corned beef." It contained Mazola. But who could have cared less, because, while we were eating Spam and scrambled eggs instead, one of the Milners' students came flying up their path. The ship! The ship! I was glad I knew what livestock Kapinga had, for that is also the way the local kids pronounce "sheep."

We left the eggs and scrambled toward the beach, where we watched the *Kaselehlia* pick its way through the channel. Soon we could see our old friends waving from the compass bridge—Tekkie Kummer, Yvette Adams, Oliver Arten, Neomy Johnny, and Captain Morrison himself. It was better than a college reunion. Elison dragged his canoe into the water, and Robbert, Lee, and I climbed in. Two of Robbert's medical assistants came along, grunting under a heavy piece of equipment that they swung aboard. It was a fogging machine, from which, as soon as we were on the big ship, spewed forth clouds of disinfectant. Robbert, after a foggy embrace with his wife, pronounced the *Kaselehlia* cleared for reentry into its home waters, and Captain Morrison invited us all to his cabin for a celebratory round of South Pacific Lager, brewed in Port Moresby.

Yvette Adams, her charter of the ship now terminated, was sulking. It seemed that she'd been paying fifteen dollars an hour for the *Kaselehlia*, and that during the night the ship had drifted off course forty miles to the southeast, or about five hours' sailing time, or about seventy-five dollars' worth of misdirection. What was more, four Micronesian merchant-marine students who'd been attending a course in the British Solomon Islands had boarded the ship at Rabaul. If they'd been classified as passengers, they'd have had to pay fare to Yvette for the Rabaul-Kapingamarangi run, but they'd been classified instead as members of the crew, which meant another fifty dollars out of, or at any rate not into, her pocket. And, finally, she'd been unable to obtain a propeller shaft for her father's boat. He needed a fourteen-footer, and Rabaul had only sixteen-footers available.

Still and all, she had acquired a good deal of merchandise. Lashed on the cargo deck were forty drums of kerosene, not to mention a new Land Rover. In the hold were trade goods of all kinds, including several dozen cases of South Pacific Lager. Captain Morrison said that whatever happened he wanted to save a case for Judge Kinnare, who would probably be parched by the time we reached Ngatik. I myself, long after we had drunk up all the potables in the Milner household, had secretly saved four ounces of vodka, as a surprise for the judge.

Everybody, it seemed, had been on a shopping spree at Rabaul. Tekkie Kummer had some new clothes, and Captain Morrison had laid in a supply of frilly French ladies' underwear. Oliver Arten had bought himself a deck chair, to loll in on the trip home. He had bought me a self-winding, waterproof, shockproof, twenty-five-jewel, German-made wristwatch, for only $23.75. He had also been commissioned by Elison, it now developed, to make a few purchases on *his* behalf: a three-cell flashlight battery, a pair of trousers, a belt, twelve yards of white cloth, and twenty-six yards of colored cloth—enough to keep a dude on top of the lava-lava heap against almost any conceivable challenge to his supremacy. Lee reported to Oliver that the Norfolk pine was in the ground and seemed to have taken hold nicely.

Robbert and I had imposed on the Milners for nine nights, and rather than wear out our welcome we moved back onto the anchored ship that afternoon. The copra-loading would begin at dawn. Kasiano calculated that the hold could accommodate sixty tons of copra in all; Kapingamarangi had seventeen tons—about seventeen hundred dollars' worth—weighed, graded, and bagged. While Captain Morrison was showing me some of his lacy purchases, the chief mate came into the master's cabin to report that he'd roused Ponape on the radio and that district headquarters had said the *Kaselehlia* could stay at Kapingamarangi as long as was necessary to get all the copra aboard. "The Judge'll be lucky if there's any beer left by the time we reach Ngatik," the captain remarked, as he summoned the mess steward to fetch him and me another bottle each of South Pacific Lager.

It took most of the next day to load the copra, along with the deck passengers—five in all—whom the Captain decided he could accommodate. There was a last-minute substitution in this group, when Dr. Kummer discovered that the baby with diarrhea, whom he had wanted to hospitalize at Ponape, wasn't aboard. Her mother had refused to make the trip, being more fearful of a voyage on the *Kaselehlia* than she was concerned about the child's survival, and Maita, the health aide, had forgotten to pass along this news to his superior. Chief Hyup, who was seeing us off, agreed to go back ashore and try to talk the mother into changing her mind, but he couldn't get anywhere with her.

So the child would have to stay, and, in Robbert's judgment, to die. He did what he could. He gave Maita twenty terramycin tablets, and instructed him to halve them and give the baby half a tablet four times daily for ten days, in syrup. (For Maita to be wakeful enough to do that, Robbert confided to me, would in his further judgment be an utterly uncharacteristic achievement.) Maita said he didn't have any syrup. Nancy Milner said she had a can of Log Cabin maple syrup in her larder that he was welcome to.

Three squealing, protesting pigs were brought aboard by the deck passengers, and were stowed in rickety wooden cages on the cargo deck, alongside the kerosene drums. Neomy Johnny, Carlos Etscheit's supercargo, seemed to be acting as housemother for the deck passengers, and as we set forth shortly before dusk, she was entertaining them with a phonograph. We slipped through the channel and away from Kapingamarangi to the strains of "Love Songs of Polynesia." It was dark by the time we circled around and passed the ocean side of Ueru. A lantern was flickering at the site of the Milners' house. They would have two or three months to catch up on their reading before they saw our ship again.

There was no particular reason to get up early the following morning, inasmuch as we weren't due to reach Nukuoro until noon, but most of us were awake before daylight. One of the pigs had broken loose, and the commotion that ensued when two seamen tried to corral it was ear-splitting and eye-opening. That morning, up on deck, I fell into conversation with one of the four merchant mariners who were homebound from the Solomons. He was a stocky, twenty-nine-year-old, eager-beaver Palauan named Elias Okamura, who while going to high school on Guam had become acquainted with a Navy chaplain. The chaplain got him a four-year scholarship at Susquehanna College, in Pennsylvania. Okamura said he was the smallest fullback Susquehanna had ever had. Later he'd gone to a celestial-navigation school on Sunset Boulevard in Los Angeles, only three blocks from Hollywood. He hoped some day to be a skilled enough seaman to command one of the Trust Territory ships, and he would seem to be well on his way toward realizing his ambition, for after I left Micronesia I learned of his appointment as second mate—replacing the new captain—on the *Kaselehlia*.

When, a few hours later, we found ourselves back ashore at familiar old Nukuoro, we were in for a surprise. The Nukuoroans, who had expected to have thirty tons of copra awaiting us, had only fifteen. They'd all been sick, and it was apparently the *Kaselehlia's* fault. Most of the natives of the Trust Territory are highly susceptible to any kind of epidemic disease, and our ship had hardly left Nukuoro a fortnight earlier when practically everyone on the atoll came down with a respiratory disease, presumably brought ashore by one of us. As a result, most of the Nukuoroans had been too weak to make copra. Vern Carroll told me this while we were taking a walk, I having some difficulty because of my oversize flapping zoris. While I was retrieving one of them, which had dropped off in a stream, I noticed that his zoris seemed much too small for him. It turned out that the only pair he had been able to get on Nukuoro were my size, and that my size fitted him perfectly. We swapped footwear on the spot.

In view of the conflict of interests that I knew beset the mess steward at Nukuoro, I was easily persuaded to dine at the Carrolls'. It was an idyllic tropical evening. A glorious golden sunset gave way to a breathtaking full moon. The moon's reflection shimmered on the nearly calm surface of the lagoon. Coconut palm fronds were gently waving. It was a made-to-order setting for Polynesian love songs, and a Nukuoroan girl did in fact turn up with a ukulele and sit in a shadowy corner of the Carrolls' porch, strumming soft background music. Captain Morrison materialized out of the night, and he sat on the porch steps, speculatively playing a flashlight on passing native girls. A few minutes later, a bell rang out. "What was that?" asked the Captain, startled. Nine o'clock curfew, Vern Carroll told him. The captain called for his whaleboat, and we rode back to the *Kaselehlia* and had a beer and went to bed.

At daybreak, I was awakened by, of all logical but unexpected summonses, a cockcrow. We'd taken on some chicken crates during the night. The albatross-like bird that had escorted us into Nukuoro before was back at its perch, ready to guide us out.

Captain Morrison wanted to make an early start for Ngatik, and he did: The last copra was loaded at six-fifty-five, and we were under way at seven. The big bird stayed with us until we cleared the lagoon channel. Then it took to the air, circled lazily over us several times, and sped off toward a bobbing canoe, with a man and boy in it, that had followed us to the outside mouth of the channel.

Just after lunch, we encountered one of those medical emergencies that can arise in an area of many square miles and few doctors. Kusaie was on the radio, requesting a conference with Dr. Kummer. But the static was so bad that none of us who were gathered at the bridge, straining our hardest to listen, could make out what was being said. So Kusaie got Ponape to relay its message, and that came in more clearly. A boy had been sick for several weeks with an intestinal virus, followed by tonsilitis and an ear infection. The virus seemed better, and the tonsils were less swollen, but the ear was still acting up, and should Kusaie try to get the boy to the Ponape hospital? (It would have required a special flight by one of the amphibian planes, assuming that either was available.) Dr. Kummer asked Ponape to ask Kusaie a few questions: What was the boy's temperature? It had been 102.6, but was normal now. What medication had he been getting? Sulfadiacin.

Robbert listened thoughtfully as the conference went crackling on, and finally scribbled a message for the ship's radio operator to transmit to Ponape to pass along to Kusaie: "Give 1.2 million units of Bicillin (4 cc.) intermuscularly every 2 days, clean ear by syringing with sterile normal saline solution every day and afterward use as ear drops a solution of 10% Chloromycetin in water. No emergency, need not remove to hospital." Roger and over and out.

Soon after dark Elias Okamura came up on deck with a sextant, to shoot stars. "I've got six now," he told me after a few minutes of action, "and I'm going to get to work and find out where we are. Excuse me, while I take a fix." With that assurance that we would not go astray, I went down to the wardroom, where Oliver

Arten was waiting to humiliate me with his cribbage board.

At six-fifteen in the morning, with Ngatik faintly visible on the horizon, Kasiano confided to me he was upset. The ship's port engine was acting up. It had begun to lose oil the second night out of Rabaul, and the chief engineer attributed this to our having grazed the reef at our first Ngatik call. "There are just too many things a field trip officer has to worry about," Kasiano told me. "Sometimes I think I'd like to settle on one of these outer islands and not have to worry about anything." It was dead low tide when we came into Ngatik, but this time we negotiated the channel without a jolt. Captain Morrison said he didn't want to try anything like that again; he was going out at high tide and would pull up anchor at one-thirty that afternoon, and any person or any copra bag that wasn't aboard by then would be out of luck. It was, accordingly, a hustling day. Two deckhands lowered a wooden platform off the starboard side, to serve as a way station for copra being transferred from canoes to the cargo deck. The supercargos hauled their trade-goods chests out of the hold and set them up, since there was no available deck space, on top of the kerosene drums. Ngatik, it was shortly to develop, had twenty tons of copra to load. Our engines had scarcely been stilled when a canoe pulled up alongside the unloading platform. The little boat had nine hundred-pound sacks of copra stacked on it, and a crew of one—a stocky, incredibly agile Ngatikese in a green baseball cap. All by himself, he transferred his nearly half-ton burden from canoe to platform, platform to deck, and deck to hold, leaping back and forth as if he were on solid ground and as if his solid merchandise were feathers. And that virtuoso solo performance proved to be merely a warmup preceding an orchestral tour de force, for as an armada of canoes converged on the *Kaselehlia*, green-cap then lent a muscular hand in the loading of at least two thirds of the two hundred bags of copra that the Ngatikese managed to get aboard before the captain ordered the cargo hatch made fast. Canoes with copra bags aboard were still coming toward us when we pulled away. The flailing paddler of one of them, I later learned, had been delayed in leaving shore because he'd been helping Judge Kinnare get his gear packed; the Ngatikese thus deprived of selling his copra may have had some private thoughts about injustice. Another canoe, bearing Elias Okamura, who had gone ashore for the morning, just barely got him back in time. Trying to clamber aboard the *Kaselehlia,* the only Palauan fullback in Susquehanna's history lost his balance and fell into the water. He was fished out and hauled on deck.

At the last minute, three more pigs were flung aboard. Captain Morrison insisted that all pigs on any ship of his had to travel in a crate, but one of the animals was let loose on the deck and made a terrible mess. Another pig was in a crate all right, but also in a sack inside the crate. It was complaining shrilly at its plight. The noise was more than the captain could bear, and he yelled to a seaman that if somebody didn't take that damned pig out of that damned sack he'd throw it overboard. The seaman, in all the confusion, misunderstood the order, removed the bagged pig from the crate, and threw the crate overboard. The pig's owner, one of the deck passengers, grabbed the pig bag, removed the pig, threw the bag overboard, and stuffed the pig into a crate already containing another pig. The resident pig attacked the newcomer. Both pigs shrieked. The chickens joined the chorus. The captain screamed at everybody, and the Kummers' infant son began to cry. Thus we sailed away from the serene atoll of Ngatik.

Judge Kinnare and Nancy Hattori, his court reporter, were in good shape after their fifteen-day sequestration. Nancy had an arm infection, but she held the atoll blameless; she had got it from a hair-dye patch test. The judge had not only run out of beer two days before, but he'd had no pipe tobacco for a week. He'd been reduced to smoking shredded cigarettes. He preferred Camels, but he'd run out of *them,* too, and had switched to Salems. I beckoned him to follow me to my cabin, and produced my hoarded vodka, which we carefully measured out in two equal portions. We had our glasses raised in a mutual toast when Oliver Arten popped in. I suppose I should have offered to cut him in, but he was a missionary and anyway he had a deck chair and we didn't. So the judge and I, greedily and gleefully, gulped our grog.

I asked Judge Kinnare how his work had gone, and he said that he had had to deal mostly with routine squabbles over land. One case involved a single taro patch. A woman named Emiso Etwin and her half-brother, Wales Etwin, had been arguing over it since 1935, when the Japanese ran Micronesia. Wales had paid a twenty-yen debt of hers, and he claimed she'd given him the patch in exchange. *She* claimed she'd merely let him use it until the debt was repaid, but that when she'd tried to repay it in 1963, twenty-eight years after she incurred it, Wales had demanded retroactive interest at the rate of ten percent a month, which she thought a mite steep.

In the course of the testimony, Judge Kinnare had had to grapple with such inscrutable documentation as one affidavit Wales had given: "It is not that I don't like to give Emiso's taro patch back but it is he [sic] who doesn't like to as he, Emiso, changed our promise after I told him that if he would change our promise he would then pay me for it." And still another document, or one-time document, had caused complications. This was a letter Emiso had ostensibly written back in 1935, which might have been germane, and the question was: Had the letter, as various witnesses asserted, been lost, stolen, or eaten by cockroaches? Judge Kinnare had ultimately ruled, after several days of testimony, that Wales, who was seventy-three, could use the taro patch as long as he lived, and that on his death it would revert to his half-sister, who was a couple of years younger.

Neomy Johnny and Kasiano Joseph had been left behind at Ngatik—she to collect from copra sellers what they owed her for trade goods she'd sold them, and he to make sure that nobody else was left behind. We hove to for a while outside the atoll, while a canoe brought Neomy alongside. The sea was running high, and she had to be tossed aboard. While her escorts were at it, they also tossed two more uncrated pigs aboard. Captain Morrison bellowed with indignation. "I'll never take another pig again!" he shouted from the bridge. A few minutes later, another canoe brought Kasiano back to us. He was being escorted by two attractive Ngatikese girls, and he looked as though he wouldn't have minded being left behind.

We steamed off at dusk. Elias Okamura, by now dried out, was at the bridge, taking a fix on the receding atoll. He told me that at fix time the night before he'd found us to be eight and a half miles off course, but that he anticipated no such further difficulty. Above us, on the compass bridge, Captain Morrison stood in solitary grandeur, with a large seagull hovering, like a winged halo, directly over his head. Maybe the gull was hoping he'd have a small pig thrown overboard. Down in the wardroom, Judge Kinnare was reading an Australian detective story and shredding a cigarette into his pipe bowl. "The next time I come to the Ponape district, I'm going to lay in a large supply of pipe tobacco and give it to Carlos Etscheit," he told me, "and stipulate that he sell it only to me." Oliver Arten had his cribbage board at the ready. Neomy sat at one end of a mess table, totting up sales slips. The wardroom steward was flirting with her, oblivious to some cockroaches that were flirting on his walls. Across the room, the second mate, an engineer, and a seaman were playing seven-card stud; possibly because they were using cards with pornographic pictures on their backs, the three players had four kibitzers. All the players, when it came their turn to deal, distributed the cards counterclockwise. It was one basic difference I discerned between Micronesian culture and our own.

At six the next morning we were all on deck, and there it was ahead of us—the huge dark bulk of Ponape! There was Madolenihmw, and there was U, and there was familiar old Kolonia! It looked big and stable, bigger maybe than Guam could possibly be, and everybody knows that Guam is a metropolis beyond compare. Nancy Hattori, who had spent only two nights aboard ship, came up on deck, looking ashen. She'd been seasick twice during the night, and was wondering how the people who'd ridden the *Kaselehlia* all the way to Rabaul and back had ever stood it. "That's a kind of torture for a very special kind of criminal," she said. Kasiano had a padlocked briefcase with him. He opened it up, and pulled forth some statistics on voter registration for the

Congressional elections: three hundred and twenty-eight Ngatikese, two hundred and three Nukuoroans, and three hundred and fifty-four Kapingamarangans, including those residing at Ponape.

When we tied up at the dock, Jack Adams came aboard to greet his wife Yvette. Adams asked me if I didn't agree, now that I'd been there, that Kapingamarangi had by far the healthiest inhabitants of any part of the entire Ponape district. I said that I didn't think that Dr. Kummer, who ought to know, would unqualifiedly concur, and in fact had been worried at the state of Kapingamarangan health. "Really?" said Adams. "Well, if Kapingamarangi worries him, he'd better not go to Pingelap. He'd drop dead of fright."

The deck passengers from Kapingamarangi were clutching their Ponape relatives in joyous family reunions, and were showing them the gifts they'd brought from home. Watching them, Judge Kinnare remarked, "I suppose the time will eventually come when a guy from Kapinga will bring his family here a ten-dollar bill instead of eighteen pandanus, six stalks of taro, a pig, and some chickens." The time may eventually come, but I would hate to have to try to set a date for it.

20.
Guam

ONE MARSHALL ISLANDS IROIJ, ON HIS FIRST VISIT TO Guam, which measures two hundred and nine square miles and has a population, including American servicemen, of seventy-odd thousand, asked to see the sights. He was taken through Agaña, a modest town with few buildings more than two stories high. He was shown a Strategic Air Command base, whence B-52 bombers have set forth for Vietnam, and a big Navy base harboring Polaris-missile-equipped submarines (with the ubiquitous Soviet trawler hovering offshore). He also got to ride in an elevator. After all these experiences, he was moved to exclaim, "Tell me, is America as big as Guam?"

Guam is a very special place to the natives of the Trust Territory. One cannot get from the headquarters at Saipan to any other part of the Trust Territory, by scheduled transportation, except by going through Guam. The economy of the Trust Territory is heavily dependent on Guam, through which port pass most of the goods that the rest of Micronesia uses. (As a gesture of independence, one of the first resolutions passed in the summer of 1965 by the Congress of Micronesia called for the bypassing of Guam on future shipments to the islands from the United States.) Guam is also a very special place on its own. Five thousand miles west of San Francisco, it must by all reasonable standards of geography be considered part of the Far East. However, Guam is also a bonafide part of the United States, having been a full-fledged territory since the end of the Spanish-American War.

Few Americans who haven't been to Guam know what it is or where it is. A couple who moved to the island from the continental United States a while ago got to wondering after a bit what could have happened to their household furnishings, which were supposed to follow them to Agaña, the capital of Guam. The shipment arrived twenty-three months late, having gone first to Accra, the capital of Ghana. At a monthly lunch of the Guam branch of the Propeller Club—a merchant-marine fraternity, of which the local president, Guam being Guam, is an airlines man—a member remarked that on his last trip to New York he had attended a national conclave of the organization. The announcement evoked only one comment. A voice from down the table called out, "Did they ask you where Guam was?"

On November 11, 1962, when Guam was devastated by a typhoon called Karen, wind velocities of two hundred miles an hour—more than twice what is regarded on the American East Coast as hurricane force—were recorded. Then the anemometers broke down. Automobiles sailed off over houses; houses—many of them quonset huts—sailed over other houses; and the air was filled with such lethal missiles as three-mile-a-minute coconuts, not to mention whole coconut trees. Much of the normally lush foliage of Guam was stripped away, and perhaps for the first time in the island's history, its trees had a bare, autumnal look.

Miraculously, only nine people were killed, but around ninety percent of the island's buildings were demolished. Not only did the power go out but so did most of the utility poles and lines; they just blew away. (The local *Times Weekly* later suggested that Guam make appropriate observance of Karen's anniversary each November by cutting off all electricity except that needed by hospitals and by the police and fire departments, but the idea did not seem to arouse much enthusiasm.) The total damage was estimated at as high as sixty million dollars—this in a territory whose annual budget is nineteen million. The continental American press paid little heed to Karen (when it comes to that, New England hurricanes do not cause much of a stir on Guam), but the administration in Washington at once declared Guam a major disaster area and allocated funds to it, first for relief and then for rehabilitation.

By the time the reconstruction is finished, Guam should be in better shape than it was before Karen. More than seventy million dollars will have been spent in all, a good part of it on up-to-date—and typhoonproof—educational facilities. Actually, Karen has proved to be an economic blessing to Guam. A construction boom that began after the war had pretty much petered out by 1962, and the outlook was bleak. Guam has never had much of an unemployment problem, largely because more than fifty percent of its labor force works for one department or another of the local and federal government. In the hot and humid climate ("Even the mildew mildews here" is a standard Guam joke), where the only air-conditioned rooms at Navy headquarters are one sheltering the admiral and one sheltering the lawbooks, the local folk have found it more agreeable to hold desk jobs than to engage in hard physical labor. Guam has reasonably fertile soil, and it once exported crops, among them pineapples, cocoa, and tobacco, but the attractiveness of white-collar jobs has all but eliminated farming as a means of livelihood. Government now occupies the work time of more than ten thousand Guamanians; agriculture, forestry, and fishing together occupy that of only five hundred. (Many Guamanians, though, tend small subsistence farms.)

Most of the skilled construction workers now busy on Guam —and there are some seven thousand of them—are Filipinos, who have been a mainstay of the labor force since 1947. Of late, the local government has begun to try to redress the imbalance of its employment situation by urging Guamanians to acquire construction skills themselves, and in the summer of 1964 the federal government announced that alien labor—a euphemism for Filipinos, since Guam has no other alien laborers to speak of—would no longer be admitted to Guam. There was an immediate howl from local contractors, who protested that the inexperienced Guamanians couldn't possibly perform up to Filipino standards, and also that their own labor costs might go up considerably if they had to make a switch, because Guamanians would probably have to be paid according to American rather than Filipino wage scales. The ban was hastily lifted. Then the government of Guam established an apprentice program in the construction trades, through which, over the next several years, it hopes to train local carpenters, plumbers, masons, electricians, and other specialists, so that the ubiquitous Filipinos can in due course be replaced.

Guam's governor and his second in command, who is invested with the title of secretary, are appointed by the President of the United States and are responsible to the Secretary of the Interior. The first native Guamanian to be named governor was Joseph Flores, a banker and the publisher of the Guam *Daily News*, whom President Eisenhower installed in 1960. Several months later, the Kennedy administration made what many Guamanians consider the greatest federal goof in history by sending over a governor, Bill Daniel, who seemed to have no qualifications other than that his brother had once been Governor of Texas.

The Guam Governor Daniel, to the mingled amusement and outrage of his involuntary constituents, changed the name of his official residence from Government House to Government Palace, brought in a number of peacocks to dress up the regal establishment, and in a burst of zoological zeal, also imported armadillos and prize bulls. The armadillos were supposed to help Guam rid itself of African snails, which migrated to Guam from Saipan and points north during the Japanese occupation, but the Guamanians were afraid that the armadillos might multiply even faster, and shortly after their arrival they mysteriously disappeared—presumably thrown into the ocean. The bulls were supposed to improve the quality of Guam's livestock, and might have been quite acceptable if the Governor hadn't escorted a pair of them into his Palace and had his picture taken with them. The Guam *Daily News* ran the photograph with the caption "The one in the middle is the Governor." Today, to identify oneself as a Texan on Guam is to invite long, searching stares.

Governor Daniel, who set out on a round-the-world jaunt before his term expired, was succeeded by Manuel Flores Leon Guerrero, a forty-nine-year-old native Guamanian. Guerrero is the son of a former musician in an American Navy band, and he has been a farmer, a businessman, a legislator, and a bureaucrat. He belongs to the Democratic Party, which is affiliated with but not identical with its namesake on the mainland. The Guam Democrats had regularly dominated the island's unicameral legislature until the 1964 elections, when the rival Territorial Party—more conservative than its opposition but by no means a political outpost of the mainland Republican Party—administered something of a drubbing to the Democrats. This upset afforded small comfort to off-island Republicans on Guam, though, because while the Guamanians are American citizens, they cannot vote in our Presidential elections. They want to, and Secretary Udall has discussed the possibility of recommending that Congress grant them that right, but this is as far as things have gone.

The Guamanians would also like to have a non-voting delegate in Congress, as Alaska and Hawaii used to have before they achieved statehood; in fact, the Guam legislature voted in 1964 to send such a representative to Washington, wishing all the while that the initiative had come from Congress. "What we've done seems awfully like inviting yourself to dinner," one Guamanian official said afterward. Apart from gaining the right to vote for President and to hang around Capitol Hill, few Guamanians have burning political aspirations. Every now and then, somebody suggests that they ought to be appended to the State of Hawaii, but Guam is far from eager to abandon its independent territorial status and become an adjunct of an entity three thousand miles away. Anyway, Hawaii itself is so far from Guam that some Honolulu businessmen believe Agaña to be the capital of a foreign country.

It has also been suggested that Guam apply for statehood, but the very idea makes Guamanians shudder; being dependent on federal funds for their very survival, they can think of nothing they would like less than to stop being an economic ward of the national government and to assume the responsibilities of a sovereign state. Their continuing enjoyment of their relatively sunny current status was further beclouded by a 1960 resolution of the United Nations to the effect that, colonialism being an inherently bad state of affairs, all non-self-governing dependencies of U.N. members should—along with Trust Territories—have a chance to indicate by plebiscite whether they wanted independence.

The notion of becoming a nation, on the order of one of the new African countries, strikes Guamanians as absurd, but the U.N., egged on by various anti-American members, periodically brings the plebiscite business up again. After a U.N. Special Committee on Ending Colonialism approved a report by one of its subcommittees that the United States grant Guam independence (the contention that the time was ripe for this libertarian gesture had originated with the Soviet Union), the Guam *Daily News* swiftly came out with an editorial saying that "we do not want independence kicked down our throats." The paper urged Guamanians to let the United Nations know that "what we have been aspiring for is closer union with the United States, not for separation."

Until 1963, when the Kennedy administration did away with a policy that had been in effect since the end of the Second World War, Guam's detachment from the rest of the United States was attributable only in part to the island's remoteness. The Navy had been running the place, and nobody had been able to visit it without Navy sanction. Now any American can inspect this farthest-flung segment of his nation. Guam remains the westernmost military bastion we can call our very own (our armed forces elsewhere in Asia are there by sufferance of other soveign nations, who—in theory, at least—could ask us to leave), but now the Navy's Guam representatives, and also those of the Strategic Air Command, are positively hospitable to civilians, and the admiral in command of the area has been doing his best to help the local government convert it into a tourist mecca comparable to Hawaii.

"Guam Is Good, but Promises to Be Better," a Navy publication recently proclaimed, and the local Chamber of Commerce, presumably in order to stimulate the imagination of visitors who would regard it as thrilling to get close to danger, boasts that Guam is "only fifteen hundred miles outside the Bamboo Curtain of Communist China"—a distinction that tourists bound for Hong Kong or Macao might find something less than hair-raising.

There has been talk for years about attracting some tourists, but Guam hasn't yet had much to offer them. Still, Guam has begun to take halting steps toward its goal. The local government allocated sixty thousand dollars for the sprucing up of a crushed-coral beach north of Agaña, a full-time tourism man was recruited from Hawaii, and there has been talk of a hundred-room Hilton hotel—or, better yet, a hundred-and-twenty-room hotel put up by local entrepreneurs, with a swimming pool and a tennis court.

In the summer of 1964, Guam was host to its first convention—seventy women from eleven countries, representing the Federation of Asian Women's Associations. In addition to conducting their business, the ladies rode carabaos and looked over the restoration of an old-fashioned thatch-roofed Chamorro village, which had been put together rather hurriedly. Prisoners were mobilized from the local jail to get coconut-palm fronds for the roofs, and the Governor's wife gave a thatching party, attended by eight hundred volunteer thatchers.

Guam's bona-fide tourists consist almost entirely of the passengers—a hundred and twenty-five of them, usually—on a small Australian cruise ship that puts in at Agaña for the day once a month. In the spring of 1965, though, a *big* Australian cruise ship, with accommodations for thirteen hundred, agreed to dock at Guam, and even before it turned up prospective greeters were agog with excitement. "It will be the greatest thing that has happened to Guam since Magellan discovered it," the Guam tourism expert said. Another government official said, less extravagantly, that the arrival of the larger vessel would certainly mark the start of a new day. "We've got to get more things here to offer tourists, though," he added. "A pretty view and nice sunsets may not be enough. Maybe we could get somebody to build some charter boats for deep-sea fishing. You hit one of those *mahimahi* or skipjacks we have out here and it's really nice. Of course, we have good shopping here, being a free port, like Hong Kong. Why, one New Zealand woman on a cruise bought two electric rotisseries here—a hundred and thirty dollars' worth in ten minutes, just like that! But we probably need a little more. Maybe we could make a pretty good tourist gimmick out of our cockfighting—without spurs, I guess."

Guam suspects that the majority of the tourists who ultimately turn up will come not from the American mainland but from Japan and Australia. Those two countries have been trading with each other at an increasingly rapid clip, and Guam lies on the path between them. Since Japan is by far the more populous of the two, it is from Japan that Guam hopes to lure a really substantial number of wayfarers. Guamanians acquired a deep loathing for everything about Japan during that country's wartime occupation of the island, but now—like mainland Americans—they are modifying their stand. In the fall of 1964, the College of Guam added a course in Japanese to its curriculum, and a few weeks after that a delegation from Guam ceremonially delivered to Japan a Zero fighter plane (the Japanese didn't have a single one left for a souvenir) that had been discovered not long before in a swamp just a quarter of a mile from the center of Agaña, where a clump of tangantangan trees had grown up around and over it. (The plane was reasonably intact and in better shape than most of the Zeros at Yap; it had apparently made a fairly smooth crash landing.) Guamanians forgive readily. They have forgiven Magellan, who, upon his landing in 1521, with most of his crew suffering from starvation and scurvy, ordered his abler-bodied seamen to murder a number of Chamorros who had paddled out to his ship with food and water for the ailing. In the summer of 1964, a Japanese newspaperman visiting the island reported coming upon a Guamanian who was willing to let bygones be bygones even though during the Second World War some Japanese had buried him alive and he had barely managed to dig himself free.

21.

Stragglers?

THE JAPANESE NEWSPAPERMAN WAS ONE OF TWO dozen reporters and photographers who came to Guam from Tokyo to cover the latest episode in a cliff-hanger serial story that had been diverting both Guamanians and Japanese for twenty years. In July of 1944, when the United States liberated Guam, the Japanese occupying garrison fled into the jungles. In accordance with the Japanese military code of that era, many committed suicide to avoid the dishonor of being taken prisoner. Many others were tracked down and shot, in subsequent months and years, by police posses who were called the Guam Combat Patrol. A few, determined never to surrender to their Emperor's Yankee enemies, escaped and hid out, sustaining themselves on the island's abundant wild fruits and on what additional provender they could steal. Early in 1962, I wrote at some length about the adventures of the two most durable known stragglers—Bunzo Minagawa and Masashi Ito, a pair of Japanese enlisted men who were captured, not without a struggle, in May, 1960. They had been leading what they conceded was a thoroughly miserable life in Guam's boondocks for just two months shy of sixteen years. Other stragglers had been flushed out of hiding places on Saipan and Peleliu; and as late as the spring of 1964 an American not normally given to flights of fancy insisted he had a brief glimpse of one still at large on a Palauan island.

Minagawa and Ito, after their return to Japan and their absorption into a strange new postwar world (both got married, sired children, and became watchmen at a motion-picture studio), often said that they had no reason to believe there might not be other stragglers still roaming miserably around Guam, unwilling to give themselves up either because they weren't sure the war was over and were determined to go on fighting if they ever got a chance to, or because they were afraid they'd be killed if they were captured, or because they were ashamed of not having committed suicide when their war was lost. And from time to time something would happen on Guam to justify Minagawa's and Ito's contention. In April, 1962, for instance, a Guamanian reported that he had shot a stragglerlike fellow out in the jungle. By the time the local constabulary found the body, it was unidentifiable, having been found by wild boars first. But when the scattered bones were assembled and examined, it was judged that they might conceivably be of Japanese origin.

Back in Tokyo, this incident was of particular interest to the Repatriation Aid Bureau of Japan's Ministry of Health and Welfare. Ever since the Japanese surrender in 1945, it has been the Bureau's task to try to find and bring home the remnants, dead or alive, of the vast and widespread Japanese expeditionary forces. On and off, in the postwar years, the Japanese government had asked the United States for permission to send a search party to Guam, on the theory that any Japanese in hiding might come out if other Japanese besought them to. (The Bureau had twice sent expeditions to Lubang, a small island of the Philippines, where there was good reason to believe that two holdouts were at large, but both expeditions had returned empty-handed.) In July, 1960, shortly after Minagawa and Ito were flushed out, the Bureau, through the Japanese Foreign Office, asked the United States to comb Guam on its behalf. That November, the United States sent word back that there were no more stragglers on Guam—an assertion that anyone familiar with Guam's tangled undergrowth and its honeycomb of caves could hardly be expected to take as definitive. In July, 1962, after the wild-boar incident, Japan once more asked the United States to look around. It was August, 1963, before a reply reached Tokyo, and the answer was the same: No more stragglers on Guam.

At 6 A.M. on August 26, 1964, a twenty-five-year-old Guamanian named José George, who drove a truck for a company that sold coral to construction firms, went to a dump at a Naval Communications Station on the northeast part of the island to deposit a load of trash. The area was off limits to Guamanians who had no business there, but, like other restricted sections of the island, it was not infrequently invaded by trespassers. Scavengers would forage in Navy dumps, and poachers would wander through woods adjacent to them, hunting deer out of season. Once, two illicit hunters fatally shot one another in such an area, each thinking he had a bead on a deer. In 1964, one Guamanian was fined two hundred dollars and given sixty days in jail for hunting at night on a military reservation (he was a second offender), and another was indicted for first-degree murder after allegedly shooting a federal Fish and Wildlife agent who had nabbed him and was trying to disarm him. (He was tried before a jury and acquitted.)

José George, however, was authorized to use the dump at the Naval Communications Station, and he often went to it. On the morning in question, he was surprised to see a scrawny, long-haired, raggedly clad figure bending over, with its back to him, and picking at the refuse. (The pickings can be good, for the Navy is prodigal with its garbage; a Guamanian policeman making a routine check of the dump found six loaves of bread, twenty pounds of sliced ham, and a mess of chicken—none of it spotless but all of it edible.) As George later recounted the story, the scavenger stood up at his approach and turned and faced him. He realized then that it was not a woman, as he had thought, but a long-haired, bearded, and—he was convinced—Japanese man.

The intruder began to run away, limping, and George leaped from his truck and took out after him. He would have caught him if he hadn't stopped at hearing a shout behind him. He looked back, and there was another man, similar in appearance to the first one, crouched behind a pile of debris and aiming a rifle at him. The crouching man pulled the trigger, but there was only a click. Now George took to *his* heels. He clambered back into his truck and sped to the nearest Navy sentry post. When he got there, he was so shaky that he had to sit down and compose himself before he could give a coherent account of what had happened.

The Guam *Daily News*, which had become blasé about straggler sightings over the years, ran the story the next day without making much of a fuss over it. The reaction in Tokyo, when the news was relayed there, was quite different. People wrote letters to the editors: If there were Japanese soldiers still at large who had committed no crime and had merely been faithful to their Emperor's injunction not to capitulate as long as the breath of life remained in them, what did the government propose to do about rescuing them from their plight and returning them to a land of peace and plenty? Whatever was to be done, it was the Repatriation Aid Bureau's job to do it, but the Bureau, being concerned with the aftermath of war, had long been a stepchild of a government trying to forget that that war had ever occurred. The Repatriation officials therefore had only limited funds at their disposal, but after examining their resources they concluded that they could allocate two and a half million yen—about six thousand dollars—for an expedition to Guam.

They wanted to make sure first, though, that such an expenditure was justified, and they addressed urgent inquiries, through the American Embassy in Tokyo, to the government of Guam. The official United States position, the Japanese learned, was unchanged. Aside from José George's unsupported testimony, there was not a shred of evidence of any stragglers. The police on Guam, however, had found George's story both unshakable and persuasive. (There had been talk of giving him a lie-detector test, but, as the Guam police pointed out, he hadn't been accused of any wrongdoing, and it would have been an affront to his feelings to subject him to polygraphic examination.) And now that Guam was no longer under tight Navy wraps, the United States had no objection to letting the Japanese look around. So on September 9th the Repatriation Aid Bureau began to organize a search party.

Since 1960, the Bureau had kept in touch with Minagawa and Ito, and now it planned to include one of them in the expedition—not both, for, as the Bureau well knew, the two men had become estranged in their long years of shared loneliness on Guam, and though they now worked for the same company in Tokyo, they hardly ever spoke to each other. Ito was a little the stronger of the two, but he had a slight stammer, which might make communication with unseen auditors in the jungle difficult, and, anyway, in the Bureau's view Minagawa was a little the smarter. So Minagawa was invited to go back to Guam. He at once agreed. His children were quite young (his daughter, Humeo, was two and his son, Yoshibumi, only a year old), but his wife and he both felt strongly that he had a duty to go—that the stragglers, if there were any still on Guam, had been his comrades-in-arms, and, just as it was the responsibility of the Japanese government to succor them as soon as possible, so it was his personal responsibility to use his jungle expertise on their behalf. "They are my brothers and they are having a wretched time," he said. "They don't deserve to suffer any longer."

The Japanese government dug up some twenty-year-old Imperial uniforms for Minagawa to wear on Guam—it was reasoned that a straggler espying him thus fraternally clad might be more likely to come out of hiding—and his wife gave him some carnations to take along and put on any Japanese graves he might come upon in his wanderings. He was scheduled to go to Guam on September 18th and search for four weeks. The Bureau sent an advance man there to make suitable arrangements for the hunt, and it prepared a batch of leaflets to be scattered around the area in which José George had spotted the two gaunt strangers. The leaflets contained pictures of the Imperial Palace in Tokyo and other nostalgic Japanese sights, and many words of comfort and encouragement, telling, in Japanese, how Minagawa and Ito had been repatriated and returned to a "happy home life with their wives and children as respectable members of society," and saying also:

> The Pacific War ended on August 15, 1945. Nineteen years have passed since the end of the war, and Japan, as a respectable country in Asia, is now on friendly terms with the United States.
>
> Learning that you are alive on Guam Island, all the people in Japan were surprised and glad about your miraculous survival, and they are praying for your early return to Japan. . . .
>
> There is absolutely no danger to your lives. You will not be treated as prisoners of war. Please answer our appeal. . . .

To facilitate a reply, it was arranged to have each leaflet encased in a plastic bag along with some up-to-date Japanese newspapers, a blank sheet of writing paper, and two pencils. The idea was that the stragglers could write their names and home addresses on the blank sheet, along with the names of their closest relatives. If any straggler did that, the Repatriation Aid Bureau planned to bring his loved ones to Guam and let them call out to him over a loudspeaker. The Repatriation Aid Bureau also assembled tapes of well-known Japanese sentimental songs, and five hundred non-governmental Japanese who wanted to help convened at the Singing Voice Coffee Shop, in the Shinjuku section of Tokyo, and made a special recording of a choral hymn that had been composed for the Tokyo Olympics. The Repatriation Aid Bureau pigeonholed the recording, however, reasoning that any Japanese who had gone into hiding on Guam in 1944 would only be confused by talk, or song, of Olympic Games, since the last information he would probably have had about any Olympics would have been about the ones that were scheduled to be held in Tokyo in 1940 but were cancelled because of the war.

While the Japanese search party was getting ready, there was a good deal of activity on Guam. On August 27th, the day after José George's upsetting encounter, a hundred and twenty-five United States Marines and thirty Guamanian policemen spent nine and a half hours tramping around the environs of the Navy dump. The police found a Japanese-type gunny sack containing a few bones, with bits of meat attached; the Marines found two camp sites that seemed to have been used not very long before. That same day, a Navy helicopter crisscrossed the area. Aboard it, calling down reassurances through a loudspeaker, was Edward G. Tsutsui, a Hawaiian-born nisei who worked in a Navy warehouse on Guam and was the island's No. 1 Japanese interpreter. (He had served as intermediary during the questioning of Minagawa and Ito immediately after they were found.) The following day, Tsutsui cruised along the northern coast of Guam aboard a Navy tug, again calling out through a loudspeaker; search parties in the jungle ashore said they could hear him clearly. To encourage any stragglers who might happen to peer out at the tugboat, the Navy agreed to pull down the Stars and Stripes that normally flew at its stern and substitute the Rising Sun. (A Japanese flag flying from an American naval vessel! What would a straggler think? What, when it came to that, might some American congressmen think?)

Without waiting for the Repatriation Aid Bureau's leaflets to arrive from Tokyo, Tsutsui wrote out messages in Japanese, which were scattered here and there. He promised the stragglers that he would drive to the dump every afternoon for twenty-one straight days, rain or shine, in a car flying two flags—that of Japan and that of the American Red Cross. He would stay there, he pledged, until sundown, and he begged the Japanese to throw their weapons away and come out with their hands up over their heads. "Do not be ashamed of this small act, and be assured that you will not be prisoners," he wrote. "May God bless you and guide you." Tsutsui's wife, also a Hawaiian-born nisei, affixed some of the messages to bowls containing rice, pickled plums, and pickled radishes. It was hoped that if these Japanese delicacies proved unalluring, the sound of a feminine Japanese voice might turn the trick, so Mrs. Tsutsui and seven other Japanese women living on Guam took turns broadcasting siren calls over a loudspeaker mounted on top of a police car. "We decided to use every means," Tsutsui said.

The chief of the Guam police, Captain José C. Quintanilla, was in charge of the hunt at the start, but then he began having trouble with an old ulcer, so he pretty much turned over his end of things to a hardboiled thirty-seven-year-old sergeant, Mariano C. Cruz, who had been a member of the Guam Combat Patrol twenty years earlier, and had been credited with a number of confirmed kills of Japanese stragglers. In those days, the police had a more forthright approach to the matter of keeping the jungle peace, and would fire in the direction of any unexpected sound. By 1964, Sergeant Cruz's attitude had changed greatly. "I feel very sorry for these Japanese," he said. "I'm always praying that they'll change their minds and come out, so we can send them home to have a good time for whatever remains of their lives. If I can ever make that possible, I'll be a proud sergeant."

The Sergeant and a squad of his men found some newly stripped coconut husks on September 4th; they thought that might mean something. Two days later, their search was interrupted by a typhoon named Sally—a mere hundred-mile-an-hour blow, but blustery enough to deter a posse. The day after that, as the winds died down, the first wave of correspondents from Tokyo hit the beaches of Guam. Their assignment meant that they would probably miss the Olympics back home, but they said buoyantly that if an honest-to-goodness live straggler materialized, they'd be on top of a story *bigger* than the Olympics. Television crews arrived from Tokyo in due course, and one channel sent Ito—stammer or no stammer—as a commentator. He stayed for a couple of weeks and went back to air his impressions, which were noncommittal.

Minagawa and two Repatriation Aid Bureau men reached Agaña on September 18th. After being given a rousing reception at the airport and paying a courtesy call on the Governor, Minagawa and his party moved out into the countryside and set up camp. Minagawa, who ought to know, thought that a likely haven for stragglers was one of the many caves that pock the cliffs along Guam's northern shoreline, and he joined forces with Cruz's patrol. The veteran Japanese straggler and the veteran killer of Japanese stragglers had a good deal in common, for they both felt at home in the jungle. Just a couple of days after Minagawa's arrival, he was making his way down the face of a cliff when a search-party colleague at the top dislodged a stone. It rolled down and caught Minagawa squarely on the forehead, and he had to be taken off to a hospital for seven stitches and two days of bed rest.

The injury—worse than any he had incurred in the sixteen years of his first stay on Guam—didn't seem to dismay Minagawa, or even to slow him down. He hadn't smoked at all while he was a straggler, and he smoked heavily now, yet he could make his way along slippery trails and through dense, clutching shrubs and vines with such agility that not even Sergeant Cruz could keep up with him. Minagawa was not impressed by his own fleetness and surefootedness. In the old days, he pointed out, he and Ito customarily carried all their possessions on their backs—the "bearded snails," they called themselves then—so why shouldn't he make good time now, when he had nothing to tote but a canteen?

The Japanese press corps, however, were taken aback at not being able to keep in sight the fellow they were supposed to be covering; the photographers ultimately had to stage many of the shots they got of him, and he was impatient about indulging them, because it took time he could have spent on his trek. This trek was a largely silent one, for he did not think that any Japanese would respond to a human voice. In his opinion, whatever stragglers there were would have to be surprised and seized, as he himself had been.

As the search went on, there were flurries of excitement. On September 29th, in a coastal cave overlooking the Air Force's bathing beach on the west side of the island, two Japanese knapsacks were discovered. The owners' names were in them. One of the men, the Repatriation Aid Bureau in Tokyo ascertained, had died in 1945, and there were witnesses to his death; the other had been reported missing on Saipan. The knapsacks contained, between them, pretty much what one would expect a soldier or sailor to carry: an undershirt, a pair of dirty handkerchiefs, a wallet, a little money, an out-of-date season railroad ticket, a good-luck charm, a toothbrush, a bandage, a cigarette case, a spoon, a piece of camouflage cloth, and the stump of a candle. The candle was wrapped in a scrap of an English-language comic strip—I saw it but I couldn't identify it from the fragment—in which one character was saying to another, "Don't be afraid, I've come to help you."

The most interesting aspect of this find was that the knapsacks and their contents were in excellent condition, and dry. Without human attention, could they have stayed that way for twenty years? Minagawa thought not. Moreover, the knapsacks were free of ants, and *that* impressed Sergeant Cruz. He told me that if he didn't check the linen closet in his house every two or three months, ants would devour his towels. "This in a cement-block house!" he said. "What would you expect in an open cave?"

Other bits of evidence—or what seemed evidence to those of the searchers who were convinced of the existence of stragglers—kept turning up. In one cave, a searcher found an old Japanese *sake* bottle filled with comparatively fresh *tuba.* In another cave, in an area that had no game and thus would logically be free of poachers, Minagawa one day discovered six palm fronds that had evidently been used, fairly recently, for bedding. Three days later, he revisited the cave, and now there were *sixteen* fronds. What was one to make of that?

And how could one account for the strange experience, not long afterward and not far off, of a Federal Aviation Agency man, Homer L. Willess, who made a sudden turn while driving home one night and transfixed in his bright headlights, only twenty yards away, a scarecrowlike, long-haired, bearded man in ragged clothes, and wearing homemade shoes, probably fashioned out of rubber tires? The man had limped off into the woods after a moment's startled pause. Willess couldn't chase him without a flashlight (that would have been a risky thing to do at best, and particularly so if the fellow had had a gun nearby), but he did report the incident to the local police. The patrolman on duty at the station tried at once to get in touch with Sergeant Cruz but he couldn't reach him (Cruz, after a hard day's searching, was at a party), and so let the matter ride until morning. Accordingly, Minagawa didn't get to the scene until almost twelve hours after Willess had seen his man. Minagawa was furious. He knew that grass trampled by feet becomes upright again quite soon. Even so, he was able to track this apparition for a while, but then the trail dwindled into nothingness.

Throughout the hunt, there was a measure of skepticism on Guam. A restaurant that normally charged three dollars for a steak posted a sign advertising a seven-course dinner for a dollar seventy-five—"For Stragglers Only." (It subsequently made a similar rib-tickling offer to crew members of the offshore Russian trawler.) The principal Repatriation Aid Bureau man on Guam thought the accumulated evidence very flimsy and the chances of finding anyone alive very slim, and he and Minagawa almost came to blows in consequence, Minagawa demanding angrily why the expedition had been mounted in the first place if there was so little confidence in its potential accomplishments. Rumor spread that the whole straggler business had been cooked up—or rehashed—by Guam's new tourist bureau, in order to attract the Japanese newspapermen, and in fact they were shepherded all around Guam and exposed to glowing commentaries on its natural charms.

A conspicuous dasher of cold water on Minagawa's hopes was a Japanese psychiatrist, Dr. Yoshiro Yase, who was on Guam doing research on amyotrophic lateral sclerosis, a neurological ailment to which Chamorros are peculiarly susceptible. Dr. Yase revealed that he had run across some victims of the disease who were quite unlike conventional Guamanians. Some of *his* people, the Doctor said, were shy and reclusive, lived in the jungle off wild fruits, never cut their hair or shaved, and dressed in tatters. "I would never have believed there were such people on Guam if I hadn't seen them," Dr. Yase said.

The original plan had been for the Japanese expedition to remain on Guam for only a month, but—in large part at Minagawa's urging—the departure date was delayed a week, until October 24th. Just before Minagawa gave up the search, he went back to one of his and Ito's old haunts to look for a rifle he had once cached. He didn't find it, but he did find some gloves of his, and some tire-rubber sandals, a bottle of salt he'd distilled from sea water, and two gunpowder barrels in which he had stored dried breadfruit. Earlier in his tireless quest, he had come upon a good many skeletons. He took one bone from each, for use in a mass symbolic funeral service back in Tokyo, and he also pinpointed the position of the rest of the bones, so that the Guamanians could retrieve them. When these were all collected, they amounted to quite a pile—two hundred pounds of bones altogether. Nobody knew quite what to do with them. Finally, our Navy packed them reverently in three big crates, with a Japanese flag wrapped around the bleak, bleached contents of each box, and sent them by ship to Japan.

Minagawa, who became a straggler at twenty-three, was sure that a man could live in and off the jungle until the age of sixty, and he stood ready to go back to Guam and search further whenever any more clues might be found. The problem, of course, is to decide what constitutes a clue. Guamanians living in remote areas periodically report the theft of chickens and bananas. Have stragglers taken them? There can be no certainty one way or another. At the end of 1964, an Air Force sergeant on a weekend outing with his wife left her in their car while he climbed a hill to take a snapshot of a handsome vista. At the summit, he flushed an odd-looking man, short, thin, and nearly naked, who dived into a clump of bushes and vanished. Other people reported spotting footprints in generally untrodden areas or wisps of smoke drifting up from unfrequented caves. Scavengers? Poachers? Sufferers from amyotrophic lateral sclerosis? In view of Minagawa's personal history, it would seem presumptuous for anyone else to declare flatly that they *couldn't* be Japanese stragglers. Minagawa had no doubt about who these jungle wraiths are. Neither had Sergeant Cruz, with twenty years of hunting—first homicidal and now humanitarian—to back up his opinion. Both were unswervingly convinced that Guam still harbored Japanese soldiers—and maybe a good many. "If these people stop wandering around and stay in one place long enough, I'll find them," Cruz said. "It makes me so mad that people who are *not* looking for them usually see them. Now, if I see them, I'm not taking any chances with them. One kid reporter from Tokyo wanted me to go out after them at night with a gun and a flashlight. I said, 'Negative.' I told him, 'You're too young to know what Japanese soldiers can be like.' All I ask God is to give me just one chance to see a straggler in daylight. I'm not going to harm him. I even had my men turn in their carbines for pistols, so that the sight of a big weapon wouldn't scare anyone. If a straggler starts running away from me, I'll chase him to kingdom come, because if anybody's going to get him back to Japan, I'd like it to be me."

Whether inspired by fact or fancy, straggler hunts on Guam may well continue for another generation or so, by which time, if the island is lucky, the place will be aswarm with tourists, their cameras loaded to record the end (if, of course, it proves to be the end) of this curious footnote to military history and this shining testimonial (if, of course, the presumptive witnesses come forth) to the toughness and tenacity of mankind.

22.

Unalterable and Inescapable Facts

"NOTHING MUCH NEW OUT HERE," AN AMERICAN official in the Trust Territory wrote not long ago to a Stateside friend. "As usual, petty crises of broken-down machinery and lack of supplies keep us from sleeping the peaceful life of the Pacific."

Both Americans and Micronesians in the Trust Territory are accustomed to living with dashed hopes. It came as no surprise to the Americans at the district headquarters on Ponape that their 1964 desk calendars, though ordered well in advance, didn't arrive until October of that year. At the start of 1964, several dozen native Ponapeans, on receiving word from Saipan that a big new generator was on its way to augment the puny electric-power facilities of their district center, went to considerable effort and expense wiring their homes. Six months later, a generator was delivered, but before it was hooked up it was packed off to Truk, which apparently had a higher priority. Late in 1965, Ponapeans got some power to hitch their wires to. For five years running, the pre-Christmas cargo ship that calls at Majuro didn't arrive before the holiday. One year, after it came in on January 8th, a store proprietor there—a man who, like most Micronesians, is usually quite pro-American—exclaimed, "If the Russians turned up here with a trade-goods ship on Christmas Eve, they could have this place."

The contemporary visitor to Micronesia's islands is likely to be struck less by their innate tropical beauty than by the shabbiness of their man-made embellishments. The natives, having different aesthetic standards from westerners, are not as offended as are Americans by the rusty tin roofs that surmount many of their homes, but indigenes and aliens alike in the area wish that so much around didn't have to look as though it had been acquired in a junk dealer's clearance sale. The Trust Territory is heavily dependent for communications on radios; many of the sets in the area are 1944 models, for which spare parts are no longer obtainable. Even the seeds the local agriculturists receive are so old they have poor yields.

The weekly newspaper at Ponape, where the resident housewives are as fond as housewives anywhere of chattering away on the phone, recently carried the notice, "Suffering from old age, our telephone switchboard now has only four active jacks available for operation. Only four calls can be connected at one time. Effective today, only business calls can be connected during working hours. Personal calls should be cut down to the minimum after 4:30 P.M. and during weekends."

Ponape has no fire engine. It had one, but its tank wouldn't hold water, and the tires gave out, and it was dumped in the sea. The only ambulance available to the Truk hospital is an Army one of Second-World-War vintage. The Majuro hospital is luckier. In 1964, it inherited an almost brand-new United States Navy ambulance. The hospital got the vehicle only because the Army had not long before superseded the Navy in charge of the missile-testing base at Kwajalein, and the Army would naturally not be caught dead in a Navy ambulance. "The reason anything is here," one American in Micronesia recently observed, perhaps a mite exaggeratedly, "is because somebody threw it out."

Even the typhoon shelters in Micronesia are second-hand. When the Palauan islands of Peleliu and Angaur were leveled by a hurricane in the fall of 1964, the emergency shelters shipped to their inhabitants were tents that had been used on Guam after its 1962 typhoon. There was one unexpected byproduct of the 1964 storm. The winds stripped Peleliu of all its vegetation, and where there had once been a tangle of growth a public-works officer espied a twenty-year-old crane boom that, after some minor rehabilitation, the Trust Territory administration was able to put into useful service.

"We spend far too much money maintaining old junk vehicles," High Commissioner Goding said in mid-1965. Maintenance is a problem anywhere in the tropics, and few Micronesians have yet become adept mechanics. Nonetheless, some of the equipment in the Trust Territory is simply too decrepit to function. When an American educator noticed that a recent visitor he was showing around the high-school grounds in Ponape was looking at the unkempt, nearly knee-high grass, the guide said, "It's kind of overgrown here. Our tractor has been out of commission for seven months." An American educator on Truk with a used jeep for sale put an ad in that district's paper that went, "Beautiful blue color, powerful engine (goes up steepest hills in second gear, when it runs). Rebuilt body. Kind of old and friendly. Especially a good buy for those who want to learn more about auto mechanics." Throughout Micronesia, there is a shortage of tires and of tire patches, too. One American at Koror has achieved a kind of celebrity by not only having set but also having tied the local record for flat tires—four in a day.

In Micronesia, inadequacy of supplies is routine. The Ponape education office got up some handsome Christmas cards, but long before the demand for them could be filled, it ran out of paper to print them on. Majuro, where housewives are accustomed to having their shops run out of paper bags, had to stop publishing its weekly newspaper for a while because it had no stencils. Adversity sometimes breeds a kind of perverse pride. While both the natives and outlanders in the Trust Territory often go out of their way to proclaim the superiority of whatever island they are on to any other island, they also set great store by dwelling on the shortages that aggravate their lives. Like hospital patients meeting in a corridor and zestfully recounting their aches and pains, old Micronesian hands enjoy regaling newcomers with tales of the time that Ponape ran out of milk, or Palau of cigarettes, or Truk, in rapid succession one especially memorable year, of fresh water, gasoline, and bandages for its hospital. The hospital at Yap, which chronically runs so low on drugs that it relies for its supplies of many of them not on shipments from the American government but on disbursements from a Catholic mission, has an encephalograph machine, but at last report nobody really knew whether it worked or not, because there was no paper to feed into it.

It is not only the insufficiency of equipment that retards material progress in the hospitals of Micronesia, as in practically all other installations, but also the dimensions of the region. At the 1965 session of the U.N. Trusteeship Council, the representative of Australia, which, having its own trust-territory headaches, is sympathetic to the United States, declared, "Constantly in considering Micronesia, one returns to the facts of the vastness of ocean and the minuteness of land, and to the immensity of the problems of administration and development posed by these unalterable and inescapable facts."

In Micronesia, there are nine hospitals—one for every ten thousand persons. (The United States ratio, for whatever the comparison may be worth, is one per thirty thousand.) Three of the Trust Territory hospitals are new, but that is deceptive. Although the one at Majuro was completed less than three years ago, its roof leaks, and its so-called emergency room, ever since its construction, has been without emergency or any other equipment. The administrators of Micronesian hospitals are plagued with special problems because, although they have limited storage space and little refrigeration, many of their patients won't eat institutional food—some Yapese can't, because their caste laws won't let them—and insist that their relatives bring them provisions, which are generally kept on the floor at bedside and inevitably attract flies, cockroaches, and rats. Some relatives, moreover, insist on staying at a hospital themselves until patients they've come to visit are released.

In his 1965 Inaugural Address, President Johnson said, "There is no room for second-class health services." Whether he had the Trust Territory specifically in mind is debatable, but in Micronesia his words have been much repeated, and the consensus there is that what he preached has not yet been practiced. To be sure, the health-services budget for the Trust Territory has tripled in the last three years. Yet deficiencies persist. Micronesians are not subject, by and large, to the same stresses as Americans—there is little variation between the blood pressures of infants and octogenarians—but an occasional one of them nonetheless does become disturbed. There are no facilities for mental patients, however, throughout the Trust Territory. When the Yap hospital found on its hands a woman whose derangement constituted a clear threat to her family, the only thing it could think of to do with her was to put her, stark naked, in a bare cement room with a small barred window and an unupholstered wooden plank for a bed. It can hardly have been what President Johnson meant, but on the other hand if anybody had tried to move the woman out of the area, her family might very well have protested.

In theory, each of the six districts has an American physician assigned to it full-time. It is not easy to get doctors to go there, though; the job of director of medical services for the whole area was vacant for eleven months not long ago before anybody could be prevailed on to take it, and the man who finally did quit after a year, following an almost non-stop vendetta with the administration. Most of the treatment in the Territory, up to and including surgery, is furnished by natives who, while commonly called "Doctor," are not Doctors of Medicine but have received the degree of Medical Practitioner, either from a school in the Fiji Islands or from one the Navy ran, just after the war, on Guam. Some of the practitioners are remarkably competent. One of them, not long after completing the Navy course, did his first Caesarian section, a successful one, on his own wife. There are several American women in Micronesia today who wouldn't dream of having anybody but a local practitioner deliver their babies. (The scarcity of transportation can be a factor. An American woman who left the island of Kusaie in September, so her child could be born six weeks later in a hospital on Guam, barely made it back home by Christmas.)

One of the practitioners is Dr. John Iaman, director of health services for the Marshall Islands. A naturalized Micronesian citizen, Dr. Iaman was born, in 1924, in the British-owned Gilbert Islands, just southeast of the Marshalls. As a boy, he wanted to be a priest, and he learned English at a mission school there. During the war, he was out in a canoe one day with some priests and nuns and other students, heading for his Gilbertese home atoll of Marakei, when a storm caught them and tossed them up on the Marshallese island of Mili. Because they were British subjects, the Japanese executed five of them. Iaman sneaked off to the shore, grabbed an empty canoe, and headed out to sea, where he was fortunate enough to be picked up by an American destroyer. The Navy used him for a while as an interpreter, and in 1946 sent him to Guam for three years' medical training. After sixteen years of surgical experience, he hoped to become a doctor, and was admitted as an undergraduate to Georgetown University, in Washington, to take a few pre-medical courses preparatory to enrolling in the university's medical school. But the academic going was understandably rough, and he withdrew without ever having had a chance to learn in a classroom some of the theory behind the profession he had been practicing nearly his entire adult life.

Doctors and practitioners in Micronesia have been much perturbed by the natives' lack of resistance, especially on isolated outer islands, to epidemics. Diseases that Americans take more or less in stride, like whooping cough and measles, can be killers, and even German measles can be serious. Since 1962, the Trust Territory administration has undertaken a sweeping program of preventive medicine, and by now, just about every reachable indigene has been inoculated against smallpox, polio, diphtheria, tetanus, typhoid, and paratyphoid. (Nearly everybody has intestinal parasites; the District Legislature of the Marianas passed a resolution in 1965 urging that all school children be dewormed at least twice annually.) Schoolteachers have been trying to inculcate in their students a respect for sanitation, and on many a classroom blackboard is chalked some such testimonial as "The reason why I have to wash my body, because it will make me clean and neat so that I do not get sick." When epidemics nonetheless do occur, the Americans in charge still sometimes use old-fashioned means of coping with them. A field-trip ship called at Satawal, in the Yap District, in the winter of 1966 and found a few natives with whooping cough. They were taken away, put ashore on an uninhabited island of the nearby Woleai atoll, and told to stay there at least two weeks, after which, if all went well, somebody would come fetch them.

As transportation has gradually improved, there has been a tendency for germs, like passengers and cargos, to skip more rapidly around Micronesia. When one district is suddenly hit by a new disease, it usually blames the district the last plane came in from. Thus when the Marshall Islands are stricken with influenza, the natives refer to their affliction as Ponape flu, the same disease that is known in Ponape as Truk flu. Not all the ailments to which the natives have succumbed can be blamed, however, on white men's means of expediting their contagiousness. It was long a custom among Yapese, for instance, to seek to acquire some of the strength embodied in their leaders by drinking the water in which their dead chiefs' bodies had been washed before burial.

23.

Anthropology and Anthropomorphism

THE YAPESE ARE THE MOST HIDEBOUND OF ALL MICRO-nesians, and they staunchly cling to many of their ancient ways. They deplore whistling in public, and they react violently to being touched without warning. Mild though they usually are, they will lash out viciously at anyone who lays unexpected hands upon them. Yap is the smallest Micronesian district. It has a population of six thousand, thirty-five hundred of whom live on a central cluster of islands that are known, like the entire district, as Yap. Yap was called Jap by the Germans and, by the Japanese, Wap, Uap, and Guap. Nobody takes spelling too seriously at Yap. One island in the main Yap group is called Map, but it appears on some maps as Maap.

Yap is Micronesia's biggest betelnut-chewing district. Nearly all Yapese adults, and a good many children, carry around straw betelnut bags. Prisoners in jail have hooks on which to hang theirs. While at school, children hang theirs on trees. If a Yapese happens to set his bag down on the ground, it is considered impolite to step over it. A betelnut kit contains nuts (a Yapese may consume fifty or sixty a day); powdered lime made by burning coral, an additive that turns the betelnut juice red; and leaves from the betel vine, a peppery plant related in name only to the nut tree. A nut is dusted with the powder, and then the chewy treat is wrapped in a leaf and popped into the mouth.

In time, an addict's teeth turn black, which is good for them; the betelnut coating protects the enamel. Those few elderly Yapese who are fitted out with dentures often hasten to stain them black; it is a Yapese legend that anyone whose teeth are unstained is liable to have them pecked out by blackbirds. The nuts play an important part in courtship. The way a girl tears a leaf or touches a boy's hand with a lime duster may significantly reveal her feelings toward him. On a date, the boy is supposed to provide the fixings, and until recently he was also expected to bring along some fresh fish for his girl's mother. Customs change. Now, a boy is apt to turn up with cigarettes and matches as well as betelnuts, and with some canned fish.

Ten years ago, no Yapese woman would have conceived of wearing Western clothes. Some of those who frequent Colonia, the district center, have changed their habits, but Colonia is also the only district center in Micronesia where women still matter-of-factly go around with nothing on but grass skirts, and where male employees in the district administrator's office sit at their desks clad only in breechclouts.

Outside Colonia, all the women go bare-breasted. Their skirts are multi-layered and ankle-length. Most Micronesians think it indecorous for a woman to expose her legs; Yapese feel most strongly about this and regard anyone who flaunts her calves as a hussy. The grass skirts are rarely made of grass. Dried and shredded banana leaf is a popular material for day-to-day wear; it doesn't smell when it gets wet. A banana-leaf skirt takes two days to make and lasts two weeks. For special occasions, like feasts and dances, hibiscus fiber dyed a variety of colors is used; a fancy-dress skirt takes two weeks to make and, unless there are an uncommon number of parties, lasts about a year. Since the skirts are made to wear, it is hard for sailors or other transients to pick one up as a souvenir. The main trading company at Yap was amused when it received an inquiry from a theatrical-supply house in Canada that wanted to order a gross of grass skirts. Recently, in an attempt to make the supply match the demand and also to provide Yapese who need it with some occupational therapy, the Yap administration has been encouraging women in the tubercular ward of the district hospital to make grass skirts for commercial sale.

Yapese girls wear their hair cropped until they menstruate. The sex of an unfamiliar Yapese child can be determined only by whether or not it is wearing a skirt. When the girls mature, they let their hair grow, by which time their sex is readily ascertainable anyway. It used to be a favorite Yapese sport to pretend to kidnap attractive young girls, after secret negotiations with their fathers, and to install them in communal men's houses. Women who had served such promiscuous apprenticeships were especially coveted as wives. While an abduction was in progress, a girl's father and her other male relatives were expected to carry on frightfully and to throw stones at the kidnappers, aiming carefully so they'd miss. In due course, suitable reparations would be made to the bereaved father in the form of the principal coin of the Yapese realm—its famous stone money.

The stone money is most commonly believed to have been the invention, more than a century ago, of a bygone chief who, admiring a full moon one night, thought it would be nice to have something similarly big and round and beautiful and durable on earth. After a while, he found an acceptable material—in the caves of the rock islands of Palau, three hundred miles to the west. It took two wars before the Palauans grudgingly gave the Yapese permission to quarry stone there. It was carved into slablike discs with a hole cut into the center of each of them, so they could be carried on poles. In time, the Yapese devised variations of the basic design—double-disc stones, for instance, or single discs with two holes in them. The value of any particular piece of money depended on its size, shape, color, quality, and the degree of difficulty in obtaining it. Some high-quality stone was once found on Map, or Maap, but the chief there at once declared it worthless because it was too accessible. In foreign-exchange terms, Yap stone money is now generally valued at twenty-five dollars per foot of diameter.

For a while, four hundred Yapese were stationed at the Palauan quarries. The money they made was shipped home precariously balanced on frail canoes. In 1879, an enterprising Irish-American sea captain, originally from Savannah, Georgia, changed all that. He was David Dean O'Keefe, who had a clipper ship, and could transport tons of money at a time. For transporting their money, the Yapese rewarded him liberally with copra and with *bêche de mer*, or trepang, a sea slug that the Chinese fancy as a soup ingredient (elsewhere, it is used for fertilizer), and that in Hong Kong would then sell for four hundred dollars a ton. Plying between Yap, Palau, and Hong Kong, Captain O'Keefe did quite nicely for himself, before he disappeared at sea in 1901. He took over one of the Yap islands as a residence, and built a comfortable home. When other English-speaking mariners came into port, he would invite them into his library to browse through his Dickens and Thackeray.

In 1929, the Japanese administrators of Yap took a census of the stone money there. They counted 13,281 pieces. The tabulation was not hard to make; Yapese customarily lean their stone money against the sides of their houses. In some villages, today as in days past, both sides of a road are lined with the stones, propped against trees or against ordinary stones. The biggest extant known piece of Yap stone money is too heavy to lift into a vertical position. Nobody knows for sure how it got where it is, but it lies flat off to the side of a dirt path on the small island of Rumung. If it could be hoisted, it would be twelve feet high, and ten feet wide, and at its middle it is a foot and a half thick. Yapese no longer make stone money, and the number of pieces has diminished since the census thirty-six years ago. During the war, the Japanese used some of them for anchors, and since the war quite a few of those flanking roads have been smashed by motor vehicles.

In Yap, dollars are now used for routine transactions, but stone money is till the proper thing to exchange when one village entertains another at an ordinary festival, called a *mit*, or a really elaborate festival, called a *mitmit*. (Since Germany occupied Yap, and the rest of Micronesia, for fifteen years at the start of the twentieth century, some linguists think that the names of these feasts derive from the German word for "with.") A *mitmit* may last a month and cost its host village the equivalent of six thousand dollars.

What accounts for a good deal of this formidable outlay is the Yapese adherence to an ancient song-and-dance ceremony called the *Tam'*, in which various groups of women—old ladies, say, or pregnant ones, or small girls—are permitted to ask for anything they want, and are supposed to have their requests granted. Some girls may invite the proprietor of a store to strip his shelves of bread for them, or of gin for their fathers. (It is considered impolite for the residents of one village to ask those of another for, say, a canoe, without first making sure that the donors have a boat to spare.) *Mitmits* used to be given in honor of recently deceased Yapese, but of late they have been held while the principal guest is still alive, on the theory that it is a shame to miss a party for oneself. Aside from the food and drink consumed, a good deal of the expenditures for a *mit* or a *mitmit* are recoverable; the exact same pieces of stone money that a host village gives to a guest village are supposed to be returned when the recipients reciprocate with a *mitmit* of their own.

For all their devotion to their ancient ways, Yapese are adaptable. Nearly every one of them, in response to an inquiry from a curious American, will profess to be a Christian. One Yapese elder who on such occasions says he is a Catholic is a sixty-four-year-old man named Ylubuan. He is also a *tamerong*, a high-ranking witch doctor. (A generation ago, *tamerongs* were buried in a sitting-up position, with their heads above ground, so they could keep an eye on things.) A much-respected dispenser of herb medicines, Ylubuan runs a small retail store, where, though he professes to be a prohibitionist, he does a lively trade in beer. Under the Japanese he was a policeman, and he was in an especially good position to maintain law and order, because a good many Yapese then were convinced, as they still are, that his father, also a *tamerong*, taught him arcane language in which he can communicate with spirits. Many Yapese believe that Ylubuan is supernatural himself. He himself believes that Adam and Eve came from Yap. His father told him so. Ylubuan's version of that part of the story of Genesis is that Adam and Eve were the offspring of a Yapese woman, though how she evolved or who if anybody was supposed to have sired her children, Ylubuan's father never got around to imparting to him. Not that that matters much: many Yapese, of high or humble rank, are of the opinion that ghosts procreate children, and, anthropologists have asserted, they have never been altogether convinced of any direct relationship between coitus and conception.

Most of Micronesia's legends have been passed along orally from generation to generation. It has been only recently that, at the urging of the American administrators, some of the natives have begun to put some of their stories on paper. Foremost among these annalists is a young Yapese, John Mangefel, the supervisor of teachers for his district. At thirty, in 1963, he became the first Yapese to earn a Bachelor of Arts degree, when he was graduated from the University of Hawaii. In Honolulu, he won fifty dollars in a literary contest, by setting down on paper some of the stories his grandmother told him before her death in 1956.

Many of the tales that Mangefel and a few others are now trying to preserve are anthropomorphic. One has to do with a Promethean rooster that was transformed into a woman and that taught the Yapese, whose lips theretofore had been perpetually sore from eating uncooked food, the art of fire. Another has to do with a Yapese boy whose tenderness toward a lonely coconut crab was rewarded when the crustacean turned into a beautiful and affectionate girl. Still another concerns a man named Gazingzing, who lived for a while with some fish. On returning to land, he underhandedly taught his fellowmen some tricks of fishing. This angered the king of the tuna, who demanded Gazingzing's life. The next time the traitor went swimming, three fish did away with him, but some others tried to share in the credit by swimming through his blood and reporting incarnate to the king that they'd had a hand in the vengeful act. For their deceitfulness, the king of the tuna punished them by making them permanently blood-colored—which is why, as any Yapese who goes along with the old-time yarns can tell you, red snappers are red.

Few Micronesians believe today that fooling around with coconut crabs is likely to have romantic anthropomorphic consequences. Many of the natives are reluctant to publicize their legends because of their wish to get into the modern swing of things and their fear that excessive circulation of their engaging but implausible tales might make other people think they are backward. Moreover, quite a few Micronesians are simply bored with their past, in part because they've resurrected it exhaustively at the urging of American anthropologists who were bent on delving into their then relatively untapped lode of lore.

When at the end of the war Micronesia came under the United States Navy, it brought with it a fleet of anthropologists, on the theory that Naval officers couldn't handle indigenes without knowledgeable intermediaries. It was the first American attempt anywhere to use anthropologists in a more or less administrative capacity, and the experiment was something less than a rollicking success, inasmuch as anthropologists, like many other scientists, tend to look upon all emissaries of all governments, including their own, with suspicion.

Still, the first postwar anthropologists had a field day doing field work. At that time, graduate students in that science were running out of out-of-the-way places where they could do research, without which it would be extremely difficult to get their Ph.D.'s. Suddenly an enormous, new, unmined area was opened up to them, and they swept upon it like a tidal wave. Enisled indigenes who had never taken any kind of examination in their lives, and didn't much care if they remained in blissful ignorance, found themselves confronted with Rorschach and thematic apperception tests. Some of the natives thought some of the anthropologists intolerably inquisitive, and wouldn't tell them anything. Others would tell them anything that came into their heads just to get them off their backs. It is customary for an anthropologist on scholarly safari to try to find one native informant in a locality, and if the informant becomes friendly and communicative, almost anything he says, up to and including pure fantasy, is apt to end up in a dissertation.

Quite a few of the anthropologists who descended upon Micronesia learned, commendably, a local language. One scientist did so without letting the natives know about it. He was shortly to be disillusioned both about the indigenes' naïveté and the validity of some of his colleagues' observations. He had an appointment with a group of village elders one day who agreed to open up their memories to him. When he arrived, the Micronesians were talking among themselves. Assuming that their visitor couldn't understand a word of their conversation, they were rehearsing an embroidered account of their lives to present for his edification and their own amusement. The reverse has also proved true. One American spent two years in the Marshall Islands and became fairly fluent in Marshallese. Then he went away for eighteen months. On his return, he had all but forgotten the language, but the natives who remembered him didn't know that and tended to be taciturn whenever he turned up.

Almost every American—scientist and non-scientist alike—who has spent any time in Micronesia believes that it is difficult to get accurate information from most of the natives, because in almost all circumstances they will politely answer a question by telling the asker whatever it is they think he wants to hear. This may be so, but the first American to perceive this truism—when, presumably, he got a "Yes" to his "Do you tell us what you think we want to hear?"—may have been told what his respondent thought he wanted to hear. In any event, many Micronesians seem to keep a good deal to themselves, which is, after all, their privilege.

Anthropologists like sex. Their treatises are as dependent on it as psychoanalysts'. One of the greatest opportunities for original research that Micronesia offered, or seemed to offer, was quickly discovered, not long after the war, on the Marshallese atoll of Arno, a lovely, prosperous cluster of fifty islands, with a total population of slightly over a thousand. Arno is rich in copra: nowadays, its average monthly output is a hundred and twenty tons. It is rich in fish: mullet and parrot fish spawn in its hundred-and-thirty-square-mile lagoon. It is impeccably clean: its old men and young girls are astir before sunup to pick up leaves that have fallen off its trees during the night. Arno wants to be up-to-date just as much as any other Micronesian community. When, in 1963, District Administrator Coleman of the Marshalls, eager as always to build roads, proposed putting one on Arno's main island, the principal trader there at once ordered a pickup truck from Japan. The truck is still the only motorized vehicle on the atoll, and its battery is enfeebled, but that inconvenience is readily circumvented. Whenever the truck's owner wants to run it, he assembles a bunch of local boys and they push it until the engine turns over.

Arno is one of the Marshall Islands' strictest Protestant outposts. Absolutely no liquor is permitted there (as a result, the community leaders consider both a jail and a constable superfluous), and the residents often sing hymns until midnight and then obediently arise for more hymns when their church bell peals commandingly at five-thirty the next morning. Incongruously, Arno also was—and there are some who say it still is—the site of a unique Micronesian institution called, by smirking Americans, the University of the Arts of Love. Its purported existence brought anthropologists there like parrot fish at spawning time. The University is the only remaining academy (if it remains) of a whole bunch of finishing schools in which older Marshallese women once taught younger ones how to make men happy. Missionaries stamped out the others, but Arno's somehow hung on. According to Marshallese who insist they have first-hand knowledge, the course of study did not involve men. Indeed, guards were posted to keep them out. The faculty simply taught the students, whose average age was around fourteen, certain libidinous dances and other rhythmic movements—many of these last patterned on the movements of waves and winds.

A couple of anthropologists somehow got permission to bring movie cameras onto the sequestered campus. During one demonstration, a story goes, a photographer grabbed a machete to lop off a tree branch that was obstructing his camera's field of vision. Holding the branch with one arm, he couldn't bring himself to take his own eyes off the girls, and as he swung the weapon almost severed his arm by mistake. The anthropologists' pictures, one hears, came close to being confiscated when they sent them in to be developed.

On Arno today, it is difficult to ascertain how much of any of this is true. Some Arnoese say there used to be some such place, but that it wasn't a school—just a brothel for Japanese colonists. Others insist that it not only did exist but that it is very much a going concern today, although they do not feel free to point out, or even hint at, its exact location. Still others suggest that the whole establishment was merely invented by transient anthropologists to titillate the United States Navy. Whatever the case, the belief persists that Arno University graduates, because of their expertise, were and are highly coveted as wives. Every now and then a Marshallese escorting a visitor around a nearby atoll will point to a passing woman and say, admiringly, "She's an Arno girl," much as, in another environment, one might say, "She's a Radcliffe girl."

"Anthropologists are almost as common as coconuts," the Yap's weekly paper has commented. "They are always with us." The United States has been running the area for so long by now that one of the best and most sensitive of the anthropologists who have specialized in Micronesia, Dr. Ward H. Goodenough of the University of Pennsylvania, has had a chance to study two generations of natives on the island of Romonum, a spit of land in the broad Truk lagoon. Goodenough was there in 1947 as a graduate student, and returned in 1964 with his wife and two young sons to live for eleven months. He had a house—with a poured-cement floor, mangrove rafters, and ivory-nut thatch—built beforehand, specifying knowledgeably that he wanted a chief's-height house. On Romonum, homes are graded according to the altitude of the major crossbeam. After a chief's-height house come, in descending order, residences known as head-just-clearing height, ducking height, dirty-knees height, and lizard's-crawl height. Having a lizard's-crawl-height house, in Truk's less halcyon days, was considered to have one advantage that compensated for its dwarfishness: there was so little headroom a homicidal intruder could not effectively wield a weapon once he got inside.

Goodenough, who is a past president of the Society for Applied Anthropology and the author of, among other works, *Cooperation in Change*, came back to Romonum, prudently carrying to that doctorless spot a year's supply of surgeon's scrubbing soap, to determine if interpersonal relationships—obligations, rights, taboos, and so forth—had an organized structure analogous to the grammar of the Trukese language, in which he became proficient on his first visit. Anybody going to Micronesia is likely to find himself pressed into extracurricular services of one kind or another. Goodenough almost at once found himself giving orientation courses to American teachers newly arrived at Truk, and working on a revision of a Trukese-English dictionary.

The scholar's research was further impeded by the curiosity of his own informant. In 1947, Goodenough's most fruitful source of information had been a chief on Romonum. By 1964, that man had died, and the scientist acquired the chief's son, who'd been just a boy the time before, as his informant. There was so little on record about the history and customs of Romonum that Goodenough spent a great deal of time acquainting the son with ancient island traditions that the dead chief had never got around to imparting to any one except the anthropologist.

Meanwhile, Mrs. Goodenough, an anthropologist in her own right, was, while not teaching her own sons, doing a study on adoption. Of the three hundred and eighteen inhabitants of Romonum, forty-one, she determined, had been adopted. Many Micronesians have double sets of parents. This is supposed to make the children more secure when they're young, and the adults more secure when they're old. One recently elected member of the Congress of Micronesia is the son of a Japanese father and a Palauan mother. At eight months, he was given in adoption to another Japanese-Palauan couple. The real father was killed at Palau during the war, and the adopted father was repatriated to Japan. The adopted mother then married a Yapese, who reared the boy. He then married a Palauan girl of part German background, and *their* first son was recently legally adopted by an American bachelor of part anthropological background.

Kinship in Micronesia is a subject broad enough and complicated enough to keep anthropologists in business forever. In the Marshalls, first cousins commonly call one another brother, and nephews call their paternal uncles, depending on their age, either older father or younger father. Everybody likes children, and some natural mothers have to fight to retain custody of their own offspring, because relatives or pseudo-relatives aspire to bring them up. With all the confusion that results as to just who is whose parent, sibling relationships sometimes outweigh all others in importance and permanence. In Truk, if a man has a fight with his wife's brother, the wife would be accounted strange indeed if she did not side with her brother against her husband.

24.

You Can Only Weld Once

Contemporary anthropologists might have made even more stimulating explorations in Micronesia had it not been for the prior dampening effect of missionaries on the innate high spirits of the area. There can be few places on earth where churchmen have more tellingly demonstrated their skill at taking the fun out of life. Micronesians are still devoted to sex, but such agreeable concomitants as singing, dancing, and general ebullience have, on many of their islands, been all but outlawed. The principal inhibiting crusaders were from the American Board of Commissioners for Foreign Missions, often known as the Boston Mission Society. These Protestant missionaries, who believed, among other things, that the wearing of Mother Hubbards in tropical climes would accelerate the salvation of womankind, first reached Micronesia in 1852, and they did much of their spiritual and sartorial work in the Marshalls. "When they stopped burning the witches in Salem, they came here," one contemporary missionary—a Catholic—recently reflected. The Marshallese island of Ebon was once called Boston, and Kusaie, in the adjoining district of Ponape, was called Strong, after a governor of Massachusetts.

Kusaie, one of the most verdant islands in Micronesia, has remained a stronghold of blue-noses—most of them nowadays being native religious leaders who are if anything more unbending than their foreign teachers ever were. It is much the same in many parts of Micronesia. In Palau, the native proprietor of one fairly isolated village's only store is so straitlaced he won't stock cigarettes. When he made known his decision, the priest at a nearby Catholic mission began buying them by the case and selling them, at cost, to his neighbors.

In the Marshalls, natives who wish to perpetuate their traditional dances are obliged to practice them in secret. The power that the Protestant church wields over the Marshallese was never better illustrated than when the district's presiding native judge, the solemn and highly respected Kabua Kabua, christened a new boat not long ago. He thought it would add a nice touch to the occasion if twelve women, wearing long-sleeved, ankle-length dresses, walked alongside the boat as it was carried to the water, each woman holding a crepe-paper tassel that had been affixed to the craft's side. The next day, the local church excommunicated the lot of them, including the judge, for dancing in public.

Today, missionaries are genuinely respected in Micronesia, because, quite apart from their religious labors, they have contributed substantially to the social, economic, and educational advancement of the region. As a kind of reward for their helpfulness, they get to ride on the Trust Territory airline at half the regular fare. Five thousand Micronesian children are now enrolled in mission schools of various sects. While their teachers usually get on well enough with one another, school spirit sometimes impels the students to excesses. In Palau, a resident Protestant missionary and a resident Catholic missionary together translated the Bible into the local language, but not long after this ecumenical collaboration there was a head-cracking rumble between two groups of teenagers whose only apparent divergency was theological. Competitiveness between rival religious factions exists in other areas, but it rarely leads to mayhem. In Majuro, for instance, there is a constant struggle for musical superiority between a Protestant children's choir and a Catholic boys' band—the latter being the only organized instrumental ensemble in Micronesia.

The band was formed, and is still energetically conducted, by a Jesuit from Buffalo, Father L. G. Hacker, who has been in the Pacific for a quarter of a century and at Majuro since 1952. On arriving there, he at once began to build a school, though he had had no construction experience. At first, his only materials were three hundred bags of cement that the American armed forces had thrown out. So he built a cellar. It was, and still is, the only cellar on Majuro. In time, he acquired some lumber and other materials, and put a superstructure on the cellar. Now he has about five hundred students. In 1954, when he had four, the armed forces who were conducting nuclear tests at Eniwetok discarded a dozen or so musical instruments. Father Hacker grabbed them. Among his parishioners were a number of adult males who had nothing to do, and the priest thought music might occupy some of their time.

Father Hacker, whose only first-hand acquaintance with any instrument had been a few boyhood scuffles with a violin, undertook to teach eight adults to play trumpets and trombones. It wasn't easy. Marshallese are sensitive, and if one of them blew a jarringly wrong note, he couldn't be told that, because he'd lose face. The mistake had to be blamed on the instrument, in which event the performer would disassemble the instrument to seek out its flaw, and might or might not be able to put it back together again.

One day, a boy student picked up a loose and intact trumpet, and blew a creditable note. Heartened at the sound, the priest decided to switch from men to boys, who were more tolerant of criticism. Within a few years he had built up a band with thirty-six instruments and dashing red tunics made by the players' mothers. Today, it would be unthinkable to hold any kind of celebration at Majuro without the brassy participation of Father Hacker's band, and when the bandsmen go to the movies and hear somebody else's rendition of a John Philip Sousa march, they nudge one another and exclaim, "What do you know, they're playing our song!"

In the history of Micronesia, there have been only two indigenous Catholic priests. One, a Ponapean, began his education under the Spanish late in the nineteenth century, and was finally ordained in Spain, in 1940. Caught in Europe when the war broke out, he had a difficult time getting home, because he was traveling, like all itinerant Micronesians of that era, on a Japanese passport. The second native priest is a young Palauan who achieved that status in 1964—the only one of ten Micronesians at a seminary in the Philippines to be ordained. He now teaches religion at a mission school in Koror, where his brother is director of secular education for the Palau district.

The alien Catholics in Micronesia, nearly all of the Jesuit order, often stay there for most of their adult lives. Last March, a priest died at Truk, at seventy-three, after thirty-nine years' service in the area. A relative newcomer, now in merely his eighteenth year out there, is perhaps the most celebrated of all the contemporary missionaries in Micronesia. He is Father Hugh Costigan, who presides over a mission at Ponape in the village of Tamori, part of the municipality of Madolenihmw, several hours by outboard motor-boat from Kolonia.

Father Costigan is a singular priest, being among other things a skilled construction man, a Sunday-school teacher in a Protestant church, and the parent, by adoption, of a Ponapean boy. Costigan, who also nonchalantly serves pork to Jews on Friday, does his Sunday-school stint at the atoll of Pingelap, where at last count the population was religiously divided into one hundred and ninety-six Protestants and four Catholics. He has so few souls of his own faith to minister to at Pingelap, whenever he visits that place, that he takes over Sunday school to give the overburdened Protestant clerics a hand. Costigan also had some construction workers on his payroll install a sink, one time, for a Protestant woman missionary. Sunday was the only day he could spare his crew, and he asked the lady if she would have any objections to their thus desecrating the Sabbath. After a moment's meditation, she replied, "Oh, we should not work on Sunday, but I do need a sink."

As for the Ponapean son, the priest acquired him through another sideline common to missionaries in remote areas—the practice of medicine. Father Costigan is especially sought out by natives who need an injection of something or other, because he uses hundred-proof vodka as a disinfectant; after the shot, the native gets to lick the liquor off his arm. One day a tubercular woman turned up at the mission with a two-month-old boy. Costigan said she had to go to the hospital at once, and when she asked what would become of the baby, the priest, who speaks fluent Ponapean, replied, "Don't worry; I'll take care of him." He shipped off the mother, and turned the child over to his own native housekeeper.

Months passed. On finally inquiring about the sick woman's condition, Costigan was surprised to hear that she'd been released from the hospital and had gone home. He asked a relative of hers why she hadn't come to reclaim her baby. "He's yours," Costigan was told. "You said you'd take care of him." The priest, aware of how embarrassing it would be for the mother to get her boy back once she thought she'd formally relinquished him, legally adopted the child.

Costigan was born in 1914 and raised in the Bronx. Before he began studying for the priesthood, he was a bricklayer and plumber; he has had a union card since high school. His father was a fire department battalion chief, and the son has good connections in important New York circles. The priest is an ex-honorary chaplain of the emergency service division of the city's police department. The head of that division, for years, was Assistant Chief Inspector Walter Klotzback, who ran a series of benefits for Costigan, and who would have enough raffle tickets sold each time to send as much as ten thousand dollars a year to the mission at Tamori. On his occasional Stateside visits, Costigan also makes a point of looking up his old friends in construction unions; a couple of years ago, the nearly fifteen hundred members of one Brooklyn plumbers' local assessed themselves a hand tool apiece for the mission. Costigan's otherwise austere bedroom at Tamori was furnished, when I last looked in on him, with a whole case of brand-new sixteen-ounce hammers.

When the *nanmwarki* of Madolenihmw learned from Costigan about the beneficent Chief Klotzback, the *nanmwarki* thought he deserved a reward for his division's emergency services to Ponape, and conferred on him the Ponapean title of *saum,* which is a high rank, though lower of course than a *nanmwarki.* When a Ponapean chief grants such an honor, he expects to be paid tribute by the lucky recipient. Every year, accordingly, Costigan takes a hundred dollars or so from the benefit funds and buys the *nanmwarki* gifts from his faithful *saum* in New York.

Costigan is on excellent terms with the *nanmwarki,* in part because the priest respects the chief's prerogatives. When the *nanmwarki* of Pingelap visited the mission, Costigan wanted to give him a feast, but he took pains first to ask permission of the Madolenihmw chief and to give *him* a feast, complete with plentiful servings of mouth-numbing *sakau,* to which the priest has become acculturated. Father Costigan would not dream of doing anything in conflict with indigenous protocol. "The Ponapeans have their ancient customs, and I think it's good for us to follow them," he says.

When Father Costigan first reached Ponape, in 1947, the district was pretty much a shambles. While he was building a school, he lived in one grass hut and said mass in another. The United States Navy was then administering Micronesia, and one Sunday several dozen officers and men, attired in crisp whites, came to a service. They were taken aback when, among the hymns the natives sang, was one hybrid of local invention. The words were Ponapean, and the music was that of "The Star-

Spangled Banner." To a man, the Navy leapt to its feet and stood stiffly at attention until the hymn was over.

Costigan moved to Tamori in 1953, and has been there ever since. His mission, approachable only by boat or on foot, is situated at the base of a hill separated by a salt-water inlet from one of the most celebrated heights of Ponape. This is a two-peaked hill that looks as though it had once been a single mountain and had been knocked about. According to a Ponapean legend, that is precisely what happened, untold years ago, when a light-skinned, Bunyanesque giant got into a contest of strength with two normal-sized orphan brothers, who were magicians. The giant was to dig a channel in the inlet with his bare hands, and the brothers were to build a mountain. The giant had his task half done when he glanced back and saw that the top of the brothers' mountain had already disappeared in the clouds. The giant got so mad he picked up a rock and threw it at the mountain, crumpling its summit.

Costigan's mission is also a short boat ride away from an indisputably man-made curiosity, the famous ruins of Nan Madol. Whenever scientists or sightseers go to look at this Micronesian counterpart of Angkor Vat, Costigan gives them a meal or a night's lodging or both, in part because he is hospitable and in part because there is no alternative. Two years ago, he was host for six weeks to the Smithsonian Institution scientists who were exploring the ruins. Costigan recruited a twenty-five-man work crew for the scientists, who since their return to Washington have been helping to stock a cooperative store he runs at the mission by supplying him with goods picked up at the department-store bargain-basement sales. When, not long ago, one Washington emporium found itself glutted with lavender bedsheets and offered them at rockbottom prices, they were acquired by the Smithsonian crowd and shipped to Tamori, where they were snatched up enthusiastically by natives who had never before had any truck with bedsheets of any color or, when it came to that, with beds.

Father Costigan is a busy man. He has a chapel at his mission and conducts mass daily, but while he conducts it reverently, he also conducts it rapidly. In five minutes, he can race through a mass that takes the average priest ten. He doesn't have much time for religiosity. "You don't judge missionary work any more by things like numbers of converts," he says. "The old 'God-and-I' concept is gone, and so is the 'Don't-do-this' approach. Man works, man recreates, and man has religion. If we take care of the whole man, we're doing our job." He construes the principal present need of the whole Ponapean man to be improved housing, and he has so unflaggingly tackled the job of filling that need that he has become known throughout Micronesia as the Building Priest. He left Ponape in 1957 long enough to study low-cost housing in, among other places, Costa Rica and Colombia. Back at Tamori, three years later, he organized a housing cooperative that the *South Pacific Bulletin* has called "a shining example of rural community development in the South Pacific."

Most Ponapeans live in grubby, unsanitary shacks. The nearly three hundred members of Father Costigan's cooperative have been building cement-block houses for their families, at a cost—their labor and the priest's guidance being free—of only a dollar and a half a square foot. The members were supposed to pay ten dollars a month each toward the ultimate expense of their homes. But quite a few of the natives didn't *have* ten dollars a month. In order to be able to pay them cash salaries, Costigan decided to branch out and go into the general construction business. In short order, he had obtained contracts to put up two hundred thousand dollars' worth of Trust Territory classrooms and teachers' homes. Since then, additional and even larger contracts have come his way. He is the biggest non-governmental employer in Micronesia today.

During the last few years, in what time he has not been devoting to projects for other people, the Building Priest has been slowly constructing a pet project of his own. Opened in the fall of 1965, it is a boys' high school called the Ponape Agriculture Trade School. Costigan picked that name because, being of Irish background, he wanted to be able to call the place "PATS." He himself has been delivering a series of lectures on business ethics, a subject to which few Ponapeans of any age have traditionally had cause to give much time or thought.

To expedite the completion of the school and of various ancillary facilities at this mission, Father Costigan borrowed a bulldozer from the Trust Territory administration. The bulldozer, like most of the available equipment in Micronesia, had seen better days, and the priest had hardly pressed it into service when its clutch gave out. When he besought a replacement from Public Works, Public Works said it didn't have any spare parts. He bought a new clutch on his own from Honolulu, prudently having it shipped by air mail, and then the oil pan cracked. Costigan proposed welding it himself, but Public Works insisted on making this repair, arguing that it didn't want anybody else fooling around with its bulldozer. Soon the oil pan cracked again, and ever since then the bulldozer has perched, a silent yellow hunk of rusting metal, halfway up a slope between Costigan's chapel and his new school. "You can only weld once," Father Costigan says, "and I guess Public Works didn't do a very good weld. There it sits, a monument to futility. Maybe I'll plant flowers around it."

There are other building priests in the Trust Territory. One of them has a broken-down truck as his futility symbol. He used it to help build a church, even though its tires were flat, its starter and brakes were inoperative, and the only way to shift from reverse to forward gear was to hit it with a rock. After a while, it collapsed utterly. The priest who lives alongside of it is bitter, and he uses words like "outrage" to describe the American administration of Micronesia. Father Costigan is more charitable. He usually says nothing more acerb than that, in his view, the United States government has had a do-nothing philosophy.

Costigan himself has a do-everything philosophy. He is one of the main participants in, and performers on, a unique mission radio network that covers a good deal of Micronesia, and over which the priests who are hooked up on it get together every evening at six-thirty to swap news and gossip. "Sometimes it's known as Catholic Hour and sometimes as Comedy Hour," Costigan says. Not infrequently, the network saves somebody's life, being the only channel of communication by means of which district centers can be appraised of a medical emergency on an outlying island, and can send a plane or a boat to the rescue. One evening at six-twenty-five, just before air time, a young man showed up at the Tamori mission, his arm pierced through by a quarter-inch barbed fishing spear. Father Costigan couldn't figure out at first how to remove the weapon, but he raised a doctor on the radio and, following his instructions (and splashing around vodka liberally as a disinfectant), managed to cope with the situation. When the priests have something confidential to transmit and don't want to be overheard by anybody in Micronesia who happens to be tuned in on their frequency, they converse in Latin.

The missionaries of all faiths who are stationed in Micronesia today are aware that making spiritual headway among the natives is a slow and uncertain process. (During the first ten years of the twentieth century, when Germany ruled Micronesia, sixty Capuchin priests were assigned to Yap, and among them made only fifteen converts to Catholicism, or one fortieth of a convert per priest per year.) Bishop Kennally, when asked by the *Jesuit Seminary News* how much of his church's missionary activity was aimed at non-members, replied, "We go along in kind of parallel lines. The Protestants and their various sects have their Bibles, and days of religious activities. Catholics go to Church, send their children to mission schools, and participate in the sacramental life of the Church. There is not much crossing of lines . . ."

A few years back, all sixteen inhabitants of the tiny Palauan-district island of Pulo Anna were avowed Catholics. Then one Pulo Anna woman went to the hospital at Koror to have a baby. On returning home, she said she'd had a vision in the big city, in the course of which she'd been directed to establish a new religion on Pulo Anna and to become its high priestess. Her fellow islanders, bedazzled at the prospect of changing the drab, unvarying pattern of their isolated lives, went along with her and at her instigation built three churches, or roughly one for every five people. Some months later, when a Catholic priest stopped off at Pulo Anna, the woman at once tried to convert him to her faith, and added that she would like to go to Rome and see the Pope and maybe win *him* over. The priest has stopped visiting Pulo Anna, because he is tired of the woman's nagging proselytism.

A good deal of more or less voodoo religion is still prevalent at Palau. One Catholic priest there cannot bring himself wholly to disbelieve the efficacy of a kind of witchcraft curse called an *cholai.* (In the Palauan language, the "ch" is silent, as is the "g" that follows the "n" in "Ngatpang," pronounced "Natpan.") As the priest tells it, an *cholai* can be invoked by a person with the magical power to make someone sick. Not long ago, a Palauan girl was hospitalized with an acute pain in her knee. There seemed to be nothing medically wrong with her, but after a while she couldn't walk, and then she couldn't eat, and she was on the point of death when it was ascertained that a man thought an uncle of hers owed him forty dollars and because the uncle wouldn't pay had vengefully invoked an *cholai* to kill the girl. On being advised of the girl's condition, the priest relates, the uncle paid the forty dollars, and the girl promptly recovered.

The Palau district is the seat also of a clandestine religious movement called Modnekngei—a pot pourri of Catholic and Protestant and Seventh Day Adventist doctrines, garnished with ancient customs and superstitions, and all in all as much a nationalist or regional movement as a theological one. Modnekngei was launched in 1912 by one Temudad, a native policeman under the Germans. He wrapped his head in a red, turban-like cloth and delivered pronouncements from on high, in the first-person singular. The voice was his own, but the sentiments, he advised his listeners, were those of their God, for whom they were expected periodically to prepare sacrificial offerings of scorched turtle meat. Once Temudad claimed to have resurrected a dead girl.

When the Japanese supplanted the Germans, they tried to suppress Temudad's religion and threw him into jail, where he died. He was not resurrected. His mantle was taken up by a man named Ongesi, who had a Black-Muslim attitude toward the rest of the world. Ongesi preached a segregated heaven, with the better section reserved for Palauans, who are the darkest-skinned and most Negroid-looking of Micronesians. Ongesi was also a faith-healer. He got into trouble when his disciples declined to give conventional therapy to one of their group who had broken a leg falling out of a tree. Eventually Ongesi committed suicide. But the Modnekngei movement, even without a publicly identified leader, has survived, and its members meet in cloistered conclaves and exchange muttered curses against the American administration and just about everything and everybody else.

25.

The Busy Palauans

Palauans are generally conceded to be the most cantankerous of Micronesians and also the most ambitious. They are full of get up and go, and Palau would probably be a fertile recruiting ground for missionary Rotarians, Elks, or Lions. Stores in Koror are apt to be bedecked with little cloth pennants that say "Buy Now," "Easy Terms," "Low Prices," and "Big Value." Although the district of Palau, with eleven thousand inhabitants, ranks below Truk, Ponape, and the Marshall Islands in population, Palauans write so many more letters than any other Micronesians that they boast the only second-class post office in the Trust Territory. Population again notwithstanding, there are more students from Palau enrolled in the Xavier High School than from any other district, including Truk, which has more than twice as many inhabitants as Palau and has Xavier to boot. So relatively sophisticated are Palauans that they were eating from handsomely carved wooden bowls (fish-shaped ones for fish courses) while most other Micronesians were still using leaves for plates. Palauans are a proud and straight-backed lot; their women are the only ones in Micronesia who habitually carry burdens on their heads.

Palau is only five hundred miles east of the Philippines, but there is no connecting transportation between the two island groups, and little contact of any sort. Palauans are oriented toward Japan. Koror was the Japanese capital in Micronesia, and a good guess would be that if Palauans were asked today if they'd like once again to be under Japanese dominion, some 30 percent of them would respond with an emphatic, affirmative "*Hai!*" The leading Palauan businessman keeps an abacus on his desk. Some Palauans still address others in Japanese fashion, adding the suffix *-san* to their surnames. One Palauan municipality, Ngiwal, on the big island of Babelthuap, has for the last fifty years been governed by an hereditary chief named Uong, whose constituents call him Uong-san. He spent four months in Tokyo in 1928 and was so beguiled with the place that ever since then one of the principal thoroughfares of Ngiwal, which has four hundred and fifty residents and no vehicles, has been called the Ginza.

One lingering vestige of Japanese influence in Micronesia is the popularity of baseball, which the natives consider a national Japanese sport. In rural Micronesian communities, it is almost as essential for an aspiring politician to have a baseball connection as it is in rural American communities to be a volunteer fireman. Year in and year out, the best ball players are Palauans, whose All-Stars regularly whip all comers, and who have consistently beaten the Guam All-Stars, even though *their* ranks are augmented by American servicemen with Stateside baseball backgrounds. In 1940, a Keio University team from Tokyo came to Micronesia for a series of exhibition games, but it was not permitted to play the leading Palauan team. The Japanese in Koror knew which one would almost certainly win, and they didn't want Keio to lose face.

It was much the same story after the war, with the Americans in charge. On the Truk lagoon island of Romonum, where the anthropologist Ward Goodenough set up housekeeping, there used to be a game every Sunday between the local boys and the United States Navy—or, at any rate, the best of the Navy then stationed in the area. Every so often the chief of Romonum would beg the natives to throw a game, fearful that Navy morale would otherwise irreparably sag. On the next lagoon island, Tol, there now lives a man named Susumu Aizawa, a Trukese who grows cacao and is also a district legislator. At the start of the war, his father, a Japanese, went back to Japan and took the boy, then a teenager, with him. Susumu, who didn't return to Truk until 1956, was at once spotted by the Japanese as a promising pitcher, and for several seasons he played professional baseball in and around Tokyo. In 1950, he pitched against a squad of American professionals, on a post-World Series barnstorming tour. Aizawa didn't exactly set them back on their heels, but he enjoys quite a celebrity at home as the only Micronesian who ever served up two home-run balls to Mickey Mantle.

Palauans are no less aesthetically than athletically inclined. The men's clubhouse, or *bai,* is perhaps their most striking artistic achievement. Practically every square inch of the steep gables and broad rafters of a *bai* is covered with pictographic ornamentation. The clubhouse at Ngiwal, for instance, has along its rafters a pictorial representation of the high spots of that municipality's history, as related by Chief Uong-san to an artist while he painted. Most prominent among the portraits in this gallery is that of a group of warriors, or *ngarchochado* (pronounced "nardo") the head of which was Uong's father, Ngirachberdong, who is shown holding a spear with the numeral 3 on it—he had killed three men with that weapon in a skirmish with a nearby village.

Some of the men shown in the *ngarchochado* have long golden hair and long golden beards; they customarily dyed themselves before going into battle. Chief Uong, who like many Japanese elders has a shaved head, was born at about the time that civil war was waged, but although he looks primitive, he speaks Japanese,

German, Spanish, and some English; and he has supervised the installation in Ngiwal of an elaborate municipal water system, with underground pipes, fed by an upland stream, that lead to every house. Thus splendidly irrigated, Ngiwal produces, and sends to market at Koror, guava, pumpkins, squash, green onions, Chinese cabbage, and a citrus fruit that tastes like a cross between orange and grapefruit but that in size resembles watermelon. Uong-san is patient but dispassionate when visitors ask him about the gory exploits of his warrior father; the chief would much rather talk about a high school he hopes to have built for his Ngiwalese teenagers.

A half century ago, when Germany governed Micronesia, Palau's artists went pretty much into eclipse. They were discouraged, for one thing, because whenever they finished decorating a building some Germans would pry off the gables and saw off the rafters and send them to European museums. The Japanese were less wreckingly acquisitive. Encouraged by a Japanese woodcarver's assurance that their *bais* would not be demolished—except possibly by typhoons—Palauans resumed their ancient skills.

Now they paint everything, including jeeps, which they decorate from bumper to bumper. Their most prolific portable output, is in the form of storyboards—carved or painted or both—which, like the *bai* rafters, relate old Palauan legends, some of these quite spicy. The best-known, and one of the blandest, is a tale of a boy who helped out his hungry foster mother by digging a littoral trench through which fish swam up to a breadfruit tree and flopped out through a hole in its trunk. When envious neighbors chopped down the fish-fruit tree, water gushed up through the spot it had occupied and drowned everyone around except the woman and the solicitous boy.

Under the American administration of Micronesia, Palauan art has taken a perhaps inevitable contemporary turn. On the front gable of a snack bar in Koror run by the West Carolines Trading Company, an artist has illustrated the identifying legend "Coffee Shop" with an ice cream cone, a sandwich, a hot dog, and a companionable man and woman. The "C" in "Coffee" evolves from steam rising from a cup the woman is holding; the "p" in "Shop" from the smoke of the man's cigarette. It is Palau's finest example of shop art.

Koror also has Micronesia's only zoo. Its chief attraction is a fifteen-foot-long crocodile. Palau has Micronesia's most diverting fauna, including a species of tree frog that emerges fully grown from eggs; a small owl, the *essuch*, which parents use as a sleep-inducer by telling children that if they don't settle down the *essuch* will come along and peck their eyes out; and an ever-growing colony of monkeys. The monkeys are not indigenous. Broad-winged bats that fly perkily around in broad daylight are among Micronesia's few native mammals, and come in two varieties—fruit-eating and carnivorous. The monkeys were imported by the Japanese and have proliferated into a nuisance. They invade taro and cassava patches just as if they owned them. Palauans would like to get rid of these animals, but they are loath to kill any creature so human in mien.

Palauans don't mind killing crocodiles, and some of them have perfected an awesome technique. They will take a motorboat into a narrow, mangrove-edged, coastal stream, stand at the stern, push the engine up to full throttle, steer the boat through a twisting channel with one foot, and somehow maintain enough balance with the other foot to aim a rifle at any crocodile they may surprise as they round a sharp bend.

The crocodiles are as unusual as their hunters. Unlike most of their kind, the animals (species *crocodylus porosus*) are sea-going critters. They are sometimes spotted in the ocean hundreds of miles off Palauan shores. Bathers have to be on the alert for them, and occasionally get chewed up by one of them. In December, 1965, the body of a fisherman who fell prey to one of them was found, in four feet of water, just outside Koror. With a few such exceptions, Palauans survive encounters with crocodiles better than many folk, being notably hardy. One Koror woman who was run through by a spear during an altercation over her affections recovered quickly, even though she couldn't receive surgical attention until a Public Works employee had sheared off part of the spear with an acetylene torch so she could be moved through the door of the local hospital's operating room.

The big crocodile in the Koror zoo was itself speared in May, 1964, near Ngeremlengui, on Babelthuap, and it recovered from its wounds after several shots of penicillin. "Having crocodiles around makes swimming a little more interesting here than elsewhere in the Trust Territory," I was told by the curator of the zoo, Robert Owen, an Oregonian who has been in Micronesia since 1949 and whose principal job is that of Trust Territory entomologist.

Owen's wife, a native of Finland who once danced with Martha Graham, is Micronesia's most celebrated non-indigenous cook. She often serves crocodile stew or crocodile shish kebab. One of her favorite dining-table centerpieces is a live crocodile nested in a clam shell—the crocodile being a baby one and the shell from one of the outsize varieties of clam that are found all over Micronesia, that reach four feet in width, and weigh as much as four hundred pounds apiece. They are formidable clams, and have the reputation, in many works of fiction, of being man-eaters.

Among the other delicacies that are served up by Mrs. Owen, who has been compiling a Micronesian cookbook that may be bought more for curiosity than for consultation, is a broth made from ginger, green onion, salt and pepper, and fruit bat. (Not all Palauans are as fond of fruit bats as Mrs. Owen is, although some eat these animals whole—they don't have to be gutted since they live cleanly on fruit juices—and insist moreover that a pinch of bat fur enhances the flavor.) Other specialties that are apt to appear on Mrs. Owen's menus are sea urchin milt, something that she calls "taro leaf mish mash," pickled bamboo shoots, and a soup made out of coconut cream and the reproductive organs of *bêche de mer*, the sea slug.

Along with its zoo, Koror has Micronesia's only operating museum—Yap has another museum under construction—of which Mrs. Owen is the main sponsor. (Her own home, a much-modified quonset hut, is so full of artifacts that transients sometimes take *it* for the museum.) Palau's museum is a trove of carved wooden monkey men, storyboards, and various kinds of native money—among these last being a bracelet, called an *ololl*, that is made from the vertebrae of the dugong and that is worn only by important men. The tighter an *ololl* fits the better; Palauans have been known to crush a few bones in their hands while forcing bracelets onto their wrists. Each Palauan clan has its own kind of money. The most precious is generally made of yellow, orange, or mustard-colored ceramic, and is worn on a cord around the neck. A single piece may be worth an entire island. Palauans, who are very materialistic, derive as much pleasure from gaping at the money in the Koror museum as Britishers do from gazing at their crown jewels in the Tower of London.

Palauans also like to stop by the museum and feast their eyes on a number of paintings of a young native boy in fancy, ruffled, eighteenth-Century English clothes. All Palauans know who *he* is—Prince Lee Boo, the second son of King Abbathule, who at the age of eighteen went to England. He was taken there by Captain Henry Wilson of the East India Company, whose ship the *Antelope*, out of Macao, hit a reef between Koror and Peleliu on August 9, 1783. At that time, the Western world thought all Palauans were cannibals. The crew of the *Antelope* were the first white men known to have put this premise to a test. King Abbathule and his subjects not only didn't eat them but succored them and helped them to build a new ship. The grateful Captain Wilson offered to take the king's son to England, where the boy created quite a stir. The British called him the Black Prince. But soon after he arrived, he caught smallpox and died, to the deep distress of Palauans then and now.

26.

The Economy

Articulate Palauans have been grumbling, this past decade, about economic inactivity. The reason for their fretfulness is simple enough: a good many of them aspire to become millionaires. Even those Palauans whose aims are relatively modest have been heartened by a recent economic development—the establishment, just outside Koror, of the first extraterritorial business venture in Micronesia since the Americans moved in. Under the terms of the trusteeship agreement with the United Nations, if commercial interests from any U.N. member nation were granted access to Micronesia, commercial interests from any other would also have to be. Thus, if Japanese or Australian capital were welcomed, Russian, say, or Indonesian capital could not be excluded. The United States, however, was a special case: the right of American capital to go into Micronesia was guaranteed by a most-favored-nation clause in the trusteeship agreement.

Even so, it was not until 1962 that the American government

—the Kennedy government at that time—thought the Trust Territory was ready for any outside enterprise, and in the ensuing years only one has appeared on the scene: a fishing operation. Palauans consider this highly appropriate, for in Japanese days Koror was a fishing port comparable, in size of catch and range of vessels, to Gloucester or New Bedford. The trail blazer is the Van Camp Sea Food Company, of Long Beach, California, which markets Chicken-of-the-Sea tuna. Palauan waters are full of tuna —mostly yellowfin and skipjack—and also have an abundant supply of baitfish.

Van Camp was not fazed by the prospect of opening up a new territory. It had already been a pioneer tuna-fisher in both Puerto Rico and American Samoa, and had accordingly had a good many dealings with the Department of the Interior. Van Camp built a million-dollar freezing plant in Palau, and in August, 1964, began fishing with a fleet of six fifteen-ton boats. (Subsequently, it acquired six more boats there, and decided to start up a similar operation at Truk.) The American resident manager for Van Camp bought a small plane for spotting schools of tuna—the only privately owned aircraft in Micronesia. The plane, carrying the Van Camp manager and a Palauan passenger, flew out to sea in December, 1965, to help search for a missing canoe with three natives aboard. The canoe was eventually picked up by a fishing boat two hundred and forty miles from the nearest Palauan island; the plane was never seen again.

In the spring of 1965, three Palauan civic leaders formed their own tuna-fishing company and imported seven additional boats from Okinawa—whence also have come a good many of the crewmen for the tuna boats, inasmuch as the techniques of mass tuna-fishing are unfamiliar to Palauans and as a lot of them, no matter how much they want to become rich, would just as soon achieve that state of grace, after twenty years of observing Americans in action, from a desk job.

The Palauan-owned company preserves its catch in the fifteen-hundred-ton-capacity Van Camp freezer until a big ship turns up to take it to a distant cannery. A short walk from this frigid oasis in the tropics is a smaller freezing room used to store reef fish caught by a Palauan fisherman's cooperative, partly for home consumption and partly for export. Many of the fish brought to this spot spoil, because the Micronesian attendants of the freezing room, even when swathed in arctic regalia, keep thinking of excuses not to go inside it.

Cooperatives are much in vogue in Micronesia. When the Yap Trading Company not long ago reorganized itself into the Yap Cooperative Association, that district's paper, under the heading "Okay, go ahead and be a capitalist!" urged all Yapese to dig up a hundred dollars some way or other and invest it, at six percent interest, in the co-op. "The French do it, the Japanese, the Americans are great at it, and even the Indians do it," said the *Rai News*. "Why shouldn't the Yapese, Ulithians, and Woleaians do it?"

There are trading companies, sometimes more than one, in each district. Some are run by Micronesians and some by Americans. The American in charge at Yap is a merchant of convictions. Being a Quaker, he frowns on smoking and drinking, and he posts signs in his store suggesting that his customers refrain from purchasing cigarettes and liquor, which are among the establishment's biggest profit-makers. The trading companies are now privately owned, but they all evolved from postwar merchandising outfits that were set up and run by the United States government. First there was something called the United States Commercial Corporation, a versatile concern that both imported ichthyologists and exported copra. It was succeeded by the Island Trading Company, a combination wholesaler and retailer that did so well—it had no transportation costs, being under Navy control and moving its merchandise in Navy bottoms—that by the time it was finally dissolved, in 1954, it had amassed a profit of around a million dollars.

There are many small businesses in Micronesia, especially outside of the district centers, where a store may consist of part of a room in a home. The proprietors make ends meet by selling goods on credit to members of their own clans and by counting on the chief of the clan (who may or may not pay for anything himself) to act as their collection agent at billing time. In the district centers, there are much larger and much more prosperous concerns. The Marshall Islands Import-Export Company now grosses over a million and a half dollars a year, and it boasts its own ocean-going freighter, the *Mieco Queen*.

One of the most successful native businessmen is a merchant at Chalan Kanoa, on Saipan, named José C. Tenorio. He is president of the Saipan Shipping Company, president of Saipan Importers, president of the Saipan Chamber of Commerce, and president of Tenorio Enterprises, Inc. José Tenorio is a common name on Saipan, like Joe Smith. The businessman long ago appropriated the nickname Joe Ten, the syllables of which also form one of his two cable addresses (no other Micronesian has more than one). The other José Tenorios on Saipan thereupon became known, not altogether to their pleasure, as Joe Three, Joe Seven, and so forth. A José Tenorio who is called Joe Eleven runs a restaurant in Chalan Kanoa and also acts as a public defender for Saipanese standing trial in the local court for minor offenses. Joe Eleven likes to say, half in jest, that he has a nice thing going: he gets people stewed at his bar at night, and gets them out of trouble the next morning. He is also jealously aware of his principal namesake's commercial eminence. "One of these days I'll be bigger than Joe Ten," Joe Eleven keeps telling his bar patrons.

Joe Ten, who had no education at all until he was twenty, began his business career as a bookkeeper for the United States Commercial Corporation, and opened a small general store of his own in 1949. Today he has a supermarket that sells everything from groceries to automobiles. He also has a ship. He has made eight trips to Japan, the source of much of his merchandise, and he took his wife to the Tokyo Olympics. Unlike most leading Micronesians, he has not participated extensively in politics: He wants to be on friendly selling terms with members of both of Saipan's hotly competitive political parties. He had a chance for international renown in 1961, when a petition he addressed to a visiting U.N. mission—he hoped that Trust Territory headquarters would be moved from Guam, where they then were, to Saipan, where they now are—was published as an annex to the mission's official report. But the petition concluded, in print, "(Signed) (illegible)." How Joe Eleven must have chuckled!

(Few official visitors leave Micronesia without having had at least one petition thrust upon them. In December, 1965, for instance, when a United States Congressional delegation made one of its periodic inspections of the Trust Territory, the Yap Islands Congress drew up a statement that said, in part, "We need not worry about the image of the United States in the world. Maintaining her image is her own problem. We may remain the last remaining Trust Territory in the world but that does not hurt so long as we obtain what we need and want in the way of development." The *Rai Review* commented: "'We cry for help when in agony and we do it out loud so someone can hear us. We cry louder when we feel someone is nearby,' so they say. The petition has been written, presented, and there is the beginning of a new chapter in Micronesian history.")

For years, Micronesia had a subsistence economy. Now it has a subsidized one. The total Trust Territory budget runs to twenty million dollars a year, and seventeen and a half million dollars of that is provided by the United States Congress. When two of the B-52's based on Guam collided in mid-air while on a bombing run to North Vietnam, the cost of the mishap was put at eighteen million dollars. It was hard for Micronesians to comprehend why a government that could take such a loss in stride could not give them at least the equivalent of a three-bomber budget.

The natives have been less eager to accept the fact that inasmuch as there are only ninety thousand of them, the federal funds they *have* been getting have come to about two hundred dollars per capita per year, which is just about what Congress has been allocating—not counting defense appropriations—for each American citizen. Moreover, as Trust Territory officials are quick to point out whenever anyone suggests that their budget might be skimpy, Australia allots its New Guinea trust territory merely fifteen dollars a native a year. To that, Micronesians can and sometimes do rejoin that the United States is a nation that traditionally spares no expense to get the helpless out of a jam. To rescue a child from a well or a dog from a crevice, Americans will call out their Police and Fire departments and the Boy Scouts and the National Guard and all their auxiliaries. In the Trust Territory, some Micronesians feel America is pretending it doesn't know there's a cat up a tree.

Nearly everyone who cares about the Trust Territory agrees that something should be done to reduce the existing imbalance between its imports—$7,090,916 in 1965, for instance, nearly half of which went for food—and its exports—$3,152,459, by far the bulk of which represented sales of copra. The second biggest export category was—notably non-industrial though the area is—scrap metal: junk from the war twenty years ago. "The sea can go a long way," High Commissioner Godding sometimes would say, meditating upon the area's economic potentialities, and he was right in more ways than one. Sixty-eight Japanese ships still lie unsalvaged on the bottom of the Truk lagoon.

The shells of just one species of local sea snail, the trochus, used to bring Micronesia hundreds of thousands of dollars a year from shirtmakers, for buttons, but trochus shell has all but priced itself out of that market. The demand was so great and the supply so limited that the value of trochus shot up, ironically, to a point where most shirtmakers decided they couldn't afford it any longer and switched to plastic buttons. Under the Japanese, Micronesia exported pearls, phosphate, and sugar cane, but there are no pearl divers left, the region's phosphate ran out ten years ago, and what sugar cane remains (the Japanese exported seven million dollars' worth a year and built railroads to expedite its shipment) is barely adequate for the native children to chew on.

Within the last couple of years, the Trust Territory administration has taken a number of steps toward stimulating economic development. Most recently, the High Commissioner engaged a Washington firm of economic consultants, at a cost of more than three hundred thousand dollars, to make an exhaustive study of Micronesia, and to ascertain, among other things, just how long a way the sea and what little land emerges from it can ultimately go.

Few Micronesian businessmen have much capital of their own. To enable the bigger ones like Joe Ten and the smaller fry as well to expand old operations or embark on new ones, the administration has a loan fund from which they may borrow reasonable sums at reasonable terms. In each of the six Trust Territory districts, moreover, at least one experimental project is under way that could some day prove profitable. Ponape hopes to become a big producer of cacao as well as pepper. Palau has begun growing ramie, a fiber admired for its smoothness and strength when woven into cloth and nets. Truk is banking in part on coir fiber, made from coconut husks and used for brushes, ropes, and floor mats. (This operation might have got under way sooner than it did had not the machinery ordered for it been one year late in arriving.) In the Marianas, where there is relatively good pasturage, beef cattle are the big thing, and the Marshalls are looking to arrowroot, which grows wild throughout that district and has the double virtue of being both edible and usable as laundry starch. Yap has been exploring the possibilities of harvesting precious deep-sea coral, the best grades of which, at last reports, fetched fifty-four dollars a pound in Japan.

On a somewhat less organized level, an American at Palau, where fifty percent of employable males are unemployed, has been exhorting the natives to sell crocodile skins. It is his estimate that crocodile culture, if it ever got going, could afford full-time employment to perhaps six Palauans. Similarly, an American on Truk, where only eight percent of the labor force is employed in any field other than subsistence agriculture, has been wondering if there might not be some sort of cash crop in that district's millipedes, which run to six inches in length and, when aroused, squirt out a highly acid liquid that turns human skin purple. That American has no notion of how many Trukese could be gainfully employed in millipede culture, but he thinks there must be a biological-supply house *somewhere* on earth that would be interested in the acid insects.

Another likely source of cash income for Micronesia would seem to be native handicrafts. The only trouble here is that, except for the Palauans, Micronesians aren't particularly creative, and, moreover, aren't particularly eager to practice what skills they have. Anxious to be modern, they shy away from old-fashioned cottage industries. They would rather dream about rug factories than sit at home making mats. There has been some desultory traffic in Palauan storyboards and monkey men, Ponapean baskets, Marshallese handbags, Yapese dolls, and Trukese love sticks. (These last, now made almost exclusively for the souvenir trade, are hand-carved, dagger-length pieces of wood with notched edges. A young man would show his love stick to a girl he was courting, and at night he would poke it through the side of her family's house and prod her with it. She could tell by the feel of its serrations whose love stick it was. If she welcomed the owner's attentions, she would tug on it, thus inviting him to crawl into the hut alongside her, or she would push the stick back out of the hut. Love sticks became anachronistic when many Trukese began occupying homes with solid walls.) A couple of years ago, hoping to spur the sale of local handicrafts, the Trust Territory administration opened a retail store, called the Micronesian Products Center, in Guam. But its proceeds weren't even enough to cover the rent.

For what relatively little activity there has been in handicrafts, local groups of Micronesian women are largely responsible. They have organized clubs and associations and in general have achieved a state of emancipation beyond anything their mothers and grandmothers could have imagined. True, there have been some female native chiefs in Micronesia (the Germans once angered the residents of one Palauan island by refusing to treat with their chief, just because she was a woman), but they were exceptions. A more typical state of affairs was that which prevailed in parts of Truk not so long ago. A woman there could not even walk past the outside of a house in which some men were sitting without making her presence known, so they would have a chance to stand up while she went by. Otherwise, she would have seemed to be looking down on them, which would never do. Now, by sharp contrast, things have reached the point where some native women even drink hard liquor at community clubs, join in the nightly conviviality there, and make jokes at the expense of their own chiefs. The Trust Territory government has lately added a Women's Interest Coordinator to its headquarters staff, and two young women from Yap are currently in training as radio announcers. In December, 1965, for the first time in the history of Truk, two women were among the twenty-seven successful candidates for seats in that district's legislature.

A generation ago, Micronesia was known as the Japanese Riviera, and its present administrators, up to and including Secretary Udall, hope that the area can achieve some kind of economic stability by once again becoming a resort. With a sultry climate, pure white sand, turquoise water, bizarre shells, centipedal clumps of mangrove and pandanus, and graceful coconut palms, not to mention the gracious natives themselves, Micronesia would seem to have in abundance the raw materials of a tourist attraction. Moreover, it is one of the few exotic places left on earth that vacationers have not yet explored en masse—the only comparable area, perhaps, being New Guinea.

When the Navy ran Micronesia, it discouraged outsiders' dropping in, and even under Interior's comparatively relaxed administration no one—American citizens included—may enter the Trust Territory without written permission from the High Commissioner. Visitors do turn up every now and then. Some come by accident. One New Zealander pulled into Saipan on a thirty-five-foot boat. He was on his way from South America to Hong Kong, and meant to stop at Wake, a thousand miles east of the Marianas, but he missed it. He didn't have an entry permit, but he was hospitably received anyway.

Another traveler who got to Micronesia more or less by mistake was an Istanbul man whose hobby was visiting out-of-the-way places. He had been to something like two hundred countries, but the Turk had never seen Truk. At a Pan American office at Istanbul, his eye lit on a printed schedule of flights connecting Guam, Truk, and other Micronesian air fields. The clerk sold the Turk a ticket that authorized him passage throughout Micronesia, and without further investigation the collector set forth for Guam and on arriving presented his paid-up ticket to a liaison officer the Trust Territory has stationed there. Having gone to all that trouble and expense, the Turk was allowed to proceed on into Micronesia.

Some of the handful of visitors to Micronesia are there to work on special projects of one sort or another—an anthropologist studying evolution on Yap, a zoologist studying shrews on Saipan, and an urbanization expert from the South Pacific Commission studying, apparently, the eventual urbanization of some of the world's most rural islands. In 1964, a retired carpet manufacturer from the suburbs of New York arranged to spend three weeks in the Trust Territory with his wife, as plain, ordinary tourists. The couple had done a good deal of traveling, and after a trip to some relatively well-trod areas of the South Pacific, like Fiji, they had chanced to share a taxi in Honolulu with a geodeticist, who when they complained that the islands they'd visited no longer seemed natural and unspoiled, replied that they should see where *he'd* just come from.

The few other tourists who have so far reached Micronesia have been inspired to try to get there mainly by memories, happy or sad, of the Second World War. Every so often, a veteran of the 1944 battles of Peleliu or Angaur will materialize to show his wife what the combat area he might have died on looks like. Since 1959, furthermore, some Japanese have been allowed to return to Micronesia, either to resettle there in their old age, or to hold memorial services for their soldier dead at the graves or the crumbling Shinto shrines of another era.

Periodically, someone turns up in search of Amelia Earhart. When the flier disappeared in 1937, she was thought to have landed, if ever she did land, somewhere in Micronesia. There are those who are certain she came down on Saipan, and who to prove their premise have as recently as 1963 engaged in exploratory digging for her grave. Another school of thought holds that she crashed in the Marshall Islands. Not long ago, the spot was described with such positiveness—a certain point in the lagoon of the Majuro atoll—that the American district administrator for the Marshalls and a native friend took a boat and some diving equipment there. They found the remains of an airplane, but it was a B-29.

Still others assert that it was Truk where Miss Earhart alit, and there are natives of that district who insist—without, however, naming names—that one Trukese man has a ring that could be identified, if he ever showed it to anybody, as the flier's. The attitude of the American authorities is that there is no evidence that Miss Earhart ever landed, dead or alive, in Micronesia, but if people are determined to dig for her grave, or any other grave, there is no objection provided they fill in their excavations.

Until recently, one hazard for all individuals contemplating a trip to Micronesia and not enjoying official-business status was their lack of a priority on the administration's airline. They would be warned that, with space at a premium, they were likely to be bumped off flights, assuming they ever got booked on one, and when they got bumped, it would mean a week's layover wherever they happened to be, before another flight was even scheduled. Now the situation has improved slightly. Two private carriers based at Guam—Micronesian Airways and Guam Airlines—make sporadic journeys to most of the Trust Territory district centers.

The High Commissioner's office at Saipan is so sanguine about a possible upturn in the tourist business that it has issued a brochure illustrated with two alluring color photographs. One shows a man and a woman strolling, alone together, on a lovely, moonlit, palm-fringed beach. The other shows a line of bare-breasted, grass-skirted native girls in a ceremonial dance. Not all Micronesians are pleased with the latter. They grumble, in effect, that here they are trying to become civilized and westernized, and there ought to be some better way of graphically depicting the big, bold, evolutionary steps they are taking than by a garden-variety parade of nubile nudity.

In view of the Trust Territory's remoteness from the American mainland, its officials, like those on Guam, expect that the bulk of the hoped-for influx of tourists will come from Japan, whose residents have a long affinity for the area and who love to travel; from Australia, whose residents would relish a chance to visit a place that wasn't as far away from their continent as most run-of-the-mill vacation areas are; and—unlike those on Guam—from Guam, where there are thousands of American servicemen who get to feeling cooped up on that tropical island and, for a change, would leap at the chance to visit other tropical islands. Some Trust Territory administrators think that Pagan, one of the northernmost of the Marianas, might make a fine tourist spot. Pagan has hot springs and a volcano that now and then still spits lava. "Most people on Guam have never seen an active volcano!" a Trust Territory official who came from Guam himself exclaimed to a recent visitor. "They'd flood the place!" Not long afterward, unfortunately, 80 percent of the buildings on Pagan were destroyed by an active typhoon.

The islands of Micronesia that do have tourist accommodations don't have many. Each district has at least one hotel, but these are fairly Spartan establishments. Truk is the most heavily populated district. Its solitary hotel has ten rooms. "We're not fancy, but we're clean!" the proprietor likes to say. The Truk hotel is in one respect indisputably modern; people keep stealing its towels. The hotel in Koror (twenty-two rooms) calls itself the Royal Palauan. Until a couple of years ago, the Trust Territory administration operated all the hostelries, but it has been encouraging indigenes to take them over. The Royal Palauan now has a native, and engagingly unpredictable, management.

Palau also has a travel bureau (one of its claims is that the local beaches are so white you can't look at the sand comfortably without dark glasses), and it has begun offering package tours to residents of Guam. Saipan has lately been making a determined bid for Guamanian tourists, with José Tenorio's Chamber of Commerce leading the way. The Saipan legislature has passed a resolution advocating the construction of an amusement park, members of the Chamber have agreed to take turns greeting tourists at the air terminal, hotels are going up apace, and a new car-rental service is in the works. This last should be a welcome change. Not long ago, a visitor who hired the only car available at an airport drive-yourself booth soon learned that it was a vehicle Avis wouldn't wish on Hertz. After he had climbed into the car and taken off along one of the island's highways, he became progressively aware that it had no mirrors, no muffler, no directional signals, no speedometer, no radio, no gas gauge, no spare tire, and no brakes. When the battery went dead, he abandoned the car in the driveway of the Assistant High Commissioner for Public Affairs. Thus in Micronesia do futility symbols become emplaced.

27.

True Progress Moves Slowly

WHILE STEPS, HOWEVER HALTING, HAVE BEEN AND are still being taken to try to provide Micronesians with more of the money they probably need and unquestionably want, there remains the problem of how many of them there are going to be to divide it among. The Trust Territory's current population of about ninety thousand is not excessive, but it is also twice what it was twenty years ago, and as more and more public-health measures are initiated in the area, there is no doubt that its inhabitants will rapidly multiply. When a recent visitor asked one thirty-five-year-old Ponapean man about the size of his family, the native replied, almost apologetically, that he had only seven children, the same number as his younger brother; there were also two older brothers, one with ten children and the other with eight. By the time the four brothers stop breeding, they will probably have fifty offspring among them. The rising birth rate and falling death rate in the Trust Territory have been of concern both to the American authorities and to the Micronesians themselves, one of whom remarked wryly that the accelerated education program introduced by the United States two years ago was nothing compared to the natives' own accelerated procreation program.

Micronesia rarely makes Stateside newspapers, but it was on the front page of *The New York Times* one day in the summer of 1965, when Secretary Udall announced that the Department of the Interior would shortly be sending birth-control information and contraceptive devices to the Indian reservations under its aegis, to American Samoa, and to the Trust Territory. Few Micronesians knew anything at all about birth control until a couple of years ago, when they heard some doctrinaire Catholic denouncements of it on the radio and concluded that anything that could get anybody so worked up must be worth looking into.

One prominent native member of the Trukese-American Woman's Association even made a public speech in favor of birth control. Her qualifications were unimpeachable. Her husband was one of sixteen siblings, she herself was one of twelve, and she was a hospital nurse among whose duties was that of deciding whether to bed down pregnant patients under fourteen in the maternity ward or the pediatric ward. The birth-control advocate, who was twenty-eight and had only five children of her own, was chided by a priest. He suggested that at subsequent meetings she address herself to less controversial topics. Secretary Udall's new policy, if it accomplishes little else, will presumably embolden the nurse and others who share her feelings to talk out as thunderously as they like about the prevention and cure of population explosions.

Micronesians are much preoccupied nowadays with all aspects of their uncertain future. Richard Taitano, the deputy high commissioner, in a recent commencement speech, said that the biggest question before local high-school graduates was "Micronesia, whither thou goest?" It is a hard question to answer. A generation hence, most Micronesians will be fluent in English. Most of today's high-school graduates already are, and wonder audibly what good it is to be bilingual if they can't get a job in any language. The younger natives, like younger people anywhere, are impatient to plunge swiftly from their placid environment into the swirling outside world. The older natives, like older people anywhere, counsel moderation. "We can't move too fast," said the venerable Chief Uong of Ngiwal, "because we're still a baby. But we're coming along little by little."

Appearing before the Trusteeship Council of the United Nations in the spring of 1963, another Palauan, Thomas Remengesau, who is an assistant district administrator in Koror, expressed his hope that the United States would "accelerate the economic infra-structure" of the Trust Territory, and he went on to say that any discussion of the future of Micronesia put him in mind of an old Palauan phrase for which there were two acceptable English translations: "You cannot hasten the ripening of a papaya fruit" and "You cannot slow down the ripening of a papaya." Both versions, he thought, were applicable and pertinent.

When the League of Nations laid down the terms of the Japanese mandate over Micronesia in 1920, there was little said about political self-determination. The United Nations, however, has been committed from the start toward fostering self-government. Many U.N. members who enjoy hectoring the United States seize every opportunity to demand that we hold a plebiscite in the Trust Territory at once and give the poor and ostensibly downtrodden Micronesians a chance to decide their future.

Some of the African nations that in theory have emerged are especially vociferous about this, and it goes without saying that the Communists join in. The Russians were demanding independence for Micronesians more than a decade ago. At one recent meeting of a U.N. General Assembly Committee that deals with colonialism and independence, the Cambodian representative—who had never been to the Trust Territory—said wildly that "he was glad to note that Micronesia possessed all the necessary resources to become a unified, prosperous, and independent nation." The Cambodian had never been there, and any Micronesian could have told him, and would probably have been glad to, that he was talking through his *mouk*, which is Cambodian for hat.

It is, of course, conceivable that Micronesia might some day become independent; after all, the U.N. has inducted into the ranks of full-fledged sovereign political entities the Maldive Islands, which have a population almost identical with the Trust Territory's. But even the few Micronesians who think they might some day enjoy governing themselves shudder at the prospect of trying it now. If in fact a plebiscite were held in Micronesia today, probably nine-tenths of the electorate would vote for some kind of continuing relationship with the United States. Just what form this might take is debatable. Many Saipanese, having family ties to nearby Guam, would like to become affiliated with that territory. Most of the seventy thousand permanent residents of Guam, on the other hand, have no more wish to abdicate their exclusive territorial status and become a minority group in a larger territory than they have to be independent.

Hawaii has seriously proposed that, Micronesians concurring, the Trust Territory islands become a far-flung county of that state. If that came to pass, Hawaiians are not unaware, their state would cut a bigger geographical swath than Alaska and Texas put together. (Goding's successor as High Commissioner, perhaps not unsignificantly, was chief administrative assistant to the governor of Hawaii.) But most Micronesians are not much impressed with a change of status that—although it would invest them, the United States Congress concurring, with both the privileges and responsibilities of American citizenship—would also see them governed not by a High Commissioner responsible to a cabinet officer in Washington, but by a County Commissioner responsible to a governor in Honolulu.

At the 1965 meeting of the U.N.'s Trusteeship Council, U Thant said at the opening session, "The most important question that has been asked today is not whether these remaining Trust Territories will ultimately attain the objectives set for them in the Charter, but when these objectives will be attained." (United Nations officials have not always seemed so eager to expedite their objectives; they first proposed a Kashmir plebiscite in 1947.) The Secretary General had apparently forgotten that a visiting mission the U.N. itself had sent to Micronesia several months before had reported back that "it must be conceded that the conditions for self-determination do not yet exist." Not even the Russians, whose appraisal of the American administration of Micronesia is apt to be studded with phrases like "brutally exploiting" and "colonial yoke," are pressing especially hard for a plebiscite there. The Russians are smart enough to realize by what a lopsided margin the natives would undoubtedly express their determination not to rock the boat that America is steering.

Nevertheless, the United States administrators are aware that some time or other there will be a plebiscite. When he was High Commissioner, Goding thought 1969 a reasonable date. Congressman Aspinall of the House Interior and Insular Affairs Committee is less optimistic; 1975 is the date he has in mind. Spokesmen for nations inimical to America suggest that *whenever* a plebiscite is held, it is bound to be unfair, unless the United States stops pouring money into Micronesia—an attitude that amuses those Micronesians who have hoped to be drenched by a fiscal spate and feel that they have, rather, merely been sprinkled. In any event, until Congressman Aspinall and his colleagues in both Houses on Capitol Hill agree in advance of a plebiscite that the United States will consider itself bound by its outcome—even if Micronesia should unforeseeably decide it wants no further truck with us—any talk of plebiscites is fairly academic.

Meanwhile, Micronesians are resigned—some more happily than others—to being dependent on Americans. "We have to lean on somebody to function," one realistic young Trukese says. "Obviously we don't have the means to support a government. When you think about our resources, it's hopeless to think about independence. And because we've come this far under the Americans, and have learned so much about America, whether we like it or not we've probably reached the point of no return and will have to continue to rely on Uncle Sam." So outspoken are many

Micronesians about the inevitability of their continuing association with their distant uncle that the United States Department of State finds their professions of dependence a mite embarrassing; after all, America is supposed to be preparing them to be, if not independent, at least non-dependent.

The extent to which Micronesians have withdrawn from self-sufficiency was indicated by a minor incident that happened not long ago at Majuro. A native's mother took ill, and he summoned an ambulance to rush her to the hospital. (In the old days there'd have been neither an ambulance nor a hospital.) Nobody saw anything wrong with that, but a good many Marshallese, along with the Americans around, were disturbed to learn that when the woman recovered, her son complained because the ambulance wouldn't also take her *home* from the hospital and he'd have to himself.

Too many Micronesians, it is glumly felt throughout the Trust Territory, are taking too many things for granted. John Mangefel, the Yapese annalist and supervisor of teachers, who in his dual roles represents a bridge between the islanders' ancient and modern ways, said not long ago, "I think it's about time that we started thinking that some things like educating our young and providing medical care for our sick are our responsibility as well as yours. I'm not saying we should take over—we simply don't have the money—but at least we ought to play a part."

An old Marshallese saying goes, "True progress moves quietly but forward." Inasmuch as neither Americans nor Micronesians have ever before been involved in a comparable evolutionary undertaking, there are no precedents on which to base an evaluation of the United States' methods of leading its wards to self-determination or self-sufficiency. Where should the Trust Territory be now, under American stewardship, relatively and absolutely? Should it have progressed as far as New York at the time of Peter Stuyvesant, or as far as California during the gold rush, or the American Indian in General Custer's era, or Texas today?

Some Micronesians have all but given up trying to answer that one. "We're accepting too much too fast and we don't really understand it," asserts Ylubuan, the beer-distributing witch doctor with his own notions about the Garden of Eden. Douglas L. Oliver, in his excellent *The Pacific Islands,* thinks it possible that "a people whose ancestors were so resourceful will be able to harmonize the cultural dissonances of the modern world into a new and equally satisfying kind of life for themselves. During the long centuries of Oceanic history they have done it before. Perhaps they will do it again."

Most Micronesians would agree that their old pattern of life has been thoroughly shattered. So perhaps the main question is: Can the United States, which in its haltingly benevolent fashion has contributed so much to Micronesia's dislocation, viably patch it up again or put a new kind of Micronesia together?

Nearly twenty years after America first assumed its odd and onerous burdens in the Trust Territory, Secretary Udall, who by virtue of his office shoulders as heavy a responsibility as anyone, said, "We obviously have to begin to move."

Index